D1593664

THE HOUSE OF FICTION

The House of Fiction

ESSAYS ON THE NOVEL BY

HENRY JAMES

Edited with an Introduction by

LEON EDEL

LIBRARY
SEMINOLE COMMUNITY COLLEGE

REC. JAN 5 1978

SANFORD, FLORIDA
32771

GREENWOOD PRESS, PUBLISHERS
WESTPORT, CONNECTICUT

Library of Congress Cataloging in Publication Data

James, Henry, 1843-1916.
  The house of fiction.

  Reprint of the 1957 ed. published by R. Hart-Davis,
London.
  CONTENTS: 1. The house of fiction: The art of
fiction, 1884. The great form, 1889. The future of
the novel, 1899. The lesson Balzac, 1905.--2. Novelists: Anthony Trollope, 1883. Robert Louis Stevenson, 1887. de Maupassant, 1888. Turgenev and
Tolstoy, 1897. Nathaniel Hawthorne, 1897. Gustave
Flaubert, 1902. Emile Zola, 1903. [etc.]

  1. Fiction--19th century--History and criticism.
I. Title.
[PN3499.J28 1973]   808.3   73-10849
ISBN 0-8371-7039-7

Originally Published in 1957
by Rupert Hart-Davis, London

Reprinted by Greenwood Press, Inc.

First Greenwood Reprinting 1973
Second Greenwood Reprinting 1976

Library of Congress Catalog Card Number 73-10849

ISBN 0-8371-7039-7

Printed in the United States of America

IN MEMORY OF
ALLAN WADE
1881–1955

Contents

Introduction   9

I THE HOUSE OF FICTION

The Art of Fiction 1884   23
The Great Form 1889   46
The Future of the Novel 1899   48
The Lesson of Balzac 1905   60

II NOVELISTS

Anthony Trollope 1883   89
Robert Louis Stevenson 1887   114
Guy de Maupassant 1888   139
Turgenev and Tolstoy 1897   168
Nathaniel Hawthorne 1897   176
Gustave Flaubert 1902   187
Emile Zola 1903   220

III NOVELS

Our Mutual Friend 1865   253
Middlemarch 1873   259
Far from the Madding Crowd 1874   268
Nana 1880   274
Bibliographical Note   281
Index   283

INTRODUCTION

In *The House of Fiction* I have brought together a number of Henry James's critical papers on novels and novelists so as to constitute a companion volume to the dramatic essays Allan Wade collected in *The Scenic Art* and the art criticism which John L. Sweeney edited in *The Painter's Eye*. My predecessors were able to assemble nearly all of James's essays on the plastic and dramatic arts, but I have had to make a choice from a much larger body of writing, indeed from a quantity sufficient to fill perhaps ten volumes. James was only occasionally a theatre or art critic; he was at every turn a critic of fiction. When it came to discussing the form he practised during all the years of his creative life he was the most voluble member of his craft. Few novelists have kept up such a constant stream of comment and criticism — and in a high style worthy of the subject — on the margin of their own creations and found time as well to weigh and discuss the creations of fellow-craftsmen. There are extant two hundred and fifty book-reviews (I speak in round figures), some thirty critical essays, a like number of 'portraits' in the manner of Sainte-Beuve, as well as a whole series of fugitive pieces, commemorative essays and various journalistic 'columns' James tossed off at the end of a day's work. These are the writings of a creator who never hesitated to use his appreciative faculties, his fine vision, his cultivated taste, in the interest of the art he followed as well as of the allied arts. Rare are the writers in whom there is such a happy coalescence of critic and creator: who produce great works and at the same time major criticism. In every century we have had but one or two — Ben Jonson and Dryden, Coleridge and Arnold, and in our time the Americans — James and Eliot.

I recognize at the outset, however, that it has been fashionable in recent years to dismiss Henry James's critical writings as the pleasant, intelligent, and urbane opinions of a wise artist, but not the work of a literary critic. This attitude has, perhaps, been influenced by the contemporary debate on the nature of criticism with its emphasis on textual explication. The best that F. W. Dupee, in his little study of James, can say of the novelist in his role of critic, is that 'as an essayist, and especially on French subjects, he was touched by that academic humanism and ready-made classicism of the cultivated American who expects literature to be at all times in the full-dress of its courtly prime and cannot forgive Flaubert for failing to be Racine'. This has undeniable charm as statement: yet how are we to reconcile Mr Dupee's Racinian James with the Henry James who championed Flaubert and Zola against a Philistine and prurient Victorian world, praising them as artists even while condemning their 'ferocious pessimism'? To invoke 'academic humanism' for a figure as critically flexible as James is like trying to place a wreath of laurel on the brow of H. G. Wells or electing Bernard Shaw to be Lord Rector of Aberdeen.

The general disparagement of James's criticism, of which Dupee's is symptomatic, seems to have its roots in certain remarks by T. S. Eliot long ago, a rather categorical and familiar dictum, as if he were speaking of a remote cousin who had failed in his career: 'Henry was not a literary critic.' Mr Eliot added to this his since much-quoted view that James was a critic who 'preyed on human beings' and had a mind too fine to be violated by an idea. Before Mr Eliot, George Moore, entering a drawing-room one evening and hearing James's voice, murmured to himself (and indeed reported his murmur to his readers): 'An extraordinarily able critic . . . a man too analytical for creation finds his job in criticism.' Mr Eliot thus considered Henry James to be too much a novelist to be a literary critic, while Moore considered him too much a critic to be a good novelist. Eliot, to be sure, speaks with more authority in critical matters than Moore, and in associating James's criticism with human beings, rather than with literature, he seems to be suggesting that the novelist approached criticism in the light of his practice of fiction.

The critical act, in the case of James, was essentially an enlargement of his action as novelist. In this he differed, for example, from Sainte-Beuve, who once wrote a novel in an effort to enlarge his action as critic. The novel was factitious, though perhaps it gave Sainte-Beuve an inkling of what the creative process might be. James was a novelist first and foremost; his critical acts were coloured constantly by his creative intelligence. To say this is to say that, in reading other novelists critically, Henry James was gaining insight into himself as novelist, and his emphasis on the importance for criticism of the writer's artistic intention is, in these circumstances, understandable. As novelist-turned-critic, he was constantly asking himself: 'What are *they* trying to do? What has been *their* intention?' and this was the surfacing of a buried question: 'How shall *I* do it?' Certainly James was not a disinterested critic, not a 'literary critic' in Eliot's sense of what literary criticism should be. But I rather suspect that when Eliot speaks of a literary critic he is, on his side, thinking more of the criticism of poetry and drama than of the novel. We take 'criticism' in general so much for granted that we forget constantly that the *ars poetica* is deeply rooted in the distant past of our civilization, whereas theory and criticism of the novel are much newer than the novel itself, which is one of the newest of literary forms. But it is not merely the antiquity of poetry and the modernism of the novel which account for the critical lag. The lag exists because the novel is elastic; it embraces all of life, including the lives of the novelist and the reader; and while a poem may be said to do so as well, it is possible for the critic to draw boundaries around poetry for the exercise upon it of his critical imagination. One draws boundaries round novels at one's peril. Poetry abstracts life, and deals with it in a highly condensed and symbolic form. The critic of poetry concerns himself with prosody and symbols; the critic of fiction is asked to accommodate himself not only to the novel's rhetoric but to the precise *field of vision* of the novelist, not to speak of his instruments of vision.

Henry James's richly-worked metaphor of the 'House of Fiction' shows us how acutely he was aware of this problem. James pictured the 'House of Fiction' as a vast front, pierced by many windows. The windows, he said, were often mere holes, makeshift points of view; but stationed at each was a figure, a pair of eyes — or at least a field glass: a unique instrument of observation. It insured to the person making use of it 'an impression distinct from every other'. The observers might watch the same show, but what they saw was never the same. One would see more while the other would see less; one would see black while the other saw white; one would see big, where the other saw small. And, not least, one would see coarse, where the other saw fine. 'There is fortunately no saying on what, for the particular pair of eyes, the window may *not* open,' said Henry James.

The view was the human scene; the aperture, the literary form; the 'posted presence of the watcher', who brought life to both, was nothing less than the whole consciousness of the artist. Such was the striking image James chose, in one of his late prefaces, to describe his characteristic art form. In the process he described also the ground upon which to establish the criticism of that art.

Henry James's essays are, therefore, not mere literary opinion; they offer us the vision of a theorist of fiction appraising, in the light of his aesthetic, the work of certain of his compeers. For our guidance James wrote a short essay on criticism itself. It was contributed originally to a symposium, of the sort held by quarterly journals from time to time, in which several voices chime in concerning the function and the destiny of the critic. The symposium was called 'The Science of Criticism' — even then! — but when the novelist reprinted his piece in *Essays in London* (1893) he more cautiously titled it 'Criticism'. I suspect that an even more accurate title would have been 'The Criticism of Fiction'.

The article began with an attack on the spurious criticism of ephemeral journals with their 'deluge of doctrine' and their 'profusion of talk'. James went on to make it clear that 'reviewing' has nothing in common with the art of criticism; it is merely a part of the machinery by which magazines, like trains, are able to fill out all their space before the journey starts at its advertised hour. Proper criticism, said James, pointing to its practice in France, is difficult and delicate; the writings to be discussed must be rigidly selected. Many books are published but few are noticed; when they are, they are handled in France with 'finer finger-tips'

than in the Anglo-Saxon world. The critical sense itself, he observed, is rare. 'We have too many small schoolmasters' — an
admirable sentence for the textual, the explanatory critics to
ponder.

Criticism, James asserts, has a high utility; but this occurs only
when it proceeds from 'the efficient combination of experience
and perception'. Then the critic can be the real 'helper of the
artist, a torch-bearing outrider, the interpreter, the brother'. There
follows a long simile by which the critic is compared to a knight
whose vigil is long, who has the piety of his chivalry and whose
act is distinctly sacrificial, for he offers himself as 'a general touch-
stone'. The requirements James enumerates would make of the
critic a rare bird indeed: his standards seem almost inhumanly
high. The critic lends himself, steeps himself, tries to *feel* until he
attains understanding so that he has 'perception at the pitch of
passion and expression as embracing as the air'. Curiosity,
patience, plasticity, an active mind, inflammability, sentience,
restlessness, the capacity to react, reciprocate, penetrate. Criticism
is the critic, just as art is the artist, and James reminds critics that
it was 'assuredly the artist who invented art and the critic who
invented criticism, and not the other way round'.

The best kind of criticism, James held, derived from the liveliest experience. The critic deals with life at second-hand as well as
at first. He deals with the experience of others which he resolves
into his own, he is concerned with the 'uncompromising swarm
of authors, the clamorous children of history'. And what should
emerge from his pen finally is a portrait, 'a text preserved by translation'. ('To criticize', James was to write some years later, 'is to
appreciate, to appropriate, to take intellectual possession, to establish in fine a relation with the criticized thing and make it one's
own.')

The statement is admirable, in the quality of its feeling and its
perception; and we must read it as the declaration of an individual
whose primary concern was the novel. James gives to the critic a
role at once significant and humble, percipient and modest, and
accords him stature as a creative being who must, however, take

his materials from another's text. The casual reader, nevertheless, may find James lacking in explicitness. Brave words, he might say, sentience and restlessness, reaction and penetration, but *how* is this done, by what rule of thumb is the critic of fiction to work? James's description of criticism suggests a high degree of subjectivity, it is hardly 'practical', it seems almost anarchistic. 'Henry was not a literary critic' for men like Eliot probably because he refused to divorce criticism from the critic and art from the artist. He refused because he believed that it is impossible to depersonalize the novel. Novels are not artifacts, like the vases of timeless civilizations, beautiful in their impersonal mystery, but are part of some original mind and consciousness, and tied by a thousand threads to the world in which they came into being. These threads in turn bind them to the reader, or to the critic, who is a more saturated and experienced reader.

Every novelist significant enough for critical discussion accordingly becomes for James a 'given case', and the reader of the essays in this volume can discover for himself how often the word 'case' is used. 'The great feast-days of all, for the restless critic', he explains, 'are those much interspaced occasions of his really meeting a "case" as he soon enough learns to call, for his convenience and assistance, any supremely contributive or determinant party to the critical question. These are recognitions that make up for many dull hours and dry contacts, many a thankless, a disconcerted gaze into faces that have proved expressionless.'

James's 'cases' are usually supreme instances, individuals who have yielded him something more than is to be found in any work-a-day novelist. And 'the critic is intelligent in proportion as he enters into that case', for 'a case is poor when the cluster of the artist's sensibilities is small'. Flaubert is 'the example and the image' of 'the intellectual case'; Zola's case is a personality that 'finely pervades and prevails'. Maupassant's case is a salient one because he writes from a direct and bold communication with his senses. James speaks almost as if he were a physician who will diagnose but not prescribe; and what he seeks, in his diagnosis, through the medium of the style and texture of the work, is the novelist's unique temperament, the range of his vision, the operation of his sensibilities, as James puts it 'the colour of the air with which this, that or the other painter of life . . . more or less unconsciously suffuses his picture'. One of the most beautiful passages in this sense is to be found in James's great lecture on Balzac, too little read in recent years, and now published for the first time on the European side of the Atlantic:

Why is it that the life that overflows in Dickens seems to me always to go on in the morning, or in the very earliest hours of the afternoon at most, and in a vast apartment that appears to have windows, large, uncurtained, and rather unwashed windows, on all sides at once? Why is it that in George Eliot the sun sinks forever to the west, and the shadows are long, and the afternoon wanes, and the trees vaguely rustle, and the colour of the day is much inclined to yellow? Why is it that in Charlotte Brontë we move through an endless autumn? Why is it that in Jane Austen we sit quite resigned in an arrested spring? Why does Hawthorne give us the afternoon hour later than any one else? — oh, late, late, quite uncannily late, and as if it were always winter outside?

This is exquisite and it is to be read in an exquisite context. It illustrates to the full what James meant when he spoke of the critic saturating himself in his medium and then finding expression 'as embracing as the air'.

To read fiction in this way is to study the novelist himself, to capture the very atmosphere of his inner being. In doing this James was at one with Sainte-Beuve, who argued that he found it difficult to judge a work 'independently of my knowledge of the man himself'. *Tel arbre, tel fruit.* Literary study, said Sainte-Beuve, led him quite naturally to the study of the mind. For 'mind' James substituted 'consciousness'. And at the same time he was extremely careful to distinguish between biographical knowledge and the material to be found below the surface of personality. 'In our opinion', James remarked, 'the life and the works are two very different matters, and an intimate knowledge of the one is not at all necessary for the genial enjoyment of the other. A writer who gives us his works is not obliged to throw his life after them. . . .' This seems indeed a rejection of Sainte-Beuve until we see the wry way in which James ended his sentence '. . . as is very apt to be assumed by persons who fail to perceive that one of the most interesting pursuits in the world is to read between the lines of the best literature.'

To this interesting pursuit Henry James was addicted all his life. There were grave risks, of course. It was all too easy for an imaginative critic to read many of his own fancies between the lines of another's work. One can learn much, however, by watching Henry James as he carries out this process in his essays on Flaubert and Zola, Maupassant and Trollope, Balzac and Hawthorne. James never makes the error of trying to read the writer's life out of the work, for it is not biography that he is seeking. 'Between the lines' there were matters far more important: the way in which the artist experienced life and people, the things he looked at closely and the things he turned away from; the situations he predicated in his novels, and how he resolved them; the moral values he drew from his experience. A remark James once made about the dramatist, Victorien Sardou, clearly illustrates what he sought 'between the lines' of a literary work. 'I can think of no writer of equal talent who put so little of himself into his writing,' James wrote. 'Search M. Sardou's plays through and you will not find a trace of personal conviction, of a moral emotion, of an intellectual temperament, of anything that makes the "atmosphere" of the work.' This was the sense in which art was the artist, and James's search for uniqueness was a search for the temperament and the 'atmosphere' of the given creative consciousness. Obviously so mechanical a creator as Sardou could show only cleverness and competence.

In other words James was concerned, in his criticism, with that part of the writer's creativity which reflected the imagination in action, which showed the tissuing together of things felt and things seen, the reflection of the artist's inner self. It was a psychological process. James wrote:

If psychology be hidden in life, as, according to M. de Maupassant, it should be in a book, the question immediately comes up, 'From whom is it hidden?' From some people, no doubt, but very much less from others; and all depends upon the observer, the nature of one's observation, and one's curiosity. For some people motives, reasons, relations, explanations, are a part of the very surface of the drama, with the foot-lights beating full upon them. For me an act, an incident, an attitude, may be a sharp, detached, isolated thing, of which I give a full account in saying that in such and such a way it came off. For you it may be hung about with implications, with relations and conditions as neces-sary to help you to recognize it as the clothes of your friends are to help you know them in the street. You feel that they would seem strange to you without petticoats and trousers.

James's essays on novelists are, in effect, essays in psychological observation and deduction. He is always concerned with implica-tions, relations, conditions and, like Balzac, with 'the other side of the tapestry'. 'The deepest quality of a work of art will always be the quality of the mind of the producer. In proportion as that intelligence is fine will the novel, the picture, the statue partake of the substance of beauty and truth. . . . No good novel will ever proceed from a superficial mind.' Or he turns it around: 'Tell me what the artist is, and I will tell you of what he has *been* conscious.

The true novelist's pen is thus a tell-tale pen, revelatory even when it takes on the multiple disguises of fiction. Indeed, the very character of the disguise reveals rather than conceals the creating consciousness. If the critic clings long enough to Proteus, he will ultimately discover the face behind the masks. The key to any given 'case' permits James to search for the 'signs and marks of the possible precious identity'. The word 'identity' like the word 'case' belongs to James's private lexicon of critical terms. If we push hard enough we can, in watching James, discover the identi-ties of other writers, gain insight into his identity as well, for while he reads between the lines of others we can discover *his* literary convictions, *his* critical standards, *his* aesthetic of the novel. We are present, so to speak, at the meeting of two con-sciousnesses, the novelist's and the critic's, and if we wish to pursue this mirror-dance we may note also that our own con-sciousness has entered upon the scene as a third party. I suppose this is what James meant, when late in life he began to speak — having long ago learned the lesson of Balzac — of 'the chemistry of criticism'.

The rationale of selection I have exercised in this volume may seem arbitrary to readers familiar with the Jamesian critical canon. Certain compromises had to be made, given the amount of material available and the fact that James's criticism was written, always, to meet the needs of the magazines. I would have liked to have a Jamesian essay on Dickens or Thackeray, on Miss Austen or the Brontës: however he wrote no essays on these writers. For Thackeray we would have to content ourselves with a late paper on *Denis Duval* and Rye, inadequate for our purposes; and for Dickens I have had to be satisfied with an early review of *Our Mutual Friend*, however much one would have preferred a review of *David Copperfield*. There was, fortunately, a review of *Middle-march*, but one is at a loss if he seeks to find in James an essay as focused and balanced on the English George as those he consecrated to the trans-Channel George, the friend of Musset and Chopin. The truth was that James wrote no essays on the English novelists comparable to those he wrote on the French, and this because he was, essentially, an interpreter of French literature to his English and American readers. There was, practically speaking, a better market in the periodicals for his French pieces; and then, too, he was drawn to the French interest in questions of art, form, manner, all that goes into their use of the word *métier*.

So too one would have liked to find essays by James on Tolstoy and Dostoievsky explaining in greater detail why he considered them to be 'fluid puddings' and poor models for writers seeking to learn the art of fiction. The best I was able to do was to exhume an essay, published in an old American anthology, giving a sketch of Turgenev and containing certain paragraphs on Tolstoy. That I have not included the splendid and moving commemorative essay on Turgenev of 1884 may strike some readers as strange; however this essay is personal and autobiographical, rather than critical, and I reserve it for a collection of James's literary 'portraits', where it would readily occupy first place.

Concerning Balzac there are no less than half a dozen essays to choose from. I have reprinted the American lecture because of the felicitous passages it contains concerning the English novelists, and because that lecture, admirable in its utterance and in its implications, was never published by James in England.

These essays, it can be seen, are offered therefore neither as 'representative', nor necessarily as 'among the best', although many of them could be so qualified. They are writings, however, which show James at large in his 'House of Fiction', pondering novels and novelists, seeking to place himself at their particular windows and to glimpse the world through their eyes. It is something to conjure with that a young novelist, emerging from the New World after the American Civil War — a world which had produced then only a Hawthorne and the unread Melville among truly great novelists — discovered in the Old World the novel at its moment of greatness, and asked the novelists to give an account of themselves. He did this without presumption; he was the scientific inquirer, the tireless searcher. No writer so authoritative was ever less doctrinaire. Henry James speaks to us eloquently, even today (when the novel has moved so much farther into the future he imagined for it in his 1900 essay), defining himself and the craft he so loyally practised. Long ago Percy Lubbock said of him that he was 'the only real *scholar* in the art' of fiction. The truth of this has been demonstrated not only in the pervading influence James has had in our century's discussion of fiction, but in the extent to which we have borrowed, for this purpose, most of his critical terminology.

LEON EDEL

New York University

PART ONE

The House of Fiction

THE ART OF FICTION

1884

I SHOULD not have affixed so comprehensive a title to these few remarks, necessarily wanting in any completeness upon a subject the full consideration of which would carry us far, did I not seem to discover a pretext for my temerity in the interesting pamphlet lately published under this name by Mr Walter Besant. Mr Besant's lecture at the Royal Institution[1] — the original form of his pamphlet — appears to indicate that many persons are interested in the art of fiction, and are not indifferent to such remarks, as those who practice it may attempt to make about it. I am therefore anxious not to lose the benefit of this favourable association, and to edge in a few words under cover of the attention which Mr Besant is sure to have excited. There is something very encouraging in his having put into form certain of his ideas on the mystery of story-telling.

It is a proof of life and curiosity — curiosity on the part of the brotherhood of novelists as well as on the part of their readers. Only a short time ago it might have been supposed that the English novel was not what the French call *discutable*. It had no air of having a theory, a conviction, a consciousness of itself behind it — of being the expression of an artistic faith, the result of choice and comparison. I do not say it was necessarily the worse for that: it would take much more courage than I possess to intimate that the form of the novel as Dickens and Thackeray (for instance) saw it had any taint of incompleteness. It was, however, *naïf* (if I may help myself out with another French word); and evidently if it be destined to suffer in any way for having lost its *naïveté* it has now an idea of making sure of the corresponding advantages.

[1] Walter Besant (1836–1901), Victorian novelist and historian, delivered the lecture at the Royal Institution 25 April 1884.

During the period I have alluded to there was a comfortable, good-humoured feeling abroad that a novel is a novel, as a pudding is a pudding, and that our only business with it could be to swallow it. But within a year or two, for some reason or other, there have been signs of returning animation — the era of discussion would appear to have been to a certain extent opened. Art lives upon discussion, upon experiment, upon curiosity, upon variety of attempt, upon the exchange of views and the comparison of standpoints; and there is a presumption that those times when no one has anything particular to say about it, and has no reason to give for practice or preference, though they may be times of honour, are not times of development — are times, possibly even, a little of dullness. The successful application of any art is a delightful spectacle, but the theory too is interesting; and though there is a great deal of the latter without the former I suspect there has never been a genuine success that has not had a latent core of conviction. Discussion, suggestion, formulation, these things are fertilizing when they are frank and sincere. Mr Besant has set an excellent example in saying what he thinks, for his part, about the way in which fiction should be written, as well as about the way in which it should be published; for his view of the 'art', carried on into an appendix, covers that too. Other labourers in the same field will doubtless take up the argument, they will give it the light of their experience, and the effect will surely be to make our interest in the novel a little more what it had for some time threatened to fail to be — a serious, active, inquiring interest, under protection of which this delightful study may, in moments of confidence, venture to say a little more what it thinks of itself.

It must take itself seriously for the public to take it so. The old superstition about fiction being 'wicked' has doubtless died out in England; but the spirit of it lingers in a certain oblique regard directed toward any story which does not more or less admit that it is only a joke. Even the most jocular novel feels in some degree the weight of the proscription that was formerly directed against literary levity: the jocularity does not always succeed in passing for orthodoxy. It is still expected, though perhaps people are ashamed to say it, that a production which is after all only a 'make believe' (for what else is a 'story'?) shall be in some degree apologetic — shall renounce the pretension of attempting really to represent life. This, of course, any sensible, wide-awake story declines to do, for it quickly perceives that the tolerance granted to it on such a condition is only an attempt to stifle it disguised in the form of generosity. The old evangelical hostility to the novel, which was as explicit as it was narrow, and which regarded it as little less favourable to our immortal part than a stage-play, was in reality far less insulting. The only reason for the existence of a novel is that it does attempt to represent life. When it relinquishes this attempt, the same attempt that we see on the canvas of the painter, it will have arrived at a very strange pass. It is not expected of the picture that it will make itself humble in order to be forgiven; and the analogy between the art of the painter and the art of the novelist is, so far as I am able to see, complete. Their inspiration is the same, their process (allowing for the different quality of the vehicle), is the same, their success is the same. They may learn from each other, they may explain and sustain each other. Their cause is the same, and the honour of one is the honour of another. The Mahometans think a picture an unholy thing, but it is a long time since any Christian did, and it is therefore the more odd that in the Christian mind the traces (dissimulated though they may be) of a suspicion of the sister art should linger to this day. The only effectual way to lay it to rest is to emphasize the analogy to which I just alluded — to insist on the fact that as the picture is reality, so the novel is history. That is the only general description (which does it justice) that we may give of the novel. But history also is allowed to represent life; it is not, any more than painting, expected to apologize. The subject-matter of fiction is stored up likewise in documents and records, and if it will not give itself away, as they say in California, it must speak with assurance, with the tone of the historian. Certain accomplished novelists have a habit of giving themselves away which must often bring tears to the eyes of people who take their fiction seriously. I was lately struck, in reading over many pages of Anthony Trollope, with his want of discretion in this particular. In a digression, a parenthesis or an aside, he concedes to the reader that he and this trusting friend are only 'making believe'. He admits that the events he narrates have not really happened, and that he can give his narrative any turn the reader may like best. Such a betrayal of a sacred office seems to me, I confess, a terrible crime; it is what I mean by the attitude of apology, and it shocks me every whit as much in Trollope as it would have shocked me in Gibbon or Macaulay. It implies that the novelist is less occupied in looking for the truth (the truth, of course I mean, that he assumes, the premises that we grant him, whatever they may be) than the historian, and in doing so it deprives him at a stroke of all his standing room. To represent and illustrate the past, the actions of men, is the task of either writer, and the only difference that I can see is, in proportion as he succeeds, to the honour of the novelist, consisting as it does in his having more difficulty in collecting his evidence, which is so far from being purely literary. It seems to me to give him a great character, the fact that he has at once so much in common with the philosopher and the painter; this double analogy is a magnificent heritage.

It is of all this evidently that Mr Besant is full when he insists upon the fact that fiction is one of the *fine* arts, deserving in its turn of all the honours and emoluments that have hitherto been reserved for the successful profession of music, poetry, painting, architecture. It is impossible to insist too much on so important a truth, and the place that Mr Besant demands for the work of the novelist may be represented, a trifle less abstractly, by saying that he demands not only that it shall be reputed artistic, but that it shall be reputed very artistic indeed. It is excellent that he should have struck this note, for his doing so indicates that there was need of it, that his proposition may be to many people a novelty. One rubs one's eyes at the thought; but the rest of Mr Besant's essay confirms the revelation. I suspect in truth that it would be possible to confirm it still further, and that one would not be far wrong in saying that in addition to the people to whom it has

never occurred that a novel ought to be artistic, there are a great
many others who, if this principle were urged upon them, would
be filled with an indefinable mistrust. They would find it difficult
to explain their repugnance, but it would operate strongly to put
them on their guard. 'Art', in our Protestant communities, where
so many things have got so strangely twisted about, is supposed
in certain circles to have some vaguely injurious effect upon those
who make it an important consideration, who let it weigh in the
balance. It is assumed to be opposed in some mysterious manner
to morality, to amusement, to instruction. When it is embodied
in the work of the painter (the sculptor is another affair!) you
know what it is: it stands there before you, in the honesty of pink
and green and a gilt frame; you can see the worst of it at a glance,
and you can be on your guard. But when it is introduced into
literature it becomes more insidious — there is danger of its hurt-
ing you before you know it. Literature should be either instructive or amusing, and there is in many minds an impression that
these artistic preoccupations, the search for form, contribute to
neither end, interfere indeed with both. They are too frivolous to
be edifying, and too serious to be diverting; and they are moreover priggish and paradoxical and superfluous. That, I think,
represents the manner in which the latent thought of many people
who read novels as an exercise in skipping would explain itself if
it were to become articulate. They would argue, of course, that a
novel ought to be 'good', but they would interpret this term in a
fashion of their own, which indeed would vary considerably from
one critic to another. One would say that being good means
representing virtuous and aspiring characters, placed in prom-
inent positions; another would say that it depends on a 'happy
ending', on a distribution at the last of prizes, pensions, husbands,
wives, babies, millions, appended paragraphs, and cheerful
remarks. Another still would say that it means being full of incident and movement, so that we shall wish to jump ahead, to see
who was the mysterious stranger, and if the stolen will was ever
found, and shall not be distracted from this pleasure by any tiresome analysis or 'description'. But they would all agree that the

'artistic' idea would spoil some of their fun. One would hold it accountable for all the description, another would see it revealed in the absence of sympathy. Its hostility to a happy ending would be evident, and it might even in some cases render any ending at all impossible. The 'ending' of a novel is, for many persons, like that of a good dinner, a course of dessert and ices, and the artist in fiction is regarded as a sort of meddlesome doctor who forbids agreeable aftertastes. It is therefore true that this conception of Mr Besant's of the novel as a superior form encounters not only negative but a positive indifference. It matters little that as a work of art it should really be as little or as much of its essence to supply happy endings, sympathetic characters, and an objective tone, as if it were a work of mechanics: the association of ideas, however incongruous, might easily be too much for it if an eloquent voice were not sometimes raised to call attention to the fact that it is at once as free and as serious a branch of literature as any other.

Certainly this might sometimes be doubted in presence of the enormous number of works of fiction that appeal to the credulity of our generation, for it might easily seem that there could be no great character in a commodity so quickly and easily produced. It must be admitted that good novels are much compromised by bad ones, and that the field at large suffers discredit from over-crowding. I think, however, that this injury is only superficial, and that the superabundance of written fiction proves nothing against the principle itself. It has been vulgarized, like all other kinds of literature, like everything else today, and it has proved more than some kinds accessible to vulgarization. But there is as much difference as there ever was between a good novel and a bad one: the bad is swept with all the daubed canvases and spoiled marble into some unvisited limbo, or infinite rubbish-yard be-neath the back-windows of the world, and the good subsists and emits its light and stimulates our desire for perfection. As I shall take the liberty of making but a single criticism of Mr Besant, whose tone is so full of the love of his art, I may as well have done with it at once. He seems to me to mistake in attempting to say so definitely beforehand what sort of an affair the good novel will be. To indicate the danger of such an error as that has been the purpose of these few pages; to suggest that certain traditions on the subject, applied *a priori*, have already had much to answer for, and that the good health of an art which undertakes so immediately to reproduce life must demand that it be perfectly free. It lives upon exercise, and the very meaning of exercise is freedom. The only obligation to which in advance we may hold a novel, without incurring the accusation of being arbitrary, is that it be interesting. That general responsibility rests upon it, but it is the only one I can think of. The ways in which it is at liberty to accomplish this result (of interesting us) strike me as innumerable, and such as can only suffer from being marked out or fenced in by prescription. They are as various as the temperament of man, and they are successful in proportion as they reveal a particular mind, different from others. A novel is in its broadest definition a personal, a direct impression of life: that, to begin with, constitutes its value, which is greater or less according to the intensity of the impression. But there will be no intensity at all, and therefore no value, unless there is freedom to feel and say. The tracing of a line to be followed, of a tone to be taken, of a form to be filled out, is a limitation of that freedom and a suppression of the very thing that we are most curious about. The form, it seems to me, is to be appreciated after the fact: then the author's choice has been made, his standard has been indicated; then we can follow lines and directions and compare tones and resemblances. Then in a word we can enjoy one of the most charming of pleasures, we can estimate quality, we can apply the test of execution. The execution belongs to the author alone; it is what is most personal to him, and we measure him by that. The advantage, the luxury, as well as the torment and responsibility of the novelist, is that there is no limit to what he may attempt as an executant — no limit to his possible experiments, efforts, discoveries, successes. Here it is especially that he works, step by step, like his brother of the brush, of whom we may always say that he has painted his picture in a manner best known to himself. His manner is his secret, not necessarily a jealous one. He cannot disclose it as a general thing if he would; he would be at a loss to teach it to others. I say this with a due recollection of having insisted on the community of method of the artist who paints a picture and the artist who writes a novel. The painter *is* able to teach the rudiments of his practice, and it is possible, from the study of good work (granted the aptitude), both to learn how to paint and to learn how to write. Yet it remains true, without injury to the *rapprochement,* that the literary artist would be obliged to say to his pupil much more than the other, 'Ah, well, you must do it as you can!' It is a question of degree, a matter of delicacy. If there are exact sciences, there are also exact arts, and the grammar of painting is so much more definite that it makes the difference.

I ought to add, however, that if Mr Besant says at the beginning of his essay that the 'laws of fiction may be laid down and taught with as much precision and exactness as the laws of harmony, perspective, and proportion', he mitigates what might appear to be an extravagance by applying his remark to 'general' laws, and by expressing most of these rules in a manner with which it would certainly be unaccommodating to disagree. That the novelist must write from his experience, that his 'characters must be real and such as might be met with in actual life'; that 'a young lady brought up in a quiet country village should avoid descriptions of garrison life', and 'a writer whose friends and personal experiences belong to the lower middle-class should carefully avoid introducing his characters into society'; that one should enter one's notes in a common-place book; that one's figures should be clear in outline; that making them clear by some trick of speech or of carriage is a bad method, and 'describing them at length' is a worse one; that English Fiction should have a 'conscious moral purpose'; that 'it is almost impossible to estimate too highly the value of careful workmanship — that is, of style'; that 'the most important point of all is the story', that 'the story is everything': these are principles with most of which it is surely impossible not to sympathize. That remark about the lower middle-class writer and his knowing his place is perhaps rather chilling;

but for the rest I should find it difficult to dissent from any one of these recommendations. At the same time, I should find it difficult positively to assent to them, with the exception, perhaps, of the injunction as to entering one's notes in a common-place book. They scarcely seem to me to have the quality that Mr Besant attributes to the rules of the novelist — the 'precision and exactness' of 'the laws of harmony, perspective, and proportion'. They are suggestive, they are even inspiring, but they are not exact, though they are doubtless as much so as the case admits of: which is a proof of that liberty of interpretation for which I just contended. For the value of these different injunctions — so beautiful and so vague — is wholly in the meaning one attaches to them. The characters, the situation, which strike one as real will be those that touch and interest one most, but the measure of reality is very difficult to fix. The reality of Don Quixote or of Mr Micawber is a very delicate shade; it is a reality so coloured by the author's vision that, vivid as it may be, one would hesitate to propose it as a model: one would expose one's self to some very embarrassing questions on the part of a pupil. It goes without saying that you will not write a good novel unless you possess the sense of reality; but it will be difficult to give you a recipe for calling that sense into being. Humanity is immense, and reality has a myriad forms; the most one can affirm is that some of the flowers of fiction have the odour of it, and others have not; as for telling you in advance how your nosegay should be composed, that is another affair. It is equally excellent and inconclusive to say that one must write from experience; to our supposititious aspirant such a declaration might savour of mockery. What kind of experience is intended, and where does it begin and end? Experience is never limited, and it is never complete; it is an immense sensibility, a kind of huge spider-web of the finest silken threads suspended in the chamber of consciousness, and catching every air-borne particle in its tissue. It is the very atmosphere of the mind; and when the mind is imaginative — much more when it happens to be that of a man of genius — it takes to itself the faintest hints of life, it converts the very pulses of the air into revelations. The young lady living in a village has only to be a damsel upon whom nothing is lost to make it quite unfair (as it seems to me) to declare to her that she shall have nothing to say about the military. Greater miracles have been seen than that, imagination assisting, she should speak the truth about some of these gentlemen. I remember an English novelist, a woman of genius,[1] telling me that she was much commended for the impression she had managed to give in one of her tales of the nature and way of life of the French Protestant youth. She had been asked where she learned so much about this recondite being, she had been congratulated on her peculiar opportunities. These opportunities consisted in her having once, in Paris, as she ascended a staircase, passed an open door where, in the household of a *pasteur*, some of the young Protestants were seated at table round a finished meal. The glimpse made a picture; it lasted only a moment, but that moment was experience. She had got her direct personal impression, and she turned out her type. She knew what youth was, and what Protestantism; she also had the advantage of having seen what it was to be French, so that she converted these ideas into a concrete image and produced a reality. Above all, however, she was blessed with the faculty which when you give it an inch takes an ell, and which for the artist is a much greater source of strength than any accident of residence or of place in the social scale. The power to guess the unseen from the seen, to trace the implication of things, to judge the whole piece by the pattern, the condition of feeling life in general so completely that you are well on your way to knowing any particular corner of it — this cluster of gifts may almost be said to constitute experience, and they occur in country and in town, and in the most differing stages of education. If experience consists of impressions, it may be said that impressions *are* experience, just as (have we not seen it?) they are the very air we breathe. Therefore, if I should certainly say to a novice, 'Write from experience and experience only,' I should feel that this was

[1] Probably Anne Thackeray, Lady Ritchie, daughter of Thackeray, whose first novel *The Story of Elizabeth* corresponds to James's description.

rather a tantalizing monition if I were not careful immediately to add, 'Try to be one of the people on whom nothing is lost!'

I am far from intending by this to minimize the importance of exactness — of truth of detail. One can speak best from one's own taste, and I may therefore venture to say that the air of reality (solidity of specification) seems to me to be the supreme virtue of a novel — the merit on which all its other merits (including that conscious moral purpose of which Mr Besant speaks) helplessly and submissively depend. If it be not there they are all as nothing, and if these be there, they owe their effect to the success with which the author has produced the illusion of life. The cultivation of this success, the study of this exquisite process, form, to my taste, the beginning and the end of the art of the novelist. They are his inspiration, his despair, his reward, his torment, his delight. It is here in very truth that he competes with life; it is here that he competes with his brother the painter in *his* attempt to render the look of things, the look that conveys their meaning, to catch the colour, the relief, the expression, the surface, the substance of the human spectacle. It is in regard to this that Mr Besant is well in-spired when he bids him take notes. He cannot possibly take too many, he cannot possibly take enough. All life solicits him, and to 'render' the simplest surface, to produce the most momentary illusion, is a very complicated business. His case would be easier, and the rule would be more exact, if Mr Besant had been able to tell him what notes to take. But this, I fear, he can never learn in any manual; it is the business of his life. He has to take a great many in order to select a few, he has to work them up as he can, and even the guides and philosophers who might have most to say to him must leave him alone when it comes to the application of precepts, as we leave the painter in communion with his palette. That his characters 'must be clear in outline', as Mr Besant says — he feels that down to his boots; but how he shall make them so is a secret between his good angel and himself. It would be absurdly simple if he could be taught that a great deal of 'description' would make them so, or that on the contrary the absence of de-scription and the cultivation of dialogue, or the absence of dialogue and the multiplication of 'incident', would rescue him from his difficulties. Nothing, for instance, is more possible than that he be of a turn of mind for which this odd, literal opposition of description and dialogue, incident and description, has little meaning and light. People often talk of these things as if they had a kind of internecine distinctness, instead of melting into each other at every breath, and being intimately associated parts of one general effort of expression. I cannot imagine composition existing in a series of blocks, nor conceive, in any novel worth discussing at all, of a passage of description that is not in its intention narrative, a passage of dialogue that is not in its intention descriptive, a touch of truth of any sort that does not partake of the nature of incident, or an incident that derives its interest from any other source than the general and only source of the success of a work of art — that of being illustrative. A novel is a living thing, all one and continuous, like any other organism, and in proportion as it lives will it be found, I think, that in each of the parts there is something of each of the other parts. The critic who over the close texture of a finished work shall pretend to trace a geography of items will mark some frontiers as artificial, I fear, as any that have been known to history. There is an old-fashioned distinction between the novel of character and the novel of incident which must have cost many a smile to the intending fabulist who was keen about his work. It appears to me as little to the point as the equally celebrated distinction between the novel and the romance — to answer as little to any reality. There are bad novels and good novels, as there are bad pictures and good pictures; but that is the only distinction in which I see any meaning, and I can as little imagine speaking of a novel of character as I can imagine speaking of a picture of character. When one says picture one says of character, when one says novel one says of incident, and the terms may be transposed at will. What is character but the determination of incident? What is incident but the illustration of character? What is either a picture or a novel that is *not* of character? What else do we seek in it and find in it? It is an incident for a woman to stand up with her hand resting on a table and look out at you in a certain way; or if it be not an incident I think it will be hard to say what it is. At the same time it is an expression of character. If you say you don't see it (character in *that — allons donc!*), this is exactly what the artist who has reasons of his own for thinking he *does* see it undertakes to show you. When a young man makes up his mind that he has not faith enough after all to enter the church as he intended, that is an incident, though you may not hurry to the end of the chapter to see whether perhaps he doesn't change once more. I do not say that these are extraordinary or startling incidents. I do not pretend to estimate the degree of interest proceeding from them, for this will depend upon the skill of the painter. It sounds almost puerile to say that some incidents are intrinsically much more important than others, and I need not take this precaution after having professed my sympathy for the major ones in remarking that the only classification of the novel that I can understand is into that which has life and that which has it not.

The novel and the romance, the novel of incident and that of character — these clumsy separations appear to me to have been made by critics and readers for their own convenience, and to help them out of some of their occasional queer predicaments, but to have little reality or interest for the producer, from whose point of view it is of course that we are attempting to consider the art of fiction. The case is the same with another shadowy category which Mr Besant apparently is disposed to set up — that of the 'modern English novel'; unless indeed it be that in this matter he has fallen into an accidental confusion of standpoints. It is not quite clear whether he intends the remarks in which he alludes to it to be didactic or historical. It is as difficult to suppose a person intending to write a modern English as to suppose him writing an ancient English novel: that is a label which begs the question. One writes the novel, one paints the picture, of one's language and of one's time, and calling it modern English will not, alas! make the difficult task any easier. No more, unfortunately, will calling this or that work of one's fellow-artist a romance — unless it be, of course, simply for the pleasantness of the thing, as for instance when Hawthorne gave this heading to his story of *Blithedale*. The French, who have brought the theory of fiction to remarkable completeness, have but one name for the novel, and have not attempted smaller things in it, that I can see, for that. I can think of no obligation to which the 'romancer' would not be held equally with the novelist; the standard of execution is equally high for each. Of course it is of execution that we are talking — that being the only point of a novel that is open to contention. This is perhaps too often lost sight of, only to produce interminable confusions and cross-purposes. We must grant the artist his subject, his idea, his *donnée*: our criticism is applied only to what he makes of it. Naturally I do not mean that we are bound to like it or find it interesting: in case we do not our course is perfectly simple — to let it alone. We may believe that of a certain idea even the most sincere novelist can make nothing at all, and the event may perfectly justify our belief; but the failure will have been a failure to execute, and it is in the execution that the fatal weakness is recorded. If we pretend to respect the artist at all, we must allow him his freedom of choice, in the face, in particular cases, of innumerable presumptions that the choice will not fructify. Art derives a considerable part of its beneficial exercise from flying in the face of presumptions, and some of the most interesting experiments of which it is capable are hidden in the bosom of common things. Gustave Flaubert has written a story[1] about the devotion of a servant-girl to a parrot, and the production, highly finished as it is, cannot on the whole be called a success. We are perfectly free to find it flat, but I think it might have been interesting; and I, for my part, am extremely glad he should have written it; it is a contribution to our knowledge of what can be done — or what cannot. Ivan Turgenev has written a tale about a deaf and dumb serf and a lap-dog,[2] and the thing is touching, loving, a little masterpiece. He struck the note of life where Gustave Flaubert missed it — he flew in the face of a presumption and achieved a victory.

[1] *Un coeur simple.*
[2] *Mumu.*

Nothing, of course, will ever take the place of the good old fashion of 'liking' a work of art or not liking it: the most improved criticism will not abolish that primitive, that ultimate test. I mention this to guard myself from the accusation of intimating that the idea, the subject, of a novel or a picture, does not matter. It matters, to my sense, in the highest degree, and if I might put up a prayer it would be that artists should select none but the richest. Some, as I have already hastened to admit, are much more remunerative than others, and it would be a world happily arranged in which persons intending to treat them should be exempt from confusions and mistakes. This fortunate condition will arrive only, I fear, on the same day that critics become purged from error. Meanwhile, I repeat, we do not judge the artist with fairness unless we say to him,

Oh, I grant you your starting-point, because if I did not I should seem to prescribe to you, and heaven forbid I should take that responsibility. If I pretend to tell you what you must not take, you will call upon me to tell you then what you must take; in which case I shall be prettily caught. Moreover, it isn't till I have accepted your data that I can begin to measure you. I have the standard, the pitch; I have no right to tamper with your flute and then criticize your music. Of course I may not care for your idea at all; I may think it silly, or stale, or unclean; in which case I wash my hands of you altogether. I may content myself with believing that you will not have succeeded in being interesting, but I shall, of course, not attempt to demonstrate it, and you will be as indifferent to me as I am to you. I needn't remind you that there are all sorts of tastes: who can know it better? Some people, for excellent reasons, don't like to read about carpenters; others, for reasons even better, don't like to read about courtesans. Many object to Americans. Others (I believe they are mainly editors and publishers) won't look at Italians. Some readers don't like quiet subjects; others don't like bustling ones. Some enjoy a complete illusion, others the consciousness of large concessions. They choose their novels accordingly, and if they don't care about your idea they won't, *a fortiori*, care about your treatment.

So that it comes back very quickly, as I have said, to the liking: in spite of M. Zola, who reasons less powerfully than he represents, and who will not reconcile himself to this absoluteness of

taste, thinking that there are certain things that people ought to
like, and that they can be made to like. I am quite at a loss to
imagine anything (at any rate in this matter of fiction) that people
ought to like or to dislike. Selection will be sure to take care of
itself, for it has a constant motive behind it. That motive is simply
experience. As people feel life, so they will feel the art that is most
closely related to it. This closeness of relation is what we should
never forget in talking of the effort of the novel. Many people
speak of it as a factitious, artificial form, a product of ingenuity,
the business of which is to alter and arrange the things that surround us, to translate them into conventional, traditional moulds.
This, however, is a view of the matter which carries us but a very
short way, condemns the art to an eternal repetition of a few
familiar *clichés*, cuts short its development, and leads us straight
up to a dead wall. Catching the very note and trick, the strange ir-
regular rhythm of life, that is the attempt whose strenuous force
keeps Fiction upon her feet. In proportion as in what she offers
us we see life *without* rearrangement do we feel that we are touching the truth; in proportion as we see it *with* rearrangement do we
feel that we are being put off with a substitute, a compromise and
convention. It is not uncommon to hear an extraordinary assurance of remark in regard to this matter of rearranging, which is
often spoken of as if it were the last word of art. Mr Besant seems
to me in danger of falling into the great error with his rather un-
guarded talk about 'selection'. Art is essentially selection, but it is
a selection whose main care is to be typical, to be inclusive. For
many people art means rose-coloured window-panes, and selection means picking a bouquet for Mrs Grundy. They will tell you
glibly that artistic considerations have nothing to do with the disagreeable, with the ugly; they will rattle off shallow commonplaces about the province of art and the limits of art till you are
moved to some wonder in return as to the province and the limits
of ignorance. It appears to me that no one can ever have made a
seriously artistic attempt without becoming conscious of an immense increase — a kind of revelation — of freedom. One perceives in that case — by the light of a heavenly ray — that the

province of art is all life, all feeling, all observation, all vision. As Mr Besant so justly intimates, it is all experience. That is a sufficient answer to those who maintain that it must not touch the sad things of life, who stick into its divine unconscious bosom little prohibitory inscriptions on the end of sticks, such as we see in public gardens — 'It is forbidden to walk on the grass; it is forbidden to touch the flowers; it is not allowed to introduce dogs or to remain after dark; it is requested to keep to the right.' The young aspirant in the line of fiction whom we continue to imagine will do nothing without taste, for in that case his freedom would be of little use to him; but the first advantage of his taste will be to reveal to him the absurdity of the little sticks and tickets. If he have taste, I must add, of course he will have ingenuity, and my disrespectful reference to that quality just now was not meant to imply that it is useless in fiction. But it is only a secondary aid; the first is a capacity for receiving straight impressions.

Mr Besant has some remarks on the question of 'the story' which I shall not attempt to criticise, though they seem to me to contain a singular ambiguity, because I do not think I understand them. I cannot see what is meant by talking as if there were a part of a novel which is the story and part of it which for mystical reasons is not — unless indeed the distinction be made in a sense in which it is difficult to suppose that any one should attempt to convey anything. 'The story', if it represents anything, represents the subject, the idea, the *donnée* of the novel; and there is surely no 'school' — Mr Besant speaks of a school — which urges that a novel should be all treatment and no subject. There must assuredly be something to treat; every school is intimately conscious of that. This sense of the story being the idea, the starting-point, of the novel, is the only one that I see in which it can be spoken of as something different from its organic whole; and since in proportion as the work is successful the idea permeates and penetrates it, informs and animates it, so that every word and every punctuation-point contribute directly to the expression, in that proportion do we lose our sense of the story being a blade which may be drawn more or less out of its sheath. The story and the novel, the

idea and the form, are the needle and thread, and I never heard of
a guild of tailors who recommended the use of the thread without
the needle, or the needle without the thread. Mr Besant is not the
only critic who may be observed to have spoken as if there were
certain things in life which constitute stories, and certain others
which do not. I find the same odd implication in an entertaining
article in the *Pall Mall Gazette*, devoted, as it happens, to Mr
Besant's lecture. 'The story is the thing!' says this graceful writer,
as if with a tone of opposition to some other idea. I should think
it was, as every painter who, as the time for 'sending in' his picture looms in the distance, finds himself still in quest of a subject
— as every belated artist not fixed about his theme will heartily
agree. There are some subjects which speak to us and others
which do not, but he would be a clever man who should undertake to give a rule — an *index expurgatorius* — by which the story
and the no-story should be known apart. It is impossible (to me
at least) to imagine any such rule which shall not be altogether
arbitrary. The writer in the *Pall Mall* opposes the delightful (as I
suppose) novel of *Margot la Balafrée* to certain tales in which
'Bostonian nymphs' appear to have 'rejected English dukes for
psychological reasons'. I am not acquainted with the romance
just designated, and can scarcely forgive the *Pall Mall* critic for
not mentioning the name of the author,[1] but the title appears to
refer to a lady who may have received a scar in some heroic adventure. I am inconsolable at not being acquainted with this episode, but am utterly at a loss to see why it is a story when the
rejection (or acceptance) of a duke is not, and why a reason,
psychological or other, is not a subject when a cicatrix is. They
are all particles of the multitudinous life with which the novel
deals, and surely no dogma which pretends to make it lawful to
touch the one and unlawful to touch the other will stand for a
moment on its feet. It is the special picture that must stand or fall,
according as it seems to possess truth or to lack it. Mr Besant does
not, to my sense, light up the subject by intimating that a story

[1] The author, fairly obviously, is James himself, and the story alluded to
clearly *An International Episode* (1879).

must, under penalty of not being a story, consist of 'adventures'. Why of adventures more than of green spectacles? He mentions a category of impossible things, and among them he places 'fiction without adventure'. Why without adventure, more than without matrimony, or celibacy, or parturition, or cholera, or hydropathy, or Jansenism? This seems to me to bring the novel back to the hapless little *rôle* of being an artificial, ingenious thing — bring it down from its large, free character of an immense and exquisite correspondence with life. And what *is* adventure, when it comes to that, and by what sign is the listening pupil to recognize it? It is an adventure — an immense one — for me to write this little article; and for a Bostonian nymph to reject an English duke is an adventure only less stirring, I should say, than for an English duke to be rejected by a Bostonian nymph. I see dramas within dramas in that, and innumerable points of view. A psychological reason is, to my imagination, an object adorably pictorial; to catch the tint of its complexion — I feel as if that idea might inspire one to Titianesque efforts. There are few things more exciting to me, in short, than a psychological reason, and yet, I protest, the novel seems to me the most magnificent form of art. I have just been reading, at the same time, the delightful story of *Treasure Island*, by Mr Robert Louis Stevenson and, in a manner less consecutive, the last tale from M. Edmond de Goncourt, which is entitled *Chérie*. One of these works treats of murders, mysteries, islands of dreadful renown, hairbreadth escapes, miraculous coincidences and buried doubloons. The other treats of a little French girl who lived in a fine house in Paris, and died of wounded sensibility because no one would marry her. I call *Treasure Island* delightful, because it appears to me to have succeeded wonderfully in what it attempts; and I venture to bestow no epithet upon *Chérie*, which strikes me as having failed deplorably in what it attempts — that is in tracing the development of the moral consciousness of a child. But one of these productions strikes me as exactly as much of a novel as the other, and as having a 'story' quite as much. The moral consciousness of a child is as much a part of life as the islands of the Spanish Main, and the one

sort of geography seems to me to have those 'surprises' of which
Mr Besant speaks quite as much as the other. For myself (since it
comes back in the last resort, as I say, to the preference of the
individual), the picture of the child's experience has the advantage
that I can at successive steps (an immense luxury, near to the
'sensual pleasure' of which Mr Besant's critic in the *Pall Mall*
speaks) say Yes or No, as it may be, to what the artist puts before
me. I have been a child in fact, but I have been on a quest for a
buried treasure only in supposition, and it is a simple accident
that with M. de Goncourt I should have for the most part to say
No. With George Eliot, when she painted that country with a far
other intelligence, I always said Yes.

The most interesting part of Mr Besant's lecture is unfortunately the briefest passage — his very cursory allusion to the 'conscious moral purpose' of the novel. Here again it is not very clear
whether he be recording a fact or laying down a principle; it is a
great pity that in the latter case he should not have developed his
idea. This branch of the subject is of immense importance, and
Mr Besant's few words point to considerations of the widest
reach, not to be lightly disposed of. He will have treated the art
of fiction but superficially who is not prepared to go every inch
of the way that these considerations will carry him. It is for this
reason that at the beginning of these remarks I was careful to
notify the reader that my reflections on so large a theme have no
pretension to be exhaustive. Like Mr Besant, I have left the question of the morality of the novel till the last, and at the last I find
I have used up my space. It is a question surrounded with difficulties, as witness the very first that meets us, in the form of a
definite question, on the threshold. Vagueness, in such a discussion, is fatal, and what is the meaning of your morality and your
conscious moral purpose? Will you not define your terms and
explain how (a novel being a picture) a picture can be either moral
or immoral? You wish to paint a moral picture or carve a moral
statue: will you not tell us how you would set about it? We are
discussing the Art of Fiction; questions of art are questions (in
the widest sense) of execution; questions of morality are quite

another affair, and will you not let us see how it is that you find it so easy to mix them up? These things are so clear to Mr Besant that he has deduced from them a law which he sees embodied in English Fiction, and which is 'a truly admirable thing and a great cause for congratulation'. It is a great cause for congratulation indeed when such thorny problems become as smooth as silk. I may add that in so far as Mr Besant perceives that in point of fact English Fiction has addressed itself preponderantly to these delicate questions he will appear to many people to have made a vain discovery. They will have been positively struck, on the contrary, with the moral timidity of the usual English novelist; with his (or with her) aversion to face the difficulties with which on every side the treatment of reality bristles. He is apt to be extremely shy (whereas the picture that Mr Besant draws is a picture of boldness), and the sign of his work, for the most part, is a cautious silence on certain subjects. In the English novel (by which of course I mean the American as well), more than in any other, there is a traditional difference between that which people know and that which they agree to admit that they know, that which they see and that which they speak of, that which they feel to be a part of life and that which they allow to enter into literature. There is the great difference, in short, between what they talk of in conversation and what they talk of in print. The essence of moral energy is to survey the whole field, and I should directly reverse Mr Besant's remark and say not that the English novel has a purpose, but that it has a diffidence. To what degree a purpose in a work of art is a source of corruption I shall not attempt to inquire; the one that seems to me least dangerous is the purpose of making a perfect work. As for our novel, I may say lastly on this score that as we find it in England today it strikes me as addressed in a large degree to 'young people', and that this in itself constitutes a presumption that it will be rather shy. There are certain things which it is generally agreed not to discuss, not even to mention, before young people. That is very well, but the absence of discussion is not a symptom of the moral passion. The purpose of the English novel — 'a truly admirable thing, and a great cause for congratulation' — strikes me therefore as rather negative.

There is one point at which the moral sense and the artistic sense lie very near together; that is in the light of the very obvious truth that the deepest quality of a work of art will always be the quality of the mind of the producer. In proportion as that intelligence is fine will the novel, the picture, the statue partake of the substance of beauty and truth. To be constituted of such elements is, to my vision, to have purpose enough. No good novel will ever proceed from a superficial mind; that seems to me an axiom which, for the artist in fiction, will cover all needful moral ground: If the youthful aspirant take it to heart it will illuminate for him many of the mysteries of 'purpose'. There are many other useful things that might be said to him, but I have come to the end of my article, and can only touch them as I pass. The critic in the *Pall Mall Gazette*, whom I have already quoted, draws attention to the danger, in speaking of the art of fiction, of generalizing. The danger that he has in mind is rather, I imagine, that of particularizing, for there are some comprehensive remarks which, in addition to those embodied in Mr Besant's suggestive lecture, might without fear of misleading him be addressed to the ingenuous student. I should remind him first of the magnificence of the form that is open to him, which offers to sight so few restrictions and such innumerable opportunities. The other arts, in comparison, appear confined and hampered; the various conditions under which they are exercised are so rigid and definite. But the only condition that I can think of attaching to the composition of the novel is, as I have already said, that it be sincere. This freedom is a splendid privilege, and the first lesson of the young novelist is to learn to be worthy of it.

Enjoy it as it deserves [I should say to him]; take possession of it, explore it to its utmost extent, publish it, rejoice in it. All life belongs to you, and do not listen either to those who would shut you up into corners of it and tell you that it is only here and there that art inhabits, or to those who would persuade you that this heavenly messenger wings her way outside of life altogether, breathing a superfine air, and turning away her head from the truth of things. There is no impression of life, no manner of seeing it and feeling it, to which the plan of the novelist may not offer a place; you have only to remember that talents so dissimilar as those of Alexandre Dumas and Jane Austen, Charles Dickens and Gustave Flaubert have worked in this field with equal glory. Do not think too much about optimism and pessimism; try and catch the colour of life itself. In France today we see a prodigious effort (that of Émile Zola, to whose solid and serious work no explorer of the capacity of the novel can allude without respect), we see an extraordinary effort vitiated by a spirit of pessimism on a narrow basis. M. Zola is magnificent, but he strikes an English reader as ignorant; he has an air of working in the dark; if he had as much light as energy, his results would be of the highest value. As for the aberrations of a shallow optimism, the ground (of English fiction especially) is strewn with their brittle particles as with broken glass. If you must indulge in conclusions, let them have the taste of a wide knowledge. Remember that your first duty is to be as complete as possible — to make as perfect a work. Be generous and delicate and pursue the prize.

THE GREAT FORM

A LETTER TO THE DEERFIELD
SUMMER SCHOOL

[*Summer 1889*]

I am afraid I can do little more than thank you for your courteous invitation to be present at the sittings of your delightfully sounding school of romance,[1] which ought to inherit happiness and honour from such a name. I am so very far away from you that I am afraid I can't participate very intelligently in your discussions, but I can only give them the furtherance of a dimly discriminating sympathy. I am not sure that I apprehend very well your apparent premise, 'the materialism of our present tendencies,' and I suspect that this would require some clearing up before I should be able (if even then) to contribute any suggestive or helpful word. To tell the truth, I can't help thinking that we already talk too much about the novel, about and around it, in proportion to the quantity of it having any importance that we produce. What I should say to the nymphs and swains who propose to converse about it under the great trees at Deerfield is: 'Oh, do something from your point of view; an ounce of example is worth a ton of generalities; do something with the great art and the great form; do something with life. Any point of view is interesting that is a direct impression of life. You each have an impression coloured by your individual conditions; make that into a picture, a picture framed by your own personal wisdom, your glimpse of the American world. The field is vast for freedom, for study, for observation, for satire, for truth.' I don't think I really do know what you mean by 'materializing tendencies' any more than I should by 'spiritualizing' or 'etherealizing'. There are no tendencies worth

---

[1] During the summer of 1889 James was invited to attend the Summer School at Deerfield, Massachusetts for a discussion of the art of the novel. He sent, instead, the letter here given, which was read during the proceedings and later published in the New York *Tribune*, 4 August 1889.

anything but to see the actual or the imaginative, which is just as visible, and to paint it. I have only two little words for the matter remotely approaching to rule or doctrine; one is life and the other freedom. Tell the ladies and gentlemen, the ingenious inquirers, to consider life directly and closely, and not to be put off with mean and puerile falsities, and be conscientious about it. It is infinitely large, various and comprehensive. Every sort of mind will find what it looks for in it, whereby the novel becomes truly multifarious and illustrative. That is what I mean by liberty; give it its head and let it range. If it is in a bad way, and the English novel is, I think, nothing but absolute freedom can refresh it and restore its self-respect. Excuse these raw brevities and please convey to your companions, my dear sir, the cordial good wishes of yours and theirs,

Henry James

THE FUTURE OF THE NOVEL

BEGINNINGS, as we all know, are usually small things, but continuations are not always strikingly great ones, and the place occupied in the world by the prolonged prose fable has become, in our time, among the incidents of literature, the most surprising example to be named of swift and extravagant growth, a development beyond the measure of every early appearance. It is a form that has had a fortune so little to have been foretold at its cradle. The germ of the comprehensive epic was more recognizable in the first barbaric chant than that of the novel as we know it today in the first anecdote retailed to amuse. It arrived, in truth, the novel, late at self-consciousness; but it has done its utmost ever since to make up for lost opportunities. The flood at present swells and swells, threatening the whole field of letters, as would often seem, with submersion. It plays, in what may be called the passive consciousness of many persons, a part that directly marches with the rapid increase of the multitude able to possess itself in one way and another of the *book*. The book, in the Anglo-Saxon world, is almost everywhere, and it is in the form of the voluminous prose fable that we see it penetrate easiest and farthest. Penetration appears really to be directly aided by mere mass and bulk. There is an immense public, if public be the name, inarticulate, but abysmally absorbent, for which, at its hours of ease, the printed volume has no other association. This public — the public that subscribes, borrows, lends, that picks up in one way and another, sometimes even by purchase — grows and grows each year, and nothing is thus more apparent than that of all the recruits it brings to the book the most numerous by far are those that it brings to the 'story'.

This number has gained, in our time, an augmentation from three sources in particular, the first of which, indeed, is perhaps but a comprehensive name for the two others. The diffusion of the rudiments, the multiplication of common schools, has had more and more the effect of making readers of women and of the very young. Nothing is so striking in a survey of this field, and nothing to be so much borne in mind, as that the larger part of the great multitude that sustains the teller and the publisher of tales is constituted by boys and girls; by girls in especial, if we apply the term to the later stages of the life of the innumerable women who, under modern arrangements, increasingly fail to marry — fail, apparently, even, largely, to desire to. It is not too much to say of many of these that they live in a great measure by the immediate aid of the novel — confining the question, for the moment, to the fact of consumption alone. The literature, as it may be called for convenience, of children is an industry that occupies by itself a very considerable quarter of the scene. Great fortunes, if not great reputations, are made, we learn, by writing for schoolboys, and the period during which they consume the compound artfully prepared for them appears — as they begin earlier and continue later — to add to itself at both ends. This helps to account for the fact that public libraries, especially those that are private and money-making enterprises, put into circulation more volumes of 'stories' than of all other things together of which volumes can be made. The published statistics are extraordinary, and of a sort to engender many kinds of uneasiness. The sort of taste that used to be called 'good' has nothing to do with the matter: we are so demonstrably in presence of millions for whom taste is but an obscure, confused, immediate instinct. In the flare of railway book-stalls, in the shop-fronts of most booksellers, especially the provincial, in the advertisements of the weekly newspapers, and in fifty places besides, this testimony to the general preference triumphs, yielding a good-natured corner at most to a bunch of treatises on athletics or sport, or a patch of theology old and new.

The case is so marked, however, that illustrations easily over-flow, and there is no need of forcing doors that stand wide open. What remains is the interesting oddity or mystery — the anomaly that fairly dignifies the whole circumstance with its strangeness:

the wonder, in short, that men, women, and children *should* have so much attention to spare for improvisations mainly so arbitrary and frequently so loose. That, at the first blush, fairly leaves us gaping. This great fortune then, since fortune it seems, has been reserved for mere unsupported and unguaranteed history, the *inexpensive* thing, written in the air, the record of what, in any particular case, has *not* been, the account that remains responsible, at best, to 'documents' with which we are practically unable to collate it. This is the side of the whole business of fiction on which it can always be challenged, and to that degree that if the general venture had not become in such a manner the admiration of the world it might but too easily have become the derision. It has in truth, I think, never philosophically met the challenge, never found a formula to inscribe on its shield, never defended its position by any better argument than the frank, straight blow: 'Why am I not so unprofitable as to be preposterous? Because I can do *that*. There!' And it throws up from time to time some purely practical masterpiece. There is nevertheless an admirable minority of intelligent persons who care not even for the masterpieces, nor see any pressing point in them, for whom the very form itself has, equally at its best and at its worst, been ever a vanity and a mockery. This class, it should be added, is beginning to be visibly augmented by a different circle altogether, the group of the formerly subject, but now estranged, the deceived and bored, those for whom the whole movement too decidedly fails to live up to its possibilities. There are people who have loved the novel, but who actually find themselves drowned in its verbiage, and for whom, even in some of its approved manifestations, it has become a terror they exert every ingenuity, every hypocrisy, to evade. The indifferent and the alienated testify, at any rate, almost as much as the omnivorous, to the reign of the great ambiguity, the enjoyment of which rests, evidently, on a primary need of the mind. The novelist can only fall back on that — on his recognition that man's constant demand for what he has to offer is simply man's general appetite for a *picture*. The novel is of all pictures the most comprehensive and the most elastic. It will

stretch anywhere — it will take in absolutely anything. All it
needs is a subject and a painter. But for its subject, magnificently,
it has the whole human consciousness. And if we are pushed a step
farther backward, and asked why the representation should be required when the object represented is itself mostly so accessible,
the answer to that appears to be that man combines with his eternal desire for more experience an infinite cunning as to getting his
experience as cheaply as possible. He will steal it whenever he can.
He likes to live the life of others, yet is well aware of the points at
which it may too intolerably resemble his own. The vivid fable,
more than anything else, gives him this satisfaction on easy terms,
gives him knowledge abundant yet vicarious. It enables him to
select, to take and to leave; so that to feel he can afford to neglect
it he must have a rare faculty, or great opportunities, for the extension of experience — by thought, by emotion, by energy —
at first hand.

Yet it is doubtless not this cause alone that contributes to the
contemporary deluge; other circumstances operate, and one of
them is probably, in truth, if looked into, something of an abatement of the great fortune we have been called upon to admire.
The high prosperity of fiction has marched, very directly, with
another 'sign of the times', the demoralisation, the vulgarisation
of literature in general, the increasing familiarity of all such
methods of communication, the making itself supremely felt, as it
were, of the presence of the ladies and children — by whom I
mean, in other words, the reader irreflective and uncritical. If the
novel, in fine, has found itself, socially speaking, at such a rate,
the book *par excellence,* so on the other hand the book has in the
same degree found itself a thing of small ceremony. So many
ways of producing it easily have been discovered that it is by no
means the occasional prodigy, for good or for evil, that it was
taken for in simpler days, and has therefore suffered a proportionate discredit. Almost any variety is thrown off and taken up,
handled, admired, ignored by too many people, and this, precisely,
is the point at which the question of its future becomes one with
that of the future of the total swarm. How are the generations to

face, at all, the monstrous multiplications? Any speculation on the further development of a particular variety is subject to the reserve that the generations may at no distant day be obliged formally to decree, and to execute, great clearings of the deck, great periodical effacements and destructions. It fills, in fact, at moments the expectant ear, as we watch the progress of the ship of civilisation — the huge splash that must mark the response to many an imperative, unanimous 'Overboard!' What at least is already very plain is that practically the great majority of volumes printed within a year cease to exist as the hour passes, and give up by that circumstance all claim to a career, to being accounted or provided for. In speaking of the future of the novel we must of course, therefore, be taken as limiting the inquiry to those types that have, for criticism, a present and a past. And it is only super- ficially that confusion seems here to reign. The fact that in Eng- land and in the United States every specimen that sees the light may look for a 'review' testifies merely to the point to which, in these countries, literary criticism has sunk. The review is in nine cases out of ten an effort of intelligence as undeveloped as the in- eptitude over which it fumbles, and the critical spirit, which knows where it is concerned and where not, is not touched, is still less compromised, by the incident. There are too many reasons why newspapers must live.

So, as regards the tangible type, the end is that in its un- defended, its positively exposed state, we continue to accept it, conscious even of a peculiar beauty in an appeal made from a footing so precarious. It throws itself wholly on our generosity, and very often indeed gives us, by the reception it meets, a useful measure of the quality, of the delicacy, of many minds. There is to my sense no work of literary, or of any other, art, that any human being is under the smallest positive obligation to 'like'. There is no woman — no matter of what loveliness — in the presence of whom it is anything but a man's unchallengeably *own* affair that he is 'in love' or out of it. It is not a question of manners; vast is the margin left to individual freedom; and the trap set by the artist occupies no different ground — Robert Louis Stevenson has admirably expressed the analogy — from the offer of her charms by the lady. There only remain infatuations that we envy and emulate. When we do respond to the appeal, when we *are* caught in the trap, we are held and played upon; so that how in the world can there *not* still be a future, however late in the day, for a contrivance possessed of this precious secret? The more we consider it the more we feel that the prose picture can never be at the end of its tether until it loses the sense of what it can do. It can do simply everything, and that is its strength and its life. Its plasticity, its elasticity are infinite; there is no colour, no extension it may not take from the nature of its subject or the temper of its craftsman. It has the extraordinary advantage — a piece of luck scarcely credible — that, while capable of giving an impression of the highest perfection and the rarest finish, it moves in a luxurious independence of rules and restrictions. Think as we may, there is nothing we can mention as a consideration outside itself with which it must square, nothing we can name as one of its peculiar obligations or interdictions. It must, of course, hold our attention and reward it, it must not appeal on false pretences; but these necessities, with which, obviously, disgust and displeasure interfere, are not peculiar to it — all works of art have them in common. For the rest it has so clear a field that if it perishes this will surely be by its fault — by its superficiality, in other words, or its timidity. One almost, for the very love of it, likes to think of its appearing threatened with some such fate, in order to figure the dramatic stroke of its revival under the touch of a life-giving master. The temperament of the artist can do so much for it that our desire for some exemplary felicity fairly demands even the vision of that supreme proof. If we were to linger on this vision long enough, we should doubtless, in fact, be brought to wondering — and still for very loyalty to the form itself — whether our own prospective conditions may not before too long appear to many critics to call for some such happy *coup* on the part of a great artist yet to come.

There would at least be this excuse for such a reverie: that speculation is vain unless we confine it, and that for ourselves the most convenient branch of the question is the state of the industry that makes its appeal to readers of English. From any attempt to measure the career still open to the novel in France I may be excused, in so narrow a compass, for shrinking. The French, as a result of having ridden their horse much harder than we, are at a different stage of the journey, and we have doubtless many of their stretches and baiting-places yet to traverse. But if the range grows shorter from the moment we drop to inductions drawn only from English and American material, I am not sure that the answer comes sooner. I should have at all events — a formidably large order — to plunge into the particulars of the question of the present. If the day *is* approaching when the respite of execution for almost any book is but a matter of mercy, does the English novel of commerce tend to strike us as a production more and more equipped by its high qualities for braving the danger? It would be impossible, I think, to make one's attempt at an answer to that riddle really interesting without bringing into the field many illustrations drawn from individuals — without pointing the moral with names both conspicuous and obscure. Such a freedom would carry us, here, quite too far, and would moreover only encumber the path. There is nothing to prevent our taking for granted all sorts of happy symptoms and splendid promises — so long, of course, I mean, as we keep before us the general truth that the future of fiction is intimately bound up with the future of the society that produces and consumes it. In a society with a great and diffused literary sense the talent at play can only be a less neglible thing than in a society with a literary sense barely discernible. In a world in which criticism is acute and mature such talent will find itself trained, in order successfully to assert itself, to many more kinds of precautionary expertness than in a society in which the art I have named holds an inferior place or makes a sorry figure. A community addicted to reflection and fond of ideas will try experiments with the 'story' that will be left untried in a community mainly devoted to travelling and shooting, to pushing trade and playing football. There are many judges, doubtless, who hold that experiments — queer and uncanny things at best — are not necessary to it, that its face has been, once for all, turned in one way, and that it has only to go straight before it. If that is what it is actually doing in England and America the main thing to say about its future would appear to be that this future will in very truth more and more define itself as negligible. For all the while the immense variety of life will stretch away to right and to left, and all the while there may be, on such lines, perpetuation of its great mistake of failing of intelligence. That mistake will be, ever, for the admirable art, the only one really inexcusable, because of being a mistake about, as we may say, its own soul. The form of novel that is stupid on the general question of its freedom is the single form that may, *a priori*, be unhesitatingly pronounced wrong.

The most interesting thing today, therefore, among ourselves is the degree in which we may count on seeing a sense of that freedom cultivated and bearing fruit. What else is this, indeed, but one of the most attaching elements in the great drama of our wide English-speaking life! As the novel is at any moment the most immediate and, as it were, admirably *treacherous* picture of actual manners — indirectly as well as directly, and by what it does not touch as well as by what it does — so its present situation, where we are most concerned with it, is exactly a reflection of our social change and chances, of the signs and portents that lay most traps for most observers, and make up in general what is most 'amusing' in the spectacle we offer. Nothing, I may say, for instance, strikes me more as meeting this description than the predicament finally arrived at, for the fictive energy, in consequence of our long and most respectable tradition of making it defer supremely, in the treatment, say, of a delicate case, to the inexperience of the young. The particular knot the coming novelist who shall prefer not simply to beg the question, will have here to untie may represent assuredly the essence of his outlook. By what it shall decide to do in respect to the 'young' the great prose fable will, from any serious point of view, practically see itself stand or fall. What is clear is that it has, among us, veritably never chosen — it has, mainly, always obeyed an unreasoning instinct of avoidance in

which there has often been much that was felicitous. While society was frank, was free about the incidents and accidents of the
human constitution, the novel took the same robust ease as society. The young then were so very young that they were not table-
high. But they began to grow, and from the moment their little
chins rested on the mahogany, Richardson and Fielding began to
go under it. There came into being a mistrust of any but the most
guarded treatment of the great relation between men and women,
the constant world-renewal, which was the conspicuous sign that
whatever the prose picture of life was prepared to take upon
itself, it was not prepared to take upon itself not to be superficial.
Its position became very much: 'There are other things, don't you
know? For heaven's sake let *that* one pass!' And to this wonderful propriety of letting it pass the business has been for these so
many years — with the consequences we see today — largely devoted. These consequences are of many sorts, not a few altogether
charming. One of them has been that there is an immense omission in our fiction — which, though many critics will always
judge that it has vitiated the whole, others will continue to speak
of as signifying but a trifle. One can only talk for one's self, and
of the English and American novelists of whom I am fond, I am
so superlatively fond that I positively prefer to take them as they
are. I cannot so much as imagine Dickens and Scott *without* the
'*love-making*' left, as the phrase is, out. They were, to my perception, absolutely right — from the moment their attention
to it could only be perfunctory — practically not to deal with
it. In all their work it is, in spite of the number of pleasant
sketches of affection gratified or crossed, the element that
matters least. Why not therefore assume, it may accordingly
be asked, that discriminations which have served their
purpose so well in the past will continue not less successfully
to meet the case? What will you have better than Scott and
Dickens?

Nothing certainly *can* be, it may at least as promptly be replied,
and I can imagine no more comfortable prospect than jogging
along perpetually with a renewal of such blessings. The difficulty

lies in the fact that two of the great conditions have changed. The novel is older, and so are the young. It would seem that everything the young can possibly do for us in the matter has been successfully done. They have kept out one thing after the other, yet there is still a certain completeness we lack, and the curious thing is that it appears to be they themselves who are making the grave discovery. 'You have kindly taken', they seem to say to the fiction-mongers, 'our education off the hands of our parents and pastors, and that, doubtless, has been very convenient for *them*, and left them free to amuse themselves. But what, all the while, pray, if it is a question of education, have you done with your own? These are directions in which you seem dreadfully untrained, and in which *can* it be as vain as it appears to apply to you for information?' The point is whether, from the moment it is a question of averting discredit, the novel can afford to take things quite so easily as it has, for a good while now, settled down into the way of doing. There are too many sources of interest neglected — whole categories of manners, whole corpuscular classes and provinces, museums of character and condition, unvisited; while it is on the other hand mistakenly taken for granted that safety lies in all the loose and thin material that keeps reappearing in forms at once ready-made and sadly the worse for wear. The simple themselves may finally turn against our simplifications; so that we need not, after all, be more royalist than the king or more childish than the children. It is certain that there is no real health for any art — I am not speaking, of course, of any mere industry — that does not move a step in advance of its farthest follower. It would be curious — really a great comedy — if the renewal were to spring just from the satiety of the very readers for whom the sacrifices have hitherto been supposed to be made. It bears on this that as nothing is more salient in English life today, to fresh eyes, than the revolution taking place in the position and outlook of women — and taking place much more deeply in the quiet than even the noise on the surface demonstrates — so we may very well yet see the female elbow itself kept in increasing activity by the play of the pen, smash with final resonance the window all this time most superstitiously closed. The particular draught that has been most deprecated will in that case take care of the question of freshness. It is the opinion of some observers that when women do obtain a free hand they will not repay their long debt to the precautionary attitude of men by unlimited consideration for the natural delicacy of the latter.

To admit, then, that the great anodyne can ever totally fail to work, is to imply, in short, that this will only be by some grave fault in some high quarter. Man rejoices in an incomparable faculty for presently mutilating and disfiguring any plaything that has helped create for him the illusion of leisure; nevertheless, so long as life retains its power of projecting itself upon his imagination, he will find the novel work off the impression better than anything he knows. Anything better for the purpose has assuredly yet to be discovered. He will give it up only when life itself too thoroughly disagrees with him. Even then, indeed, may fiction not find a second wind, or a fiftieth, in the very portrayal of that collapse? Till the world is an unpeopled void there will be an image in the mirror. What need more immediately concern us, therefore, is the care of seeing that the image shall continue various and vivid. There is much, frankly, to be said for those who, in spite of all brave pleas, feel it to be considerably menaced, for very little reflection will help to show us how the prospect strikes them. They see the whole business too divorced on the one side from observation and perception, and on the other from the art and taste. They get too little of the first-hand impression, the effort to penetrate — that effort for which the French have the admirable expression to *fouiller* — and still less, if possible, of any science of composition, any architecture, distribution, proportion. It is not a trifle, though indeed it is the concomitant of an edged force, that 'mystery' should, to so many of the sharper eyes, have disappeared from the craft, and a facile flatness be, in place of it, in acclaimed possession. But these are, at the worst, even for such of the disconcerted, signs that the novelist, not that the novel, has dropped. So long as there is a subject to be treated, so long will it depend wholly on the treatment to rekindle the fire. Only the ministrant must really approach the altar; for if the novel *is* the treatment, it is the treatment that is essentially what I have called the anodyne.

THE LESSON OF BALZAC[1]

1905

I HAVE found it necessary, at the eleventh hour, to sacrifice to the
terrible question of time a very beautiful and majestic approach
that I had prepared to the subject on which I have the honour of
addressing you. I recognize it as impossible to ask you to linger
with me on that pillared portico — paved with marble, I beg you
to believe, and overtwined with charming flowers. I must invite
you to pass straight into the house and bear with me there as if I
had already succeeded in beginning to interest you. Let us assume,
therefore, that we have exchanged some ideas on the question of
the beneficent play of criticism, and that I have even ingeniously
struck it off that criticism is the only gate of appreciation, just as
appreciation is, in regard to a work of art, the only gate of enjoyment. You may wonder perhaps why I speak as if we were possessed, in our conditions, of a literary court of appeal, and I hasten
to say that the appeal I think of is precisely from the general judgment, and not to it; is to the particular judgment altogether: by
which I mean to that quantity of opinion, very small at all times,
but at all times infinitely precious, that is capable of giving some
intelligible account of itself. Where, among us, at this time of day,
this element of the lucid report of impressions received, of estimates formed, of intentions understood, of values attached, is
exactly to be looked for — that is another branch of the question,
to which I am afraid I should have to devote quite another discourse. I do not propose for a moment to invite you to blink the
fact that our huge Angle-Saxon array of producers and readers —
and especially our vast cis-Atlantic multitude — presents produc-

[1] A lecture delivered for the first time before the Contemporary Club of Phila-
delphia, 12 January 1905, and repeated on various occasions elsewhere. Several
passages omitted in delivery — one of considerable length — were restored by James.

tion uncontrolled, production untouched by criticism, unguided, unlighted, uninstructed, unashamed, on a scale that is really a new thing in the world. It is all the complete reversal of any proportion, between the elements, that was ever seen before. It is the biggest flock straying without shepherds, making its music without a sight of the classic crook, beribboned or other, without a sound of the sheepdog's bark — wholesome note, once in a way — that has ever found room for pasture. The very opposite has happened from what might have been expected to happen. The shepherds have diminished as the flock has increased — quite as if number and quantity had got beyond them, or even as if their charge had turned, by some uncanny process, to a pack of ravening wolves. Let us none the less assume that we may still find two or three of the fraternity hiding under a hedge or astride of some upper limb of a tree; let us even assume that if we set rightly, if we set tactfully about it, we may establish again some friendly connection with them.

Putting, on this basis, then, all our heads together, we may become aware of an intelligent gratitude, deep within our breasts, to any author who consents to fit with a certain fullness of presence and squareness of solidity into one of the conscious categories of our attention. There are literary figures in plenty that scarce fill out even the smaller of these critical receptacles; there are others, on the contrary, that almost strain the larger to breaking. It is to these latter that interested contemplation most fondly attaches itself — to that degree, really, that there seems, on any good occasion, more and more about them to be said. They have the great sign that their immediate presence causes our ideas, whether about life in general or about the art they have exemplified in particular, to revive and breathe again, to multiply, more or less to swarm. I must profess that no Novelist — since we are by common consent confining our attention to that great Company — no Novelist, to my sense, so rewards consideration as he or she (and I emphasize the liberality of my 'she') who offers the critical spirit this opportunity for a certain intensity of educative practice. The lesson of Balzac, whom we thus march straight up to, is that he offers it as no other members of the company can pretend to do.

For there are members of the company who scarce produce the effect in question at all. Take, to begin with, close at Balzac's side, his illustrious contemporary Mme George Sand, so suggestive, so affirmative, so instructive, as a dealer with life, as an eloquent exponent of her own, as what we call today a Personality equipped and armed, but of an artistic complexion so comparatively smooth and simple, so happily harmonious, that her work, taken together, presents about as few pegs for analysis to hang upon as if it were a large, polished, gilded Easter egg, the pride of a sweet shop if not the treasure of a museum. Let me add, further — so far as it is a question of the nameable sisterhood too — that Jane Austen, with all her light felicity, leaves us hardly more curious of her process, or of the experience in her that fed it, than the brown thrush who tells his story from the garden bough; and this, I freely confess, in spite of her being one of those of the shelved and safe, for all time, of whom I should have liked to begin by talking; one of those in whose favour discrimination has long since practically operated. She is in fact a signal instance of the way it does, with all its embarrassments, at last infallibly operate. A sharp short cut, one of the sharpest and shortest achieved, in this field, by the general judgment, came out, betimes, straight at her feet. Practically overlooked for thirty or forty years after her death, she perhaps really stands there for us as the prettiest possible example of that rectification of estimate, brought about by some slow clearance of stupidity, the half-century or so is capable of working round to. This tide has risen high on the opposite shore, the shore of appreciation — risen rather higher, I think, than the high-water mark, the highest, of her intrinsic merit and interest; though I grant indeed — as a point to be made — that we are dealing here in some degree with the tides so freely driven up, beyond their mere logical reach, by the stiff breeze of the commercial, in other words of the special bookselling spirit; an eager, active, interfering force which has a great many confusions of apparent value, a great many wild and wandering estimates, to answer for. For these distinctively mechanical and overdone reactions, of course, the critical spirit, even in its most relaxed mood, is not responsible. Responsible, rather, is the body of publishers, editors, illustrators, producers of the pleasant twaddle of magazines; who have found their 'dear', our dear, everybody's dear, Jane so infinitely to their material purpose, so amenable to pretty reproduction in every variety of what is called tasteful, and in what seemingly proves to be saleable, form.

I do not, naturally, mean that she would be saleable if we had not more or less — beginning with Macaulay, her first slightly ponderous amoroso — lost our hearts to her; but I cannot help seeing her, a good deal, as in the same lucky box as the Brontës — lucky for the ultimate guerdon; a case of popularity (that in especial of the Yorkshire sisters), a beguiled infatuation, a sentimentalized vision, determined largely by the accidents and circumstances originally surrounding the manifestation of the genius — only with the reasons for the sentiment, in this latter connection, turned the other way. The key to Jane Austen's fortune with posterity has been in part the extraordinary grace of her facility, in fact of her unconsciousness: as if, at the most, for difficulty, for embarrassment, she sometimes, over her work basket, her tapestry flowers, in the spare, cool drawing-room of other days, fell a-musing, lapsed too metaphorically, as one may say, into woolgathering, and her dropped stitches, of these pardonable, of these precious moments, were afterwards picked up as little touches of human truth, little glimpses of steady vision, little master-strokes of imagination. The romantic tradition of the Brontës, with posterity, has been still more essentially helped, I think, by a force independent of any one of their applied faculties — by the attendant image of their dreary, their tragic history, their loneliness and poverty of life. That picture has been made to hang before us as insistently as the vividest page of *Jane Eyre* or of *Wuthering Heights*. If these things were 'stories', as we say, and stories of a lively interest, the medium from which they sprang was above all in itself a story, such a story as has fairly elbowed out the rights of appreciation, as has come at last to impose itself as an expression of the power concerned. The personal position of the three sisters, of the two in particular, had been marked, in short, with so sharp an accent that this accent has become for us the very tone of their united production. It covers and supplants their matter, their spirit, their style, their talent, their taste; it embodies, really, the most complete intellectual muddle, if the term be not extravagant, ever achieved, on a literary question, by our wonderful public. The question has scarce indeed been accepted as belonging to literature at all. Literature is an objective, a projected result; it is life that is the unconscious, the agitated, the struggling, floundering cause. But the fashion has been, in looking at the Brontës, so to confound the cause with the result that we cease to know, in the presence of such ecstasies, what we have hold of or what we are talking about. They represent, the ecstasies, the high-water mark of sentimental judgment.

These are but glimmering lanterns, however, you will say, to hang in the great dusky and deserted avenue that leads up to the seated statue of Balzac; and you are so far right, I am bound to admit, as that I place them there, no doubt, in a great measure, just to render the darkness visible. We do, collectively, with all our dimness of view, arrive at rough discriminations, and by one of the roughest of these the author of the *Comédie Humaine* has in a manner profited; we have for many a year taken his greatness for granted; but in the graceless and nerveless fashion of those who edge away from a classic or a bore. 'Oh, yes, he is as "great" as you like — so let us not talk of him!' My purpose has been to 'talk' of him, and I find this form of greeting, therefore, and still more this form of parting, not at all adequate; failing as I do to point my moral unless I show that a really paying acquaintance with a writer can never take place if our recognition remains perfunctory. Our indolence and our ignorance may prefer the empty form; but the penalty and the humiliation come for us with the perception that when the consecration really takes place we have been excluded, so to speak, from the fun. I see no better proof that the great interesting art of which Balzac remains the greatest master is practically, round about us, a bankrupt and discredited art (discredited, of course, I mean, for any directed and motived attention), than this very fact that we are so ready to beg off from knowing anything about him. Perfunctory rites, even, at present, are seldom rendered; and, amid the flood of verbiage for which the thousand new novels of the season find themselves a pretext in the newspapers, the name of the man who is really the father of us all, as we stand, is scarcely more mentioned than if he were not of the family.

I may at once intimate that the family strikes me as likely to recover its wasted heritage, and pull itself together for another chance, on condition only of shutting itself up, for an hour of wholesome heart-searching, with the image of its founder. He labours, I know, under the drawback of not being presentable as a classic — which is precisely why there would have seemed to be the less furtherance for regarding him as a bore. His situation in this respect is all his own: it was not given him to flower, for our convenience, into a single supreme felicity. His 'successes' hang so together that analysis is almost baffled by his consistency, by his density. Even *Eugénie Grandet* is not a supreme felicity in the sense that this particular bloom is detachable from the cluster. The cluster is too thick, the stem too tough; before we know it, when we begin to pull, we have the whole branch about our heads — or it would indeed be more just to say we have the whole tree, if not the whole forest. It tells against a great worker, for free reference, that we must take his work in the mass; for, unfortunately, the circumstance that nothing of it surpassingly stands forth to represent the rest, to symbolize the whole, suggests a striking resemblance to work of other sorts. Of the mediocrities, and the bunglers too is it true that *they* do not supremely flower — as well as, further, of certain happy geniuses who have flowed in an uncontrolled, an undirected, above all in an unfiltered, current.

But the difference is that, for the most part, these loose and easy producers, the great resounding improvisatori, have not, in general, ended by imposing themselves; when we deal with them conclusively and, as I have said, for clearance of the slate, we deal with them by simplification, by elimination: which may very well be the revenge that time takes upon them to make up for the amount of space they happened immediately to occupy. They are still there, evidently: but they are there under this condition, which enters into account, as every instant, in any pious inquiry about them, and which is attached, intimately, to the appearance they finally wear for us, that the looseness and ease showing as their main sign in the time of their freshness is now a quality still more striking and often still more disconcerting. The weak sides in an artist are weakened with time, and the strong sides strengthened; so that it is never amiss, for duration, to have as many strong sides as possible. It is the only way we have yet made out — even in this age of superlative study of the cheap and easy — not to have so many weak ones as will eventually betray us. Balzac stands almost alone as an extemporizer achieving closeness and weight, and whom closeness and weight have preserved. My reason for speaking of him as an extemporizer I shall presently mention; but let me meanwhile frankly say that I speak of him, and can only speak, as a man of his own craft, an emulous fellow-worker, who has learned from him more of the lessons of the engaging mystery of fiction than from any one else, and who is conscious of so large a debt to repay that it has had positively to be discharged in installments; as if one could never have at once all the required cash in hand.

When I am tempted, on occasion, to ask myself why we should, after all, so much as talk about the Novel, the wanton fable, against which, in so many ways, so showy an indictment may be drawn, I seem to see that the simplest plea is not to be sought in any attempted philosophy, in any abstract reason for our perversity or our levity. The real gloss upon these things is reflected from some great practitioner, some concrete instance of the art, some ample cloak under which we may gratefully crawl. It comes back, of course, to the example and the analogy of the Poet — with the abatement, however, that the Poet is most the Poet when he is preponderantly lyrical, when he speaks, laughing or crying, most directly from his individual heart, which throbs under the impressions of life. It is not the *image* of life that he thus expresses, so much as life itself, in its sources — so much as his own intimate, essential states and feelings. By the time he has begun to collect anecdotes, to tell stories, to represent scenes, to concern himself, that is, with the states and feelings of others, he is well on the way not to be the Poet pure and simple. The lyrical element, all the same, abides in him, and it is by this element that he is connected with what is most splendid in his expression. The lyrical instinct and tradition are immense in Shakespeare; which is why, great storyteller, great dramatist and painter, great lover, in short, of the image of life though he was, we need not press the case of his example. The lyrical element is not great, is in fact not present at all, in Balzac, in Scott (the Scott of the voluminous prose), nor in Thackeray, nor in Dickens — which is precisely why they are so essentially novelists, so almost exclusively lovers of the image of life. It *is* great, or it is at all events largely present, in such a writer as George Sand — which is doubtless why we take her for a novelist in a much looser sense than the others we have named. It is considerable in that bright particular genius of our own day, George Meredith, who so strikes us as hitching winged horses to the chariot of his prose — steeds who prance and dance and caracole, who strain the traces, attempt to quit the ground, and yearn for the upper air. Balzac, with huge feet fairly ploughing the sand of our desert, is on the other hand the very type and model of the projector and creator; so that when I think, either with envy or with terror, of the nature and the effort of the Novelist, I think of something that reaches its highest expression in him. That is why those of us who, as fellow-craftsmen, have once caught a glimpse of this value in him, can never quite rest from hanging about him; that is why he seems to have all that the others have to tell us, with more, besides, that is all his own. He lived and breathed in his medium, and the fact that he was able to achieve in it, as man and as artist, so crowded a career, remains for us one of the most puzzling problems — I scarce know whether to say of literature or of life. He is himself a figure more extraordinary than any he drew, and the fascination may still be endless of all the questions he puts to us and of the answers for which we feel ourselves helpless.

He died, as we sufficiently remember, at fifty — worn out with work and thought and passion; the passion, I mean, that he had put into his mighty plan and that had ridden him like an infliction of the gods. He began, a friendless and penniless young provincial, to write early, and to write very badly, and it was not till well toward his thirtieth year, with the conception of the *Comédie Humaine*, as we all again remember, that he found his right ground, found his feet and his voice. This huge distributed, divided and subdivided picture of the life of France in his time, a picture bristling with imagination and information, with fancies and facts and figures, a world of special and general insight, a rank tropical forest of detail and specification, but with the strong breath of genius forever circulating through it and shaking the treetops to a mighty murmur, got itself hung before us in the space of twenty short years. The achievement remains one of the most inscrutable, one of the unfathomable, final facts in the history of art, and if, as I have said, the author himself has his own surpassing objectivity, it is just because of this challenge his figure constitutes for any other painter of life, inflamed with ingenuity, who should feel the temptation to represent or explain him. How represent, how explain him, as a concrete active energy? How depict him, we ask ourselves, *at* his huge conceived and accepted task, how reconcile such dissemination with such intensity, the collection and possession of so vast a number of facts with so rich a presentation of each? The elements of the world he set up before us, with all its insistent particulars, these elements were not, for him, a direct revelation — of so large a part of life is it true that we can know it only by living, and that living is the process that, in our mortal span, makes the largest demand on our time. How could a man have lived at large so much if, in the service of art, he had so much abstracted and condensed himself? How could he have so much abstracted and condensed himself if, in the service of life, he had felt and fought and acted, had laboured and suffered, so much as a private in the ranks? The wealth and strength of his temperament indeed partly answer the question and partly obscure it. He could so extend his existence partly because he vibrated to so many kinds of contact and curiosity. To vibrate intellectually was his motive, but it magnified, all the while, it multiplied his experience. He could live at large, in short, because he was always living in the particular necessary, the particular intended connection — was always astride of his imagination, always charging, with his heavy, his heroic lance in rest, at every object that sprang up in his path. But as he was at the same time always fencing himself in against the personal adventure, the personal experience, in order to preserve himself for converting it into history, how did experience, in the immediate sense, still get itself saved? — or, to put it as simply as possible, where, with so strenuous a conception of the use of material, was material itself so strenuously quarried? Out of what mines, by what innumerable tortuous channels, in what endless winding procession of laden chariots and tugging teams and marching elephants, did the immense consignments required for his work reach him?

The point at which the emulous admirer, however diminished by comparison, may most closely approach him is, it seems to me, through the low portal of envy, so irresistibly do we lose ourselves in the vision of the quantity of life with which his imagination communicated. Quantity and intensity are at once and together his sign; the truth being that his energy did not press hard in some places only to press lightly in others, did not lay it on thick here or there to lay it on thin elsewhere, did not seek the appearance of extent and number by faintness of evocation, by shallow soundings, or by the mere sketchiness of suggestion that dispenses, for reference and verification, with the book, the total collection of human documents, with what we call 'chapter and verse'. He never throws dust in our eyes, save only the fine gold-dust through the haze of which his own romantic vision operates; never does it, I mean, when he is pretending not to do it, pretending to give us the full statement of his case, to deal with the facts of the spectacle surrounding him. Then he goes in, as we say, for a portentous clearness, a reproduction of the real on the scale of the real — with a definiteness actually proportionate; though a clearness that in truth sometimes fails (like the sight of the forest of the adage, which fails for the presence of the trees), through the positive monstrosity of his effort. He sees and presents too many facts, — facts of history, of property, of genealogy, of topography, of sociology, and has too many ideas and images about them; their value is thus threatened with submersion by the flood of general reference in which they float, by their quantity of indicated relation to other facts, which break against them like waves of a high tide. He may thus at times become obscure from his very habit of striking too many matches; or we may at least say of him, out of our wondering loyalty, that the light he produces is, beyond that of any other corner of the great planted garden of romance, thick and rich and heavy — interesting, so to speak, on its own account.

There would be much to say, I think, had we only a little more time, on this question of the projected light of the individual strong temperament in fiction — the colour of the air with which this, that or the other painter of life (as we call them all), more or less unconsciously suffuses his picture. I say unconsciously because I speak here of an effect of atmosphere largely, if not wholly, distinct from the effect sought on behalf of the special subject to be treated; something that proceeds from the contemplative mind itself, the very complexion of the mirror in which the material is reflected. This is of the nature of the man himself — an emanation of his spirit, temper, history; it springs from his very presence, his spiritual presence, in his work, and is, in so far, not a matter of calculation and artistry. All a matter of his own, in a word, for each seer of visions, the particular tone of the medium in which each vision, each clustered group of persons and places and objects, is bathed. Just how, accordingly, does the light of the world, the projected, painted, peopled, poetized, realized world, the furnished and fitted world into which we are beguiled for the holiday excursion, cheap trips or dear, of the eternally amusable, eternally dupeable voyaging mind — just how does this strike us as different in Fielding and in Richardson, in Scott

and in Dumas, in Dickens and in Thackeray, in Hawthorne and
in Meredith, in George Eliot and in George Sand, in Jane Austen
and in Charlotte Brontë? Do we not feel the general landscape
evoked by each of the more or less magical wands to which I have
given name, not to open itself under the same sun that hangs over
the neighbouring scene, not to receive the solar rays at the same
angle, not to exhibit its shadows with the same intensity or the
same sharpness; not, in short, to seem to belong to the same time
of day or same state of the weather? Why is it that the life that
overflows in Dickens seems to me always to go on in the morning, or in the very earliest hours of the afternoon at most, and in a
vast apartment that appears to have windows, large, uncurtained,
and rather unwashed windows, on all sides at once? Why is it that
in George Eliot the sun sinks forever to the west, and the shadows
are long, and the afternoon wanes, and the trees vaguely rustle,
and the colour of the day is much inclined to yellow? Why is it
that in Charlotte Brontë we move through an endless autumn?
Why is it that in Jane Austen we sit quite resigned in an arrested
spring? Why does Hawthorne give us the afternoon hour later
than any one else? — oh, late, late, quite uncannily late, and as if
it were always winter outside? But I am wasting the very minutes
I pretended, at the start, to cherish, and am only sustained through
my levity by seeing you watch for the time of day or season of
the year or state of the weather that I shall fasten upon the complicated clock-face of Thackeray. I do, I think, see his light also —
see it very much as the light (a different thing from the mere dull
dusk) of rainy days in 'residential' streets; but we are not, after all,
talking of him, and, though Balzac's waiting power has proved
itself, this half-century, immense, I must not too much presume
upon it.

The question of the colour of Balzac's air and the time of *his*
day would indeed here easily solicit our ingenuity — were I at
liberty to say more than one thing about it. It is rich and thick,
the mixture of sun and shade diffused through the *Comédie
Humaine* — a mixture richer and thicker and representing an absolutely greater quantity of 'atmosphere' than we shall find pre-

vailing within the compass of any other suspended frame. That is
how we see him, living in his garden, and it is by reason of the
restless energy with which he circulated there that I hold his fortune and his privilege, in spite of the burden of his toil and the
brevity of his immediate reward, to have been before any others
enviable. It is strange enough, but what most abides with us, as
we follow his steps, is a sense of the intellectual luxury he enjoyed.
To focus him at all, for a single occasion, we have to simplify,
and this wealth of his vicarious experience forms the side, moreover, on which he is most attaching for those who take an interest
in the real play of the imagination. From the moment our imagination plays at all, of course, and from the moment we try to
catch and preserve the pictures it throws off, from that moment
we too, in our comparatively feeble way, live vicariously — succeed in opening a series of dusky passages in which, with a more
or less childlike ingenuity, we can romp to and fro. Our passages
are mainly short and dark, however; we soon come to the end of
them — dead walls, without resonance, in presence of which the
candle goes out and the game stops, and we have only to retrace
our steps. Balzac's luxury, as I call it, was in the extraordinary
number and length of his radiating and ramifying corridors — the
labyrinth in which he finally lost himself. What it comes back to,
in other words, is the intensity with which we live — and his
intensity is recorded for us on every page of his work.

It is a question, you see, of *penetrating* into a subject; his corridors always went further and further and further; which is but
another way of expressing his inordinate passion for detail. It
matters nothing — nothing for my present contention — that
this extravagance is also his great fault; in spite, too, of its all being
detail vivified and related, characteristic and constructive, essentially prescribed by the terms of his plan. The relations of parts to
each other are at moments multiplied almost to madness — which
is at the same time just why they give us the measure of his hallucination, make up the greatness of his intellectual adventure. His
plan was to handle, primarily, not a world of ideas, animated by
figures representing these ideas; but the packed and constituted,

the palpable, proveable world before him, by the study of which ideas would inevitably find themselves thrown up. If the happy fate is accordingly to *partake* of life, actively, assertively, not passively, narrowly, in mere sensibility and sufferance, the happiness has been greatest when the faculty employed has been largest. We employ different faculties — some of us only our arms and our legs and our stomach; Balzac employed most what he possessed in largest quantity. This is where his work ceases in a manner to mystify us — this is where we make out how he did quarry his material: it is the sole solution to an otherwise baffling problem. He collected his experience within himself; no other economy explains his achievement; this thrift alone, remarkable yet thinkable, embodies the necessary miracle. His system of cellular confinement, in the interest of the miracle, was positively that of a Benedictine monk, leading his life within the four walls of his convent and bent, the year round, over the smooth parchment on which, with wondrous illumination and enhancement of gold and crimson and blue, he inscribed the glories of the faith and the legends of the saints. Balzac's view of himself was indeed in a manner the monkish one; he was most at ease, while he wrought, in the white gown and cowl — an image of him that the friendly art of his time has handed down to us. Only, as happened, his subject of illumination was the legends not merely of the saints, but of the much more numerous uncanonized strugglers and sinners, an acquaintance with whose attributes was not all to be gathered in the place of piety itself; not even from the faintest ink of old records, the mild lips of old brothers, or the painted glass of church windows.

This is where envy does follow him, for to have so many other human cases, so many other personal predicaments to get into, up to one's chin, is verily to be able to get out of one's own box. And it was up to his chin, constantly that he sank in his illusion — not, as the weak and timid in this line do, only up to his ankles or his knees. The figures he sees begin immediately to bristle with all their characteristics. Every mark and sign, outward and inward, that they possess; every virtue and every vice, every strength and every weakness, every passion and every habit, the sound of their voices, the expression of their eyes, the tricks of feature and limb, the buttons on their clothes, the food on their plates, the money in their pockets, the furniture in their houses, the secrets in their breasts, are all things that interest, that concern, that command him, and that have, for the picture, significance, relation and value. It is a prodigious multiplication of values, and thereby a prodigious entertainment of the vision — on the condition the vision can bear it. Bearing it — that is *our* bearing it — is a serious matter; for the appeal is truly to that faculty of attention out of which we are educating ourselves, as hard as we possibly can; educating ourselves with such complacency, with such boisterous high spirits, that we may already be said to have practically lost it — with the consequence that any work of art or of criticism making a demand on it is by that fact essentially discredited. It takes attention not only to thread the labyrinth of the *Comédie Humaine*, but to keep our author himself in view, in the relations in which we thus image him. But if we can muster it, as I say, in sufficient quantity, we thus walk with him in the great glazed gallery of his thought; the long, lighted and pictured ambulatory where the endless series of windows, on one side, hangs over his revolutionized, ravaged, yet partly restored and reinstated garden of France, and where, on the other, the figures and the portraits we fancy stepping down to meet him climb back into their frames, larger and smaller, and take up position and expression as he desired they shall look out and compose.

We have lately had a literary case of the same general family as the case of Balzac, and in presence of which some of the same speculations come up: I had occasion, not long since, after the death of Émile Zola, to attempt an appreciation of *his* extraordinary performance — his series of the *Rougon-Macquart* constituting in fact, in the library of the fiction that can hope in some degree to live, a monument to the idea of plenitude, of comprehension and variety, second only to the *Comédie Humaine*. The question presented itself, in respect to Zola's ability and Zola's career, with a different proportion and value, I quite recognize, and wearing a much less distinguished face; but it was there to be met, none the less, on the very threshold, and all the more because this was just where he himself had placed it. His idea had been, from the first, in a word, to lose no time — as if one could have experience, even the mere amount requisite for showing others as having it, *without* losing time! — and yet the degree in which he too, so handicapped, has achieved valid expression is such as still to stagger us. He had had inordinately to simplify — had had to leave out the life of the soul, practically, and confine himself to the life of the instincts, of the more immediate passions, such as can be easily and promptly caught in the fact. He had had, in a word, to confine himself almost entirely to the impulses and agitations that men and women are possessed by in common, and to take them as exhibited in mass and number, so that, being writ larger, they might likewise be more easily read. He met and solved, in this manner, his difficulty — the difficulty of knowing, and of showing, of life, only what his 'notes' would account for. But it is in the *waste*, I think, much rather — the waste of time, of passion, of curiosity, of contact — that true initiation resides; so that the most wonderful adventures of the artist's spirit are those, immensely quickening for his 'authority', that are yet not reducible to his notes. It is exactly here that we get the difference between such a solid, square, symmetrical structure as *Les Rougon-Macquart*, vitiated, in a high degree, by its mechanical side, and the monument left by Balzac — without the example of which, I surmise, Zola's work would not have existed. The mystic process of the crucible, the transformation of the material under aesthetic heat, is, in the *Comédie Humaine*, thanks to an intenser and more submissive fusion, completer, and also finer; for if the commoner and more wayside passions and conditions are, in the various episodes there, at no time gathered into so large and so thick an illustrative bunch, yet on the other hand they are shown much more freely at play in the individual case — and the individual case it is that permits of supreme fineness. It is hard to say where Zola is fine; whereas it is often, for pages together, hard to say where Balzac is, even under the weight of his too ponderous personality, not. The most fundamental and general sign of the novel, from one desperate experiment to another, is its being everywhere an effort at *representation* — this is the beginning and the end of it: wherefore it was that one could say at last, with account taken of everything, that Zola's performance, on his immense scale, was an extraordinary show of representation imitated. The imitation, in places — notably and admirably, for instance, in *L'Assommoir* — breaks through into something that we take for reality; but, for the most part, the separating rift, the determining difference, holds its course straight, prevents the attempted process from becoming the sound, straight, whole thing that is given us by those who have really *bought* their information. This is where Balzac remains unshaken — in our feeling that, with all his faults of pedantry, ponderosity, pretentiousness, bad taste and charmless form, his spirit has somehow paid for its knowledge. His subject is again and again the complicated human creature or human condition; and it is with these complications as if he knew them, as Shakespeare knew them, by his charged consciousness, by the history of his soul and the direct exposure of his sensibility. This source of supply he found, forever — and one may indeed say he mostly left — sitting at his fireside; where it constituted the company with which I see him shut up, and his practical intimacy with which, during such orgies and debauches of intellectual passion, might earn itself that name of high personal good fortune that I have applied.

Let me say, definitely, that I hold several of his faults to be grave, and that if there were any question of time for it I should like to speak of them; but let me add, as promptly, that they are faults, on the whole, of execution, flaws in the casting, accidents of the process: they never come back to that fault in the artist, in the novelist, that amounts most completely to a failure of dignity, the absence of saturation with his idea. When saturation fails no other presence really avails; as when, on the other hand, it operates, no failure of method fatally interferes. There is never in Balzac that damning interference which consists of the painter's not seeing, not possessing, his image; not having fixed and held his creature and his creature's conditions. 'Balzac aime sa Valérie', says Taine, in his great essay — so much the finest thing ever written on our author — speaking of the way in which the awful little Mme Marneffe of *Les Parents Pauvres* is drawn, and of the long rope, for her acting herself out, that her creator's participation in her reality assures her. He has been contrasting her, as it happens, with Thackeray's Becky Sharp or rather with Thackeray's attitude toward Becky, and the marked jealousy of her freedom that Thackeray exhibits from the first. I remember reading at the time of the publication of Taine's study — though it was long, long ago — a phrase in an English review of the volume which seemed to my limited perception, even in extreme youth, to deserve the highest prize ever bestowed on critical stupidity undisguised. If Balzac loved his Valérie, said this commentator, that only showed Balzac's extraordinary taste; the truth being really, throughout, that it was just through this love of each seized identity, and of the sharpest and liveliest identities most, that Mme Marneffe's creator was able to marshal his array at all. The love, as we call it, the joy in their communicated and exhibited movement, in their standing on their feet and going of themselves and acting out their characters, was what rendered possible the saturation I speak of; what supplied him, through the inevitable gaps of his preparation and the crevices of his prison, his long prison of labour, a short cut to the knowledge he required. It was by loving them — as the terms of his subject and the nuggets of his mine — that he knew them; it was not by knowing them that he loved.

He at all events robustly loved the sense of another explored, assumed, assimilated identity — enjoyed it as the hand enjoys the glove when the glove ideally fits. My image indeed is loose; for what he liked was absolutely to get into the constituted consciousness, into all the clothes, gloves and whatever else, into the very skin and bones, of the habited, featured, coloured, articulated form of life that he desired to present. How do we know given persons, for any purpose of demonstration, unless we know their situation for themselves, unless we see it from their point of vision, that is, from their point of pressing consciousness or

sensation? — without our allowing for which there is no appreciation. Balzac loved his Valérie then as Thackeray did not love
his Becky, or his Blanche Amory in *Pendennis*. But his prompting
was not to expose her; it could only be, on the contrary — intensely aware as he was of all the lengths she might go and
paternally, maternally alarmed about them — to cover her up and
protect her, in the interest of her special genius and freedom. All
his impulse was to *la faire valoir*, to give her all her value, just as
Thackeray's attitude was the opposite one, a desire positively to
expose and desecrate poor Becky — to follow her up, catch her
in the act, and bring her to shame: though with a mitigation, an
admiration, an inconsequence, now and then wrested from him
by an instinct finer, in his mind, than the so-called 'moral' eager-
ness. The English writer wants to make sure, first of all, of your
moral judgment; the French is willing, while it waits a little, to
risk, for the sake of his subject and its interest, your spiritual
salvation. Mme Marneffe, detrimental, fatal as she is, is 'exposed',
so far as anything in life, or in art, may be, by the working-out of
the situation and the subject themselves; so that when they have
done what they would, what they logically had to, with her, we
are ready to take it from them. We do not feel, very irritatedly,
very lecturedly, in other words with superfluous edification, that
she has been sacrificed. Who can say, on the contrary, that
Blanche Amory, in *Pendennis*, with the author's lash about her
little bare white back from the first — who can feel that she has
not been sacrificed, or that her little bareness and whiteness, and
all the rest of her, have been, by such a process, presented as they
had a right to demand?

It all comes back, in fine, to that respect for the liberty of the
subject which I should be willing to name as *the* great sign of the
painter of the first order. Such a witness to the human comedy
fairly holds his breath for fear of arresting or diverting that natural license; the witness who begins to breathe so uneasily in
presence of it that his respiration not only warns off the little
prowling or playing creature he is supposed to be studying, but
drowns, for our ears, the ingenuous sounds of the animal, as well

as the general, truthful hum of the human scene at large — this demonstrator has no sufficient warrant for his task. And if such an induction as this is largely the moral of our renewed glance at Balzac, there is a lesson, of a more essential sort, I think, folded still deeper within — the lesson that there is no convincing art that is not ruinously expensive. I am unwilling to say, in the presence of such of his successors as George Eliot and Tolstoy and Zola (to name, for convenience, only three of them), that he was the last of the novelists to do the thing handsomely; but I will say that we get the impression at least of his having had more to spend. Many of those who have followed him affect us as doing it, in the vulgar phrase, 'on the cheap'; by reason mainly, no doubt, of their having been, all helplessly, foredoomed to cheapness. Nothing counts, of course, in art, but the excellent; nothing exists, however briefly, for estimation, for appreciation, but the superlative — always in its kind; and who shall declare that the severe economy of the vast majority of those apparently emulous of the attempt to 'render' the human subject and the human scene proceeds from anything worse than the conscious-ness of a limited capital? This flourishing frugality operates happily, no doubt — given all the circumstances — for the novel-ist; but it has had terrible results for the novel, so far as the novel is a form with which criticism may be moved to concern itself. Its misfortune, its discredit, what I have called its bankrupt state among us, is the not unnatural consequence of its having ceased, for the most part, to be artistically interesting. It has become an object of easy manufacture, showing on every side the stamp of the machine; it has become the article of commerce, produced in quantity, and as we so see it we inevitably turn from it, under the rare visitations of the critical impulse, to compare it with those more precious products of the same general nature that we used to think of as belonging to the class of the hand-made.

The lesson of Balzac, under this comparison, is extremely various, and I should prepare myself much too large a task were I to attempt a list of the separate truths he brings home. I have to choose among them, and I choose the most important; the three or four that more or less include the others. In reading him over, in opening him almost anywhere today, what immediately strikes us is the part assigned by him, in any picture, to the *conditions* of the creatures with whom he is concerned. Contrasted with him other prose painters of life scarce seem to see the conditions at all. He clearly held pretended portrayal as nothing, as less than nothing, as a most vain thing, unless it should be, in spirit and intention, the art of complete representation. 'Complete' is of course a great word, and there is no art at all, we are often reminded, that is not on too many sides an abject compromise. The element of compromise is always there; it is of the essence; we live with it, and it may serve to keep us humble. The formula of the whole matter is sufficiently expressed perhaps in a reply I found myself once making to an inspired but discouraged friend, a fellow-craftsman who had declared in his despair that there was no use trying, that it was a form, the novel, absolutely too difficult. 'Too difficult indeed; yet there is one way to master it — which is to pretend consistently that it isn't.' We are all of us, all the while, pretending — as consistently as we can — that it isn't, and Balzac's great glory is that he pretended hardest. He never had to pretend so hard as when he addressed himself to that evocation of the medium, that distillation of the natural and social air, of which I speak, the things that most require on the part of the painter preliminary possession — so definitely require it that, terrified at the requisition, when conscious of it, many a painter prefers to beg the whole question. He has thus, this ingenious person, to invent some *other* way of making his characters interesting — some other way, that is, than the arduous way, demanding so much consideration, of presenting them to us. They are interesting, in fact, as subjects of fate, the figures round whom a situation closes, in proportion as, sharing their existence, we feel where fate comes in and just how it gets at them. In the void they are not interesting — and Balzac, like Nature herself, abhorred a vacuum. Their situation takes hold of us because it is theirs, not because it is somebody's, any one's, that of creatures unidentified. Therefore it is not superfluous that their identity shall first be established for us, and their adventures, in that measure, have a relation to it, and therewith an appreciability. There is no such thing in the world as an adventure pure and simple; there is only mine and yours, and his and hers — it being the greatest adventure of all, I verily think, just to *be* you or I, just to be he or she. To Balzac's imagination that was indeed in itself an immense adventure — and nothing appealed to him more than to show *how* we all are, and how we are placed and built-in for being so. What befalls us is but another name for the way our circumstances press upon us — so that an account of what befalls us is an account of our circumstances.

Add to this, then, that the fusion of all the elements of the picture, under his hand, is complete — of what people are with what they do, of what they do with what they are, of the action with the agents, of the medium with the action, of all the parts of the drama with each other. Such a production as *Le Père Goriot* for example, or as *Eugénie Grandet*, or as *Le Curé de Village*, has, in respect to this fusion, a kind of inscrutable perfection. The situation sits shrouded in its circumstances, and then, by its inner expansive force, emerges from them, the action marches, to the rich rustle of this great tragic and ironic train, the embroidered heroic mantle, with an art of keeping together that makes of *Le Père Goriot* in especial a supreme case of composition, a model of that high virtue that we know as economy of effect, economy of line and touch. An inveterate sense of proportion was not, in general, Balzac's distinguishing mark; but with great talents one has great surprises, and the effect of this large handling of the conditions was more often than not to make the work, whatever it might be, appear admirably composed. Of all the costly charms of a 'story' this interest derived from composition is the costliest — and there is perhaps no better proof of our present penury than the fact that, in general, when one makes a plea for it, the plea might seemingly (for all it is understood!) be for trigonometry or osteology. 'Composition? — what may that happen to *be*, and, whatever it is, what has it to do with the matter?' I shall take for granted here that every one perfectly knows, for without that assumption I shall not be able to wind up, as I must immediately do. The presence of the conditions, when really presented, when made vivid, provides for the action — which is, from step to step, constantly implied in them; whereas the process of suspending the action in the void and dressing it there with the tinkling bells of what is called dialogue only makes no provision at all for the other interest. There are two elements of the art of the novelist which, as they present, I think, the greatest difficulty, tend thereby most to fascinate us: in the first place that mystery of the foreshortened procession of facts and figures, of appearances of whatever sort, which is in some lights but another name for the picture governed by the principle of composition, and which has at any rate as little as possible in common with the method now usual among us, the juxtaposition of items emulating the column of numbers of a schoolboy's sum in addition. It is the art of the brush, I know, as opposed to the art of the slate-pencil; but to the art of the brush the novel must return, I hold, to recover whatever may be still recoverable of its sacrificed honour.

The second difficulty that I commend for its fascination, at all events, the most attaching when met and the most rewarding when triumphantly met — though I hasten to add that it also strikes me as not only the least 'met', in general, but the least suspected — this second difficulty is that of representing, to put it simply, the lapse of time, the duration of the subject: representing it, that is, more subtly than by a blank space, or a row of stars, on the historic page. With the blank space and the row of stars Balzac's genius had no affinity, and he is therefore as unlike as possible those narrators — so numerous, all round us, it would appear, today in especial — the succession of whose steps and stages, the development of whose action, in the given case, affects us as occupying but a week or two. No one begins, to my sense, to handle the time-element and produce the time-effect with the authority of Balzac in his amplest sweeps — by which I am far from meaning in his longest passages. That study of the foreshortened image, of the neglect of which I suggest the ill consequence, is precisely the enemy of the tiresome procession of would-be narrative items, seen all in profile, like the rail-heads of a fence; a substitute for the baser device of accounting for the time-quantity by mere quantity of statement. Quality and manner of statement account for it in a finer way — always assuming, as I say, that unless it is accounted for nothing else really is. The fashion of our day is to account for it almost exclusively by an inordinate abuse of the colloquial resource, of the report, from page to page, from chapter to chapter, from beginning to end, of the talk, between the persons involved, in which situation and action may be conceived as registered. Talk between persons is perhaps, of all the parts of the novelist's plan, the part that Balzac most scrupulously weighed and measured and kept in its place; judging it, I think, — though he perhaps even had an undue suspicion of its possible cheapness, as feeling it the thing that can least afford to be cheap — a precious and supreme resource, the very flower of illustration of the subject and thereby not to be inconsiderately discounted. It was his view, discernibly, that the flower must keep its bloom, or in other words not be too much handled, in order to have a fragrance when nothing but its fragrance will serve.

It was his view indeed positively that there is a *law* in these things, and that, admirable for illustration, functional for illustration, dialogue has its function perverted, and therewith its life destroyed, when forced, all clumsily, into the constructive office. It is in the drama, of course, that it is constructive; but the drama lives by a law so different, verily, that everything that is right for it seems wrong for the prose picture, and everything that is right for the prose picture addressed directly, in turn, to the betrayal of the 'play'. These are questions, however, that bore deep — if I have successfully braved the danger that they absolutely do bore; so that I must content myself, as a glance at this point, with the claim for the author of *Le Père Goriot* that colloquial illustration, in his work, suffers less, on the whole, than in any other I know, from its attendant, its besetting and haunting penalty of springing, unless watched, a leak in its effect. It is as if the master of the ship were keeping his eye on the pump; the pump, I mean, of relief and alternation, the pump that keeps the vessel free of too much water. We must always remember that, save in the cases where 'dialogue' is organic, is the very law of the game — in which case, as I say, the game is another business altogether — it is essentially the fluid element: as, for instance (to cite, conveniently, Balzac's most eminent prose contemporary) was strikingly its character in the elder Dumas: just as its character in the younger, the dramatist, illustrates supremely what I call the other game. The current, in old Dumas, the large, loose, facile flood of talked movement, talked interest, as much as you will, is, in virtue of this fluidity, a current indeed, with so little of wrought texture that we float and splash in it; feeling it thus resemble much more some capacious tepid tank than the figured tapestry, all over-scored with objects in fine perspective, which symbolizes to me (if one may have a symbol) the last word of the achieved fable. Such a tapestry, with its wealth of expression of its subject, with its myriad ordered stitches, its harmonies of tone and felicities of taste, is a work, above all, of closeness — and therefore the more pertinent image here, as it is in the name of closeness that I am inviting you to let Balzac once more appeal to you.

It will strike you perhaps that I speak as if we all, as if you all, without exception were novelists, haunting the back shop, the laboratory, or, more nobly expressed, the inner shrine of the temple; but such assumptions, in this age of print — if I may not say this age of poetry — are perhaps never too wide of the mark, and I have at any rate taken your interest sufficiently for granted to ask you to close up with me for an hour at the feet of the master of us all. Many of us may stray, but he always remains — he is fixed by virtue of his weight. Do not look too knowing at that — as a hint that you were already conscious he is heavy, and that if this is what I have mainly to suggest my lesson might have been spared. He is, I grant, too heavy to be moved; many of us may stray and straggle, as I say — since we have not his inaptitude largely to circulate. There is none the less such an odd condition as circulating without motion, and I am not so sure that even in our own way we do move. We do not, at any rate, get away from him; he is behind us, at the worst, when he is not before, and I feel that any course about the country we explore is ever best held by keeping him, through the trees of the forest, in sight. So far as we do move, we move round him; every road comes back to him; he sits there, in spite of us, so massively, for orientation. 'Heavy' therefore if we like, but heavy because weighted with his fortune; the extraordinary fortune that has survived all the extravagance of his career, his twenty years of royal intellectual spending, and that has done so by reason of the rare value of the original property — the high, prime genius so tied-up from him that that was safe. And 'that', through all that has come and gone, has steadily, has enormously appreciated. Let us then also, if we see him, in the sacred grove, as our towering idol, see him as gilded thick, with so much gold — plated and burnished and bright, in the manner of towering idols. It is for the lighter and looser and poorer among us to be gilded thin!

PART TWO

Novelists

ANTHONY TROLLOPE

1883

WHEN, a few months ago, Anthony Trollope laid down his pen for the last time, it was a sign of the complete extinction of that group of admirable writers who, in England, during the preceding half century, had done so much to elevate the art of the novelist. The author of *The Warden*, of *Barchester Towers*, of *Framley Parsonage*, does not, to our mind, stand on the very same level as Dickens, Thackeray and George Eliot; for his talent was of a quality less fine than theirs. But he belonged to the same family — he had as much to tell us about English life; he was strong, genial and abundant. He published too much; the writing of novels had ended by becoming, with him, a perceptibly mechanical process. Dickens was prolific, Thackeray produced with a freedom for which we are constantly grateful; but we feel that these writers had their periods of gestation. They took more time to look at their subject; relatively (for today there is not much leisure, at best, for those who undertake to entertain a hungry public), they were able to wait for inspiration. Trollope's fecundity was prodigious; there was no limit to the work he was ready to do. It is not unjust to say that he sacrificed quality to quantity. Abundance, certainly, is in itself a great merit; almost all the greatest writers have been abundant. But Trollope's fertility was gross, importunate; he himself contended, we believe, that he had given to the world a greater number of printed pages of fiction than any of his literary contemporaries. Not only did his novels follow each other without visible intermission, overlapping and treading on each other's heels, but most of these works are of extraordinary length. *Orley Farm*, *Can You Forgive Her?*, *He Knew He Was Right*, are exceedingly voluminous tales. *The Way We Live Now* is one of the longest of modern novels. Trollope produced, moreover, in the intervals of larger labour a great number of short stories, many of them charming, as well as various books of travel, and two or three biographies. He was the great *improvisatore* of these latter years. Two distinguished story-tellers of the other sex — one in France and one in England — have shown an extraordinary facility of composition; but Trollope's pace was brisker even than that of the wonderful Mme Sand and the delightful Mrs Oliphant. He had taught himself to keep this pace, and had reduced his admirable faculty to a system. Every day of his life he wrote a certain number of pages of his current tale, a number sacramental and invariable, independent of mood and place. It was once the fortune of the author of these lines to cross the Atlantic in his company, and he has never forgotten the magnificent example of plain persistence that it was in the power of the eminent novelist to give on that occasion. The season was unpropitious, the vessel overcrowded, the voyage detestable; but Trollope shut himself up in his cabin every morning for a purpose which, on the part of a distinguished writer who was also an invulnerable sailor, could only be communion with the muse. He drove his pen as steadily on the tumbling ocean as in Montague Square; and as his voyages were many, it was his practice before sailing to come down to the ship and confer with the carpenter, who was instructed to rig up a rough writing-table in his small sea-chamber. Trollope has been accused of being deficient in imagination, but in the face of such a fact as that the charge will scarcely seem just. The power to shut one's eyes, one's ears (to say nothing of another sense), upon the scenery of a pitching Cunarder and open them upon the loves and sorrows of Lily Dale or the conjugal embarrassments of Lady Glencora Palliser, is certainly a faculty which could take to itself wings. The imagination that Trollope possessed he had at least thoroughly at his command. I speak of all this in order to explain (in part) why it was that, with his extraordinary gift, there was always in him a certain infusion of the common. He abused his gift, overworked it, rode his horse too hard. As an artist he never took himself seriously; many people will say this was why he was so delightful.

The people who take themselves seriously are prigs and bores; and Trollope, with his perpetual 'story', which was the only thing he cared about, his strong good sense, hearty good nature, generous appreciation of life in all its varieties, responds in perfection to a certain English ideal. According to that ideal it is rather dangerous to be explicitly or consciously an artist — to have a system, a doctrine, a form. Trollope, from the first, went in, as they say, for having as little form as possible; it is probably safe to affirm that he had no 'views' whatever on the subject of novel writing. His whole manner is that of a man who regards the practice as one of the more delicate industries, but has never troubled his head nor clogged his pen with theories about the nature of his business. Fortunately he was not obliged to do so, for he had an easy road to success; and his honest, familiar, deliberate way of treating his readers as if he were one of them, and shared their indifference to a general view, their limitations of knowledge, their love of a comfortable ending, endeared him to many persons in England and America. It is in the name of some chosen form that, of late years, things have been made most disagreeable for the novel reader, who has been treated by several votaries of the new experiments in fiction to unwonted and bewildering sensations. With Trollope we were always safe; there were sure to be no new experiments.

His great, his inestimable merit was a complete appreciation of the usual. This gift is not rare in the annals of English fiction; it would naturally be found in a walk of literature in which the feminine mind has laboured so fruitfully. Women are delicate and patient observers; they hold their noses close, as it were, to the texture of life. They feel and perceive the real with a kind of personal tact, and their observations are recorded in a thousand delightful volumes. Trollope, therefore, with his eyes comfortably fixed on the familiar, the actual, was far from having invented a new category; his great distinction is that in resting there his vision took in so much of the field. And then he *felt* all daily and immediate things as well as saw them; felt them in a simple, direct, salubrious way, with their sadness, their gladness, their

charm, their comicality, all their obvious and measurable mean-
ings. He never wearied of the pre-established round of English
customs — never needed a respite or a change — was content to
go on indefinitely watching the life that surrounded him, and holding up his mirror to it. Into this mirror the public, at first especially, grew very fond of looking — for it saw itself reflected in
all the most credible and supposable ways, with that curiosity
that people feel to know how they look when they are represented, 'just as they are', by a painter who does not desire to put
them into an attitude, to drape them for an effect, to arrange his
light and his accessories. This exact and on the whole becoming
image, projected upon a surface without a strong intrinsic tone,
constitutes mainly the entertainment that Trollope offered his
readers. The striking thing to the critic was that his robust and
patient mind had no particular bias, his imagination no light of its
own. He saw things neither pictorially and grotesquely like
Dickens; nor with that combined disposition to satire and to
literary form which gives such 'body', as they say of wine, to the
manner of Thackeray; nor with anything of the philosophic, the
transcendental cast — the desire to follow them to their remote
relations — which we associate with the name of George Eliot.
Trollope had his elements of fancy, of satire, of irony; but these
qualities were not very highly developed, and he walked mainly
by the light of his good sense, his clear, direct vision of the things
that lay nearest, and his great natural kindness. There is something remarkably tender and friendly in his feeling about all
human perplexities; he takes the good-natured, temperate, con-
ciliatory view — the humorous view, perhaps, for the most part,
yet without a touch of pessimistic prejudice. As he grew older,
and had sometimes to go farther afield for his subjects, he acquired a savour of bitterness and reconciled himself sturdily to
treating of the disagreeable. A more copious record of disagreeable matters could scarcely be imagined, for instance, than *The
Way We Live Now*. But, in general, he has a wholesome mistrust
of morbid analysis, an aversion to inflicting pain. He has an infinite love of detail, but his details are, for the most part, the in-

numerable items of the expected. When the French are disposed to pay a compliment to the English mind they are so good as to say that there is in it something remarkably *honnête*. If I might borrow this epithet without seeming to be patronising, I should apply it to the genius of Anthony Trollope. He represents in an eminent degree this natural decorum of the English spirit, and represents it all the better that there is not in him a grain of the mawkish or the prudish. He writes, he feels, he judges like a man, talking plainly and frankly about many things, and is by no means destitute of a certain saving grace of coarseness. But he has kept the purity of his imagination and held fast to old-fashioned reverences and preferences. He thinks it a sufficient objection to several topics to say simply that they are unclean. There was nothing in his theory of the storyteller's art that tended to convert the reader's or the writer's mind into a vessel for polluting things. He recognized the right of the vessel to protest, and would have regarded such a protest as conclusive. With a considerable turn for satire, though this perhaps is more evident in his early novels than in his later ones, he had as little as possible of the quality of irony. He never played with a subject, never juggled with the sympathies or the credulity of his reader, was never in the least paradoxical or mystifying. He sat down to his theme in a serious, businesslike way, with his elbows on the table and his eye occasionally wandering to the clock.

To touch successively upon these points is to attempt a portrait, which I shall perhaps not altogether have failed to produce. The source of his success in describing the life that lay nearest to him, and describing it without any of those artistic perversions that come, as we have said, from a powerful imagination, from a cynical humour or from a desire to look, as George Eliot expresses it, for the suppressed transitions that unite all contrasts, the essence of this love of reality was his extreme interest in character. This is the fine and admirable quality in Trollope, this is what will preserve his best works in spite of those flatnesses which keep him from standing on quite the same level as the masters. Indeed this quality is so much one of the finest (to my mind at

least), that it makes me wonder the more that the writer who had it
so abundantly and so naturally should not have just that distinction which Trollope lacks, and which we find in his three brilliant
contemporaries. If he was in any degree a man of genius (and I
hold that he was), it was in virtue of this happy, instinctive perception of human varieties. His knowledge of the stuff we are
made of, his observation of the common behaviour of men and
women, was not reasoned nor acquired, not even particularly
studied. All human doings deeply interested him, human life, to
his mind, was a perpetual story; but he never attempted to take
the so-called scientific view, the view which has lately found ingenious advocates among the countrymen and successors of
Balzac. He had no airs of being able to tell you *why* people in a
given situation would conduct themselves in a particular way; it
was enough for him that he felt their feelings and struck the right
note, because he had, as it were, a good ear. If he was a knowing
psychologist he was so by grace; he was just and true without
apparatus and without effort. He must have had a great taste for
the moral question; he evidently believed that this is the basis of
the interest of fiction. We must be careful, of course, in attributing convictions and opinions to Trollope, who, as I have said,
had as little as possible of the pedantry of his art, and whose occasional chance utterances in regard to the object of the novelist and
his means of achieving it are of an almost startling simplicity. But
we certainly do not go too far in saying that he gave his practical
testimony in favour of the idea that the interest of a work of fiction is great in proportion as the people stand on their feet. His
great effort was evidently to make them stand so; if he achieved
this result with as little as possible of a flourish of the hand it was
nevertheless the measure of his success. If he had taken sides on
the droll, bemuddled opposition between novels of character and
novels of plot, I can imagine him to have said (except that he
never expressed himself in epigrams), that he preferred the former
class, inasmuch as character in itself is plot, while plot is by no
means character. It is more safe indeed to believe that his great
good sense would have prevented him from taking an idle contro-

versy seriously. Character, in any sense in which we can get at it, is action, and action is plot, and any plot which hangs together, even if it pretend to interest us only in the fashion of a Chinese puzzle, plays upon our emotion, our suspense, by means of personal references. We care what happens to people only in proportion as we know what people are. Trollope's great apprehension of the real, which was what made him so interesting, came to him through his desire to satisfy us on this point — to tell us what certain people were and what they did in consequence of being so. That is the purpose of each of his tales; and if these things produce an illusion it comes from the gradual abundance of his testimony as to the temper, the tone, the passions, the habits, the moral nature, of a certain number of contemporary Britons.

His stories, in spite of their great length, deal very little in the surprising, the exceptional, the complicated; as a general thing he has no great story to tell. The thing is not so much a story as a picture; if we hesitate to call it a picture it is because the idea of composition is not the controlling one and we feel that the author would regard the artistic, in general, as a kind of affectation. There is not even much description, in the sense which the present votaries of realism in France attach to that word. The painter lays his scene in a few deliberate, not especially pictorial strokes, and never dreams of finishing the piece for the sake of enabling the reader to hang it up. The finish, such as it is, comes later, from the slow and somewhat clumsy accumulation of small illustrations. These illustrations are sometimes of the commonest; Trollope turns them out inexhaustibly, repeats them freely, unfolds them without haste and without rest. But they are all of the most obvious sort, and they are none the worse for that. The point to be made is that they have no great spectacular interest (we beg pardon of the innumerable love affairs that Trollope has described), like many of the incidents, say, of Walter Scott and of Alexandre Dumas: if we care to know about them (as repetitions of a usual case), it is because the writer has managed, in his candid, literal, somewhat lumbering way, to tell us that about the men and women concerned which has already excited on their

96 THE HOUSE OF FICTION

behalf the impression of life. It is a marvel by what homely arts, by what imperturbable button-holing persistence, he contrives to excite this impression. Take, for example, such a work as *The Vicar of Bullhampton*. It would be difficult to state the idea of this slow but excellent story, which is a capital example of interest produced by the quietest conceivable means. The principal persons in it are a lively, jovial, high-tempered country clergyman, a young woman who is in love with her cousin, and a small, rather dull squire who is in love with the young woman. There is no connection between the affairs of the clergyman and those of the two other persons, save that these two are the Vicar's friends. The Vicar gives countenance, for Christian charity's sake, to a young countryman who is suspected (falsely, as it appears) of murder, and also to the lad's sister, who is more than suspected of leading an immoral life. Various people are shocked at his indiscretion, but in the end he is shown to have been no worse a clergyman because he is a good fellow. A cantankerous nobleman, who has a spite against him, causes a Methodist conventicle to be erected at the gates of the vicarage; but afterward, finding that he has no title to the land used for this obnoxious purpose, causes the conventicle to be pulled down, and is reconciled with the parson, who accepts an invitation to stay at the castle. Mary Lowther, the heroine of *The Vicar of Bullhampton*, is sought in marriage by Mr Harry Gilmore, to whose passion she is unable to respond; she accepts him, however, making him understand that she does not love him, and that her affections are fixed upon her kinsman, Captain Marrable, whom she would marry (and who would marry her), if he were not too poor to support a wife. If Mr Gilmore will take her on these terms she will become his spouse; but she gives him all sorts of warnings. They are not superfluous; for, as Captain Marrable presently inherits a fortune, she throws over Mr Gilmore, who retires to foreign lands, heartbroken, inconsolable. This is the substance of *The Vicar of Bullhampton*; the reader will see that it is not a very tangled skein. But if the interest is gradual it is extreme and constant, and it comes altogether from excellent portraiture. It is essentially a moral, a social interest. There is something masterly in the large-fisted grip with which, in work of this kind, Trollope handles his brush. The Vicar's nature is thoroughly analysed and rendered, and his monotonous friend the Squire, a man with limitations, but possessed and consumed by a genuine passion, is equally near the truth.

Trollope has described again and again the ravages of love, and it is wonderful to see how well, in these delicate matters, his plain good sense and good taste serve him. His story is always primarily a love story, and a love story constructed on an inveterate system. There is a young lady who has two lovers, or a young man who has two sweethearts; we are treated to the innumerable forms in which this predicament may present itself and the consequences, sometimes pathetic, sometimes grotesque, which spring from such false situations. Trollope is not what is called a colourist; still less is he a poet: he is seated on the back of heavy-footed prose. But his account of those sentiments which the poets are supposed to have made their own is apt to be as touching as demonstrations more lyrical. There is something wonderfully vivid in the state of mind of the unfortunate Harry Gilmore, of whom I have just spoken; and his history, which has no more pretensions to style than if it were cut out of yesterday's newspaper, lodges itself in the imagination in all sorts of classic company. He is not handsome, nor clever, nor rich, nor romantic, nor distinguished in any way; he is simply rather a dense, narrow-minded, stiff, obstinate, commonplace, conscientious modern Englishman, exceedingly in love and, from his own point of view, exceedingly ill-used. He is interesting because he suffers and because we are curious to see the form that suffering will take in that particular nature. Our good fortune, with Trollope, is that the person put before us will have, in spite of opportunities not to have it, a certain particular nature. The author has cared enough about the character of such a person to find out exactly what it is. Another particular nature in *The Vicar of Bullhampton* is the surly sturdy, skeptical old farmer Jacob Brattle, who doesn't want to be patronised by the parson, and in his dumb, dusky, half-brutal, half-spiritual melancholy, surrounded by domestic troubles, financial embarrassments and a puzzling world, declines altogether to be won over to clerical optimism. Such a figure as Jacob Brattle, purely episodical though it be, is an excellent English portrait. As thoroughly English, and the most striking thing in the book, is the combination, in the nature of Frank Fenwick — the delightful Vicar — of the patronizing, conventional, clerical element with all sorts of manliness and spontaneity; the union, or to a certain extent the contradiction, of official and personal geniality. Trollope touches these points in a way that shows that he knows his man. Delicacy is not his great sign, but when it is necessary he can be as delicate as any one else.

I alighted, just now, at a venture, upon the history of Frank Fenwick; it is far from being a conspicuous work in the immense list of Trollope's novels. But to choose an example one must choose arbitrarily, for examples of almost anything that one may wish to say are numerous to embarrassment. In speaking of a writer who produced so much and produced always in the same way, there is perhaps a certain unfairness in choosing at all. As no work has higher pretensions than any other, there may be a certain unkindness in holding an individual production up to the light. 'Judge me in the lump', we can imagine the author saying; 'I have only undertaken to entertain the British public. I don't pretend that each of my novels is an organic whole.' Trollope had no time to give his tales a classic roundness; yet there is (in spite of an extraordinary defect) something of that quality in the thing that first revealed him. *The Warden* was published in 1855. It made a great impression; and when, in 1857, *Barchester Towers* followed it, every one saw that English literature had a novelist the more. These were not the works of a young man, for Anthony Trollope had been born in 1815. It is remarkable to reflect, by the way, that his prodigious fecundity (he had published before *The Warden* three or four novels which attracted little attention) was enclosed between his fortieth and his sixty-seventh years. Trollope had lived long enough in the world to learn a good deal about it; and his maturity of feeling and evidently large know-

edge of English life were for much in the effect produced by the
two clerical tales. It was easy to see that he would take up room.
What he had picked up, to begin with, was a comprehensive,
various impression of the clergy of the Church of England and
the manners and feelings that prevail in cathedral towns. This,
for a while, was his speciality, and, as always happens in such
cases, the public was disposed to prescribe to him that path. He
knew about bishops, archdeacons, prebendaries, precentors, and
about their wives and daughters; he knew what these dignitaries
say to each other when they are collected together, aloof from
secular ears. He even knew what sort of talk goes on between a
bishop and a bishop's lady when the august couple are enshrouded
in the privacy of the episcopal bedroom. This knowledge, somehow, was rare and precious. No one, as yet, had been bold enough
to snatch the illuminating torch from the very summit of the
altar. Trollope enlarged his field very speedily — there is, as I
remember that work, as little as possible of the ecclesiastical in the
tale of *The Three Clerks*, which came after *Barchester Towers*. But
he always retained traces of his early divination of the clergy; he
introduced them frequently, and he always did them easily and
well. There is no ecclesiastical figure, however, so good as the
first — no creation of this sort so happy as the admirable Mr
Harding. *The Warden* is a delightful tale, and a signal instance of
Trollope's habit of offering us the spectacle of a character. A
motive more delicate, more slender, as well as more charming,
could scarcely be conceived. It is simply the history of an old
man's conscience.

The good and gentle Mr Harding, precentor of Barchester
Cathedral, also holds the post of warden of Hiram's Hospital, an
ancient charity where twelve old paupers are maintained in comfort. The office is in the gift of the bishop, and its emoluments are
as handsome as the duties of the place are small. Mr Harding has
for years drawn his salary in quiet gratitude; but his moral repose
is broken by hearing it at last begun to be said that the wardenship
is a sinecure, that the salary is a scandal, and that a large part, at
least, of his easy income ought to go to the pensioners of the

hospital. He is sadly troubled and perplexed, and when the great London newspapers take up the affair he is overwhelmed with confusion and shame. He thinks the newspapers are right — he perceives that the warden is an overpaid and rather a useless functionary. The only thing he can do is to resign the place. He has no means of his own — he is only a quiet, modest, innocent old man, with a taste, a passion, for old church-music and the violoncello. But he determines to resign, and he does resign in spite of the sharp opposition of his friends. He does what he thinks right, and goes to live in lodgings over a shop in the Barchester High Street. That is all the story, and it has exceeding beauty. The question of Mr Harding's resignation becomes a drama, and we anxiously wait for the catastrophe. Trollope never did anything happier than the picture of this sweet and serious little old gentleman, who on most of the occasions of life has shown a lamblike softness and compliance, but in this particular matter opposes a silent, impenetrable obstinacy to the arguments of the friends who insist on his keeping his sinecure — fixing his mild, detached gaze on the distance, and making imaginary passes with his fiddle-bow while they demonstrate his pusillanimity. The subject of *The Warden*, exactly viewed, is the opposition of the two natures of Archdeacon Grantley and Mr Harding, and there is nothing finer in all Trollope than the vividness with which this opposition is presented. The archdeacon is as happy a portrait as the precentor — an image of the full-fed, worldly churchman, taking his stand squarely upon his rich temporalities, and regarding the church frankly as a fat social pasturage. It required the greatest tact and temperance to make the picture of Archdeacon Grantley stop just where it does. The type, impartially considered, is detestable, but the individual may be full of amenity. Trollope allows his archdeacon all the virtues he was likely to possess, but he makes his spiritual grossness wonderfully natural. No charge of exaggeration is possible, for we are made to feel that he is conscientious as well as arrogant, and expansive as well as hard. He is one of those figures that spring into being all at once, solidifying in the author's grasp. These two capital portraits are what we carry away from

The Warden, which some persons profess to regard as our writer's masterpiece. We remember, while it was still something of a novelty, to have heard a judicious critic say that it had much of the charm of *The Vicar of Wakefield*. Anthony Trollope would not have accepted the compliment, and would not have wished this little tale to pass before several of its successors. He would have said, very justly, that it gives too small a measure of his knowledge of life. It has, however, a certain classic roundness, though, as we said a moment since, there is a blemish on its fair face. The chapter on Dr Pessimist Anticant and Mr Sentiment would be a mistake almost inconceivable if Trollope had not in other places taken pains to show us that for certain forms of satire (the more violent, doubtless), he had absolutely no gift. Dr Anticant is a parody of Carlyle, and Mr Sentiment is an exposure of Dickens: and both these little *jeux d'esprit* are as infelicitous as they are misplaced. It was no less luckless an inspiration to convert Archdeacon Grantley's three sons, denominated respectively Charles James, Henry and Samuel, into little effigies of three distinguished English bishops of that period, whose well-known peculiarities are reproduced in the description of these unnatural urchins. The whole passage, as we meet it, is a sudden disillusionment; we are transported from the mellow atmosphere of an assimilated Barchester to the air of ponderous allegory.

I may take occasion to remark here upon a very curious fact — the fact that there are certain precautions in the way of producing that illusion dear to the intending novelist which Trollope not only habitually scorned to take, but really, as we may say, asking pardon for the heat of the thing, delighted wantonly to violate. He took a suicidal satisfaction in reminding the reader that the story he was telling was only, after all, a make-believe. He habitually referred to the work in hand (in the course of that work) as a novel, and to himself as a novelist, and was fond of letting the reader know that this novelist could direct the course of events according to his pleasure. Already, in *Barchester Towers*, he falls into this pernicious trick. In describing the wooing of Eleanor Bold by Mr Arabin he has occasion to say that the lady might

have acted in a much more direct and natural way than the way he
attributes to her. But if she had, he adds, 'where would have been
my novel?' The last chapter of the same story begins with the
remark, 'The end of a novel, like the end of a children's dinner
party, must be made up of sweetmeats and sugar-plums.' These
little slaps at credulity (we might give many more specimens) are
very discouraging, but they are even more inexplicable; for they
are deliberately inartistic, even judged from the point of view of
that rather vague consideration of form which is the only canon
we have a right to impose upon Trollope. It is impossible to
imagine what a novelist takes himself to be unless he regard himself as an historian and his narrative as a history. It is only as an
historian that he has the smallest *locus standi*. As a narrator of
fictitious events he is nowhere; to insert into his attempt a back-
bone of logic, he must relate events that are assumed to be real.
This assumption permeates, animates all the work of the most
solid storytellers; we need only mention (to select a single instance) the magnificent historical tone of Balzac, who would as
soon have thought of admitting to the reader that he was deceiv-
ing him, as Garrick or John Kemble would have thought of pull-
ing off his disguise in front of the footlights. Therefore, when
Trollope suddenly winks at us and reminds us that he is telling us
an arbitrary thing, we are startled and shocked in quite the same
way as if Macaulay or Motley were to drop the historic mask and
intimate that William of Orange was a myth or the Duke of Alva
an invention.

It is a part of this same ambiguity of mind as to what constitutes
evidence that Trollope should sometimes endow his people with
such fantastic names. Dr Pessimist Anticant and Mr Sentiment
make, as we have seen, an awkward appearance in a modern
novel; and Mr Neversay Die, Mr Stickatit, Mr Rerechild and Mr
Fillgrave (the two last the family physicians) are scarcely more
felicitous. It would be better to go back to Bunyan at once. There
is a person mentioned in *The Warden* under the name of Mr
Quiverful — a poor clergyman, with a dozen children, who holds
the living of Puddingdale. This name is a humorous allusion to

his overflowing nursery, and it matters little so long as he is not
brought to the front. But in *Barchester Towers*, which carries on
the history of Hiram's Hospital, Mr Quiverful becomes, as a
candidate for Mr Harding's vacant place, an important element,
and the reader is made proportionately unhappy by the primitive
character of this satiric note. A Mr Quiverful with fourteen children (which is the number attained in *Barchester Towers*) is too
difficult to believe in. We can believe in the name and we can
believe in the children; but we cannot manage the combination. It
is probably not unfair to say that if Trollope derived half his inspiration from life, he derived the other half from Thackeray; his
earlier novels, in especial, suggest an honourable emulation of the
author of *The Newcomes*. Thackeray's names were perfect; they
always had a meaning, and (except in his absolutely jocose productions, where they were still admirable) we can imagine, even
when they are most figurative, that they should have been borne
by real people. But in this, as in other respects, Trollope's hand
was heavier than his master's; though when he is content not to be
too comical his appellations are sometimes fortunate enough. Mrs
Proudie is excellent, for Mrs Proudie, and even the Duke of
Omnium and Gatherum Castle rather minister to illusion than
destroy it. Indeed, the names of houses and places, throughout
Trollope, are full of colour.

I would speak in some detail of *Barchester Towers* if this did
not seem to commit me to the prodigious task of appreciating
each of Trollope's works in succession. Such an attempt as that is
so far from being possible that I must frankly confess to not
having read everything that proceeded from his pen. There came
a moment in his vigorous career (it was even a good many years
ago) when I renounced the effort to 'keep up' with him. It ceased
to seem obligatory to have read his last story; it ceased soon to be
very possible to know which was his last. Before that, I had been
punctual, devoted; and the memories of the earlier period are
delightful. It reached, if I remember correctly, to about the publication of *He Knew He Was Right*; after which, to my recollection
(oddly enough, too, for that novel was good enough to encourage

a continuance of past favours, as the shop-keepers say), the picture becomes dim and blurred. The author of *Orley Farm* and
The Small House at Allington ceased to produce individual works;
his activity became a huge 'serial'. Here and there, in the vast
fluidity, an organic particle detached itself. *The Last Chronicle of
Barset*, for instance, is one of his most powerful things; it contains the sequel of the terrible history of Mr Crawley, the starving
curate — an episode full of that literally truthful pathos of which
Trollope was so often a master, and which occasionally raised
him quite to the level of his two immediate predecessors in the
vivid treatment of English life — great artists whose pathetic
effects were sometimes too visibly prepared. For the most part,
however, he should be judged by the productions of the first half
of his career; later the strong wine was rather too copiously
watered. His practice, his acquired facility, were such that his
hand went of itself, as it were, and the thing looked superficially
like a fresh inspiration. But it was not fresh, it was rather stale;
and though there was no appearance of effort, there was a fatal
dryness of texture. It was too little of a new story and too much
of an old one. Some of these ultimate compositions — *Phineas
Redux* (*Phineas Finn* is much better), *The Prime Minister, John
Caldigate, The American Senator, The Duke's Children* — betray
the dull, impersonal rumble of the mill wheel. What stands Trollope always in good stead (in addition to the ripe habit of writing)
is his various knowledge of the English world — to say nothing
of his occasionally laying under contribution the American. His
American portraits, by the way (they are several in number), are
always friendly; they hit it off more happily than the attempt to
depict American character from the European point of view is
accustomed to do: though, indeed, as we ourselves have not yet
learned to represent our types very finely — are not apparently
even very sure what our types are — it is perhaps not to be
wondered at that transatlantic talent should miss the mark. The
weakness of transatlantic talent in this particular is apt to be want
of knowledge; but Trollope's knowledge has all the air of being
excellent, though not intimate, Had he indeed striven to learn the

way to the American heart? No less than twice, and possibly even
oftener, has he rewarded the merit of a scion of the British aristocracy with the hand of an American girl. The American girl was
destined sooner or later to make her entrance into British fiction,
and Trollope's treatment of this complicated being is full of good
humour and that of fatherly indulgence, that almost motherly
sympathy, which characterizes his attitude throughout toward
the youthful feminine. He has not mastered all the springs of her
delicate organism nor sounded all the mysteries of her conversation. Indeed, as regards these latter phenomena, he has observed
a few of which he has been the sole observer. 'I got to be thinking
if any one of them should ask me to marry him', words attributed
to Miss Boncassen, in *The Duke's Children*, have much more the
note of English American than of American English. But, on the
whole, in these matters Trollope does very well. His fund of acquaintance with his own country — and indeed with the world at
large — was apparently inexhaustible, and it gives his novels a
spacious, geographical quality which we should not know where
to look for elsewhere in the same degree, and which is the sign of
an extraordinary difference between such an horizon as his and
the limited world-outlook, as the Germans would say, of the
brilliant writers who practise the art of realistic fiction on the
other side of the Channel. Trollope was familiar with all sorts and
conditions of men, with the business of life, with affairs, with the
great world of sport, with every component part of the ancient
fabric of English society. He had travelled more than once all
over the globe, and for him, therefore, the background of the
human drama was a very extensive scene. He had none of the
pedantry of the cosmopolite; he remained a sturdy and sensible
middle-class Englishman. But his work is full of implied reference
to the whole arena of modern vagrancy. He was for many years
concerned in the management of the Post Office; and we can imagine no experience more fitted to impress a man with the diversity
of human relations. It is possibly from this source that he derived
his fondness for transcribing the letters of his lovelorn maidens
and other embarrassed persons. No contemporary storyteller deals

so much in letters; the modern English epistle (very happily imitated, for the most part) is his unfailing resource.

There is perhaps little reason in it, but I find myself comparing this tone of allusion to many lands and many things, and whatever it brings us of easier respiration, with that narrow vision of humanity which accompanies the strenuous, serious work lately offered us in such abundance by the votaries of art for art who sit so long at their desks in Parisian *quatrièmes*. The contrast is complete, and it would be interesting, had we space to do so here, to see how far it goes. On one side a wide, good-humoured, superficial glance at a good many things; on the other a gimlet-like consideration of a few. Trollope's plan, as well as Zola's, was to describe the life that lay near him; but the two writers differ immensely as to what constitutes life and what constitutes nearness. For Trollope the emotions of a nursery governess in Australia would take precedence of the adventures of a depraved *femme du monde* in Paris or London. They both undertake to do the same thing — to depict French and English manners; but the English writer (with his unsurpassed industry) is so occasional, so accidental, so full of the echoes of voices that are not the voice of the muse. Gustave Flaubert, Émile Zola, Alphonse Daudet, on the other hand, are nothing if not concentrated and sedentary. Trollope's realism is as instinctive, as inveterate as theirs; but nothing could mark more the difference between the French and English mind than the difference in the application, on one side and the other, of this system. We say system, though on Trollope's part it is none. He has no visible, certainly no explicit care for the literary part of the business; he writes easily, comfortably, and profusely, but his style has nothing in common either with the minute stippling of Daudet or the studied rhythms of Flaubert. He accepted all the common restrictions, and found that even within the barriers there was plenty of material. He attaches a preface to one of his novels — *The Vicar of Bullhampton*, before mentioned — for the express purpose of explaining why he has introduced a young woman who may, in truth, as he says, be called a 'castaway'; and in relation to this episode he remarks that it is the object of the novelist's art to entertain the young people of both sexes. Writers of the French school would, of course, protest indignantly against such a formula as this, which is the only one of the kind that I remember to have encountered in Trollope's pages. It is meagre, assuredly; but Trollope's practice was really much larger than so poor a theory. And indeed any theory was good which enabled him to produce the works which he put forth between 1856 and 1869, or later. In spite of his want of doctrinal richness I think he tells us, on the whole, more about life than the 'naturalists' in our sister republic. I say this with a full consciousness of the opportunities an artist loses in leaving so many corners unvisited, so many topics untouched, simply because I think his perception of character was naturally more just and liberal than that of the naturalists. This has been from the beginning the good fortune of our English providers of fiction, as compared with the French. They are inferior in audacity, in neatness, in acuteness, in intellectual vivacity, in the arrangement of material, in the art of characterizing visible things. But they have been more at home in the moral world; as people say today they know their way about the conscience. This is the value of much of the work done by the feminine wing of the school — work which presents itself to French taste as deplorably thin and insipid. Much of it is exquisitely human, and that after all is a merit. As regards Trollope, one may perhaps characterize him best, in opposition to what I have ventured to call the sedentary school, by saying that he was a novelist who hunted the fox. Hunting was for years his most valued recreation, and I remember that when I made in his company the voyage of which I have spoken, he had timed his return from the Antipodes exactly so as to be able to avail himself of the first day on which it should be possible to ride to hounds. He 'worked' the hunting field largely; it constantly reappears in his novels; it was excellent material.

But it would be hard to say (within the circle in which he revolved) what material he neglected. I have allowed myself to be detained so long by general considerations that I have almost forfeited the opportunity to give examples. I have spoken of *The*

Warden not only because it made his reputation, but because, taken in conjunction with *Barchester Towers*, it is thought by many people to be his highest flight. *Barchester Towers* is admirable; it has an almost Thackerayan richness. Archdeacon Grantley grows more and more into life, and Mr Harding is as charming as ever. Mrs Proudie is ushered into a world in which she was to make so great an impression. Mrs Proudie has become classical; of all Trollope's characters she is the most often referred to. She is exceedingly true; but I do not think she is quite so good as her fame, and as several figures from the same hand that have not won so much honour. She is rather too violent, too vixenish, too sour. The truly awful female bully — the completely fatal episcopal spouse — would have, I think, a more insidious form, a greater amount of superficial padding. The Stanhope family, in *Barchester Towers*, are a real *trouvaille*, and the idea of transporting the Signora Vesey-Neroni into a cathedral town was an inspiration. There could not be a better example of Trollope's manner of attaching himself to character than the whole picture of Bertie Stanhope. Bertie is a delightful creation; and the scene in which, at the party given by Mrs Proudie, he puts this majestic woman to rout is one of the most amusing in all the chronicles of Barset. It is perhaps permitted to wish, by the way, that this triumph had been effected by means intellectual rather than physical; though, indeed, if Bertie had not despoiled her of her drapery we should have lost the lady's admirable 'Unhand it, sir!' Mr Arabin is charming, and the henpecked bishop has painful truth; but Mr Slope, I think, is a little too arrant a scamp. He is rather too much the old game; he goes too coarsely to work, and his clamminess and cant are somewhat overdone. He is an interesting illustration, however, of the author's dislike (at that period at least) of the bareness of evangelical piety. In one respect *Barchester Towers* is (to the best of our recollection) unique, being the only one of Trollope's novels in which the interest does not centre more or less upon a simple maiden in her flower. The novel offers us nothing in the way of a girl; though we know that this attractive object was to lose nothing by waiting. Eleanor Bold is a charming and natural person, but Eleanor Bold is not in her flower. After this, however, Trollope settled down steadily to the English girl; he took possession of her, and turned her inside out. He never made her a subject of heartless satire, as cynical fabulists of other lands have been known to make the shining daughters of those climes; he bestowed upon her the most serious, the most patient, the most tender, the most copious consideration. He is evidently always more or less in love with her, and it is a wonder how under these circumstances he should make her so objective, plant her so well on her feet. But, as I have said, if he was a lover, he was a paternal lover; as competent as a father who has had fifty daughters. He has presented the British maiden under innumerable names, in every station and in every emergency in life, and with every combination of moral and physical qualities. She is always definite and natural. She plays her part most properly. She has always health in her cheek and gratitude in her eye. She has not a touch of the morbid, and is delightfully tender, modest and fresh. Trollope's heroines have a strong family likeness, but it is a wonder how finely he discriminates between them. One feels, as one reads him, like a man with 'sets' of female cousins. Such a person is inclined at first to lump each group together; but presently he finds that even in the groups there are subtle differences. Trollope's girls, for that matter, would make delightful cousins. He has scarcely drawn, that we can remember, a disagreeable damsel. Lady Alexandrina de Courcy is disagreeable, and so is Amelia Roper, and so are various provincial (and indeed metropolitan) spinsters, who set their caps at young clergymen and government clerks. Griselda Grantley was a stick; and considering that she was intended to be attractive, Alice Vavasor does not commend herself particularly to our affections. But the young women I have mentioned had ceased to belong to the blooming season; they had entered the bristling, or else the limp, period. Not that Trollope's more mature spinsters invariably fall into these extremes. Miss Thorne of Ullathorne, Miss Dunstable, Miss Mackenzie, Rachel Ray (if she may be called mature), Miss Baker and Miss Todd, in *The Bertrams*, Lady Julia Guest, who comforts poor

John Eames: these and many other amiable figures rise up to contradict the idea. A gentleman who had sojourned in many lands was once asked by a lady (neither of these persons was English), in what country he had found the women most to his taste. 'Well, in England', he replied. 'In England?' the lady repeated. 'Oh yes,' said her interlocutor; 'they are so affectionate!' The remark was fatuous, but it has the merit of describing Trollope's heroines. They are so affectionate. Mary Thorne, Lucy Robarts, Adela Gauntlet, Lily Dale, Nora Rowley, Grace Crawley, have a kind of clinging tenderness, a passive sweetness, which is quite in the old English tradition. Trollope's genius is not the genius of Shakespeare, but his heroines have something of the fragrance of Imogen and Desdemona. There are two little stories to which, I believe, his name has never been affixed, but which he is known to have written, that contain an extraordinarily touching representation of the passion of love in its most sensitive form. In *Linda Tressel* and *Nina Balatka* the vehicle is plodding prose, but the effect is none the less poignant. And in regard to this I may say that in a hundred places in Trollope the extremity of pathos is reached by the homeliest means. He often achieved a conspicuous intensity of the tragical. The long, slow process of the conjugal wreck of Louis Trevelyan and his wife (in *He Knew He Was Right*), with that rather lumbering movement which is often characteristic of Trollope, arrives at last at an impressive completeness of misery. It is the history of an accidental rupture between two stiff-necked and ungracious people — 'the little rift within the lute' — which widens at last into a gulf of anguish. Touch is added to touch, one small, stupid, fatal aggravation to another; and as we gaze into the widening breach we wonder at the vulgar materials of which tragedy sometimes composes itself. I have always remembered the chapter called 'Casalunga', towards the close of *He Knew He Was Right*, as a powerful picture of the insanity of stiff-neckedness. Louis Trevelyan, separated from his wife, alone, haggard, suspicious, unshaven, undressed, living in a desolate villa on a hilltop near Siena and returning doggedly to his fancied wrong, which he has nursed until it becomes an hallucination, is a picture worthy of Balzac. Here and in several other places Trollope has dared to be thoroughly logical; he has not sacrificed to conventional optimism; he has not been afraid of a misery which should be too much like life. He has had the same courage in the history of the wretched Mr Crawley and in that of the much-to-be-pitied Lady Mason. In this latter episode he found an admirable subject. A quiet, charming, tender-souled English gentlewoman who (as I remember the story of *Orley Farm*) forges a codicil to a will in order to benefit her son, a young prig who doesn't appreciate immoral heroism, and who is suspected, accused, tried, and saved from conviction only by some turn of fortune that I forget; who is furthermore an object of high-bred, respectful, old-fashioned gallantry on the part of a neighbouring baronet, so that she sees herself dishonoured in his eyes as well as condemned in those of her boy: such a personage and such a situation would be sure to yield, under Trollope's handling, the last drop of their reality.

There are many more things to say about him than I am able to add to these very general observations, the limit of which I have already passed. It would be natural, for instance, for a critic who affirms that his principal merit is the portrayal of individual character, to enumerate several of the figures that he has produced. I have not done this, and I must ask the reader who is not acquainted with Trollope to take my assertion on trust; the reader who knows him will easily make a list for himself. No account of him is complete in which allusion is not made to his practice of carrying certain actors from one story to another — a practice which he may be said to have inherited from Thackeray, as Thackeray may be said to have borrowed it from Balzac. It is a great mistake, however, to speak of it as an artifice which would not naturally occur to a writer proposing to himself to make a general portrait of a society. He has to construct that society, and it adds to the illusion in any given case that certain other cases correspond with it. Trollope constructed a great many things — a clergy, an aristocracy, a middle-class, an administrative class, a little replica of the political world. His political novels are distinctly dull, and I confess I have not been able to read them. He evidently took a good deal of pains with his aristocracy; it makes its first appearance, if I remember right, in *Doctor Thorne*, in the person of the Lady Arabella de Courcy. It is difficult for us in America to measure the success of that picture, which is probably, however, not absolutely to the life. There is in *Doctor Thorne* and some other works a certain crudity of reference to distinctions of rank — as if people's consciousness of this matter were, on either side, rather inflated. It suggests a general state of tension. It is true that, if Trollope's consciousness had been more flaccid he would perhaps not have given us Lady Lufton and Lady Glencora Palliser. Both of these noble persons are as living as possible, though I see Lady Lufton, with her terror of Lucy Robarts, the best. There is a touch of poetry in the figure of Lady Glencora, but I think there is a weak spot in her history. The actual woman would have made a fool of herself to the end with Burgo Fitzgerald; she would not have discovered the merits of Plantagenet Palliser — or if she had, she would not have cared about them. It is an illustration of the businesslike way in which Trollope laid out his work that he always provided a sort of underplot to alternate with his main story — a strain of narrative of which the scene is usually laid in a humbler walk of life. It is to his underplot that he generally relegates his vulgar people, his disagreeable young women; and I have often admired the perseverance with which he recounts these less edifying items. Now and then, it may be said, as in *Ralph the Heir*, the story appears to be all underplot and all vulgar people. These, however, are details. As I have already intimated, it is difficult to specify in Trollope's work, on account of the immense quantity of it; and there is sadness in the thought that this enormous mass does not present itself in a very portable form to posterity.

Trollope did not write for posterity; he wrote for the day, the moment; but these are just the writers whom posterity is apt to put into its pocket. So much of the life of his time is reflected in his novels that we must believe a part of the record will be saved; and the best parts of them are so sound and true and genial, that readers with an eye to that sort of entertainment will always be sure, in a certain proportion, to turn to them. Trollope will remain one of the most trustworthy, though not one of the most eloquent, of the writers who have helped the heart of man to know itself. The heart of man does not always desire this knowledge; it prefers sometimes to look at history in another way — to look at the manifestations, without troubling about the motives. There are two kinds of taste in the appreciation of imaginative literature: the taste for emotions of surprise, and the taste for emotions of recognition. It is the latter that Trollope gratifies, and he gratifies it the more that the medium of his own mind, through which we see what he shows us, gives a confident direction to our sympathy. His natural rightness and purity are so real that the good things he projects must be real. A race is fortunate when it has a good deal of the sort of imagination — of imaginative feeling — that had fallen to the share of Anthony Trollope; and in this possession our English race is not poor.

ROBERT LOUIS STEVENSON

1887

If there be a writer of our language at the present moment who has the effect of making us regret the extinction of the pleasant fashion of the literary portrait, it is certainly the bright particular genius whose name is written at the head of these remarks. Mr Stevenson fairly challenges portraiture, as we pass him on the highway of literature (if that be the road, rather than some wandering, sun-chequered by-lane that he may be said to follow), just as the possible model, in local attire, challenges the painter who wanders through the streets of a foreign town looking for subjects. He gives us new ground to wonder why the effort to fix a face and figure, to seize a literary character and transfer it to the canvas of the critic, should have fallen into such discredit among us and have given way to the mere multiplication of little private judgment-seats, where the scales and the judicial wig, both of them considerably awry, and not rendered more august by the company of a vicious-looking switch, have taken the place, as the symbols of office, of the kindly, disinterested palette and brush. It has become the fashion to be effective at the expense of the sitter, to make some little point, or inflict some little dig, with a heated party air, rather than to catch a talent in the fact, follow its line, and put a finger on its essence: so that the exquisite art of criticism, smothered in grossness, finds itself turned into a question of 'sides'. The critic industriously keeps his score, but it is seldom to be hoped that the author, criminal though he may be, will be apprehended by justice through the handbills given out in the case; for it is of the essence of a happy description that it shall have been preceded by a happy observation and a free curiosity; and desuetude, as we say, has overtaken these amiable, uninvidious faculties, which have not the glory of organs and chairs.

I hasten to add that it is not the purpose of these few pages to restore their lustre, or to bring back the more penetrating vision of which we lament the disappearance. No individual can bring it back, for the light that we look at things by is, after all, made by all of us. It is sufficient to note, in passing, that if Mr Stevenson had presented himself in an age, or in a country, of portraiture, the painters would certainly each have had a turn at him. The easels and benches would have bristled, the circle would have been close, and quick, from the canvas to the sitter, the rising and falling of heads. It has happened to all of us to have gone into a studio, a studio of pupils, and seen the thick cluster of bent backs and the conscious model in the midst. It has happened to us to be struck, or not to be struck, with the beauty or the symmetry of this personage, and to have made some remark which, whether expressing admiration or disappointment, has elicited from one of the attentive workers the exclamation, 'Character — character is what he has!' These words may be applied to Mr Robert Louis Stevenson; in the language of that art which depends most on direct observation, character, character is what he has. He is essentially a model, in the sense of a sitter; I do not mean, of course, in the sense of a pattern or a guiding light. And if the figures who have a life in literature may also be divided into two great classes, we may add that he is conspicuously one of the draped; he would never, if I may be allowed the expression, pose for the nude. There are writers who present themselves before the critic with just the amount of drapery that is necessary for decency; but Mr Stevenson is not one of these — he makes his appearance in an amplitude of costume. His costume is part of the character of which I just now spoke; it never occurs to us to ask how he would look without it. Before all things he is a writer with a style — a model with a complexity of curious and picturesque garments. It is by the cut and the colour of this rich and becoming frippery — I use the term endearingly, as a painter might — that he arrests the eye and solicits the brush.

That is, frankly, half the charm he has for us, that he wears a dress and wears it with courage, with a certain cock of the hat and

tinkle of the supererogatory sword; or, in other words, that he is
curious of expression, and regards the literary form not simply as
a code of signals, but as the keyboard of a piano and as so much
plastic material. He has that vice deplored by Mr Herbert Spencer,
a manner — a manner for manner's sake it may sometimes doubtless be said. He is as different as possible from the sort of writer
who regards words as numbers, and a page as the mere addition
of them; much more, to carry out our image, the dictionary stands
for him as a wardrobe, and a proposition as a button for his coat.
Mr William Archer, in an article[1] so gracefully and ingeniously
turned that the writer may almost be accused of imitating even
while he deprecates, speaks of him as a votary of 'lightness of
touch' at any cost, and remarks that 'he is not only philosophically
content, but deliberately resolved, that his readers shall look first
to his manner and only in the second place to his matter'. I shall
not attempt to gainsay this: I cite it rather, for the present, because it carries out our own sense. Mr Stevenson delights in a
style, and his own has nothing accidental or diffident; it is eminently conscious of its responsibilities and meets them with a kind
of gallantry — as if language were a pretty woman and a person
who proposes to handle it had of necessity to be something of a
Don Juan. This bravery of gesture is a noticeable part of his
nature, and it is rather odd that at the same time a striking feature
of that nature should be an absence of care for things feminine.
His books are for the most part books without women, and it is
not women who fall most in love with them. But Mr Stevenson
does not need, as we may say, a petticoat to inflame him; a happy
collocation of words will serve the purpose, or a singular image,
or the bright eye of a passing conceit, and he will carry off a pretty
paradox without so much as a scuffle. The tone of letters is in him
— the tone of letters as distinct from that of philosophy, or of
those industries whose uses are supposed to be immediate. Many
readers, no doubt, consider that he carries it too far; they manifest
an impatience for some glimpse of his moral message. They may

[1] 'R. L. Stevenson: his Style and Thought', *Time*, November 1885.

be heard to ask what it is he proposes to demonstrate, with such a variety of paces and graces.

The main thing that he demonstrates, to our own perception, is that it is a delight to read him, and that he renews this delight by a constant variety of experiment. Of this anon, however; and meanwhile, it may be noted as a curious characteristic of current fashions that the writer whose effort is perceptibly that of the artist is very apt to find himself thrown on the defensive. A work of literature is a form, but the author who betrays a consciousness of the responsibilities involved in this circumstance not rarely perceives himself to be regarded as an uncanny personage. The usual judgment is that he may be artistic, but that he must not be too much so; that way, apparently, lies something worse than madness. This queer superstition has so successfully imposed itself that the mere fact of having been indifferent to such a danger constitutes in itself an originality. How few they are in number and how soon we could name them, the writers of English prose, at the present moment, the quality of whose prose is personal, expressive, renewed at each attempt! The state of things that would have expected to be the rule has become the exception, and an exception for which, most of the time, an apology appears to be thought necessary. A mill that grinds with regularity and with a certain commercial fineness — that is the image suggested by the manner of a good many of the fraternity. They turn out an article for which there is a demand, they keep a shop for a speciality, and the business is carried on in accordance with a useful, well-tested prescription. It is just because he has no speciality that Mr Stevenson is an individual, and because his curiosity is the only receipt by which he produces. Each of his books is an independent effort — a window opened to a different view. *Doctor Jekyll and Mr Hyde* is as dissimilar as possible from *Treasure Island*; *Virginibus Puerisque* has nothing in common with *The New Arabian Nights*, and I should never have supposed *A Child's Garden of Verses* to be from the hand of the author of *Prince Otto*.

Though Mr Stevenson cares greatly for his phrase, as every writer should who respects himself and his art, it takes no very attentive reading of his volumes to show that it is not what he cares for most, and that he regards an expressive style only, after all, as a means. It seems to me the fault of Mr Archer's interesting paper that it suggests too much that the author of these volumes considers the art of expression as an end — an ingenious game of words. He finds that Mr Stevenson is not serious, that he neglects a whole side of life, that he has no perception, and no consciousness, of suffering; that he speaks as a happy but heartless pagan, living only in his senses (which the critic admits to be exquisitely fine), and that in a world full of heaviness he is not sufficiently aware of the philosophic limitations of mere technical skill. In sketching these aberrations Mr Archer himself, by the way, displays anything but ponderosity of hand. He is not the first reader, and will not be the last, who shall have been irritated by Mr Stevenson's jauntiness. That jauntiness is an essential part of his genius; but, to my sense it ceases to be irritating — it indeed becomes positively touching and constitutes an appeal to sympathy and even to tenderness — when once one has perceived what lies beneath the dancing-tune to which he mostly moves. Much as he cares for his phrase, he cares more for life, and for a certain transcendently lovable part of it. He feels, as it seems to us, and that is not given to every one; this constitutes a philosophy which Mr Archer fails to read between his lines — the respectable, desirable moral which many a reader doubtless finds that he neglects to point. He does not feel everything equally, by any manner of means; but his feelings are always his reason. He regards them, whatever they may be, as sufficiently honourable, does not disguise them in other names or colours, and looks at whatever he meets in the brilliant candle-light that they shed. As in his extreme artistic vivacity he seems really disposed to try everything he has tried once, by way of a change, to be inhuman, and there is a hard glitter about *Prince Otto* which seems to indicate that in this case too he has succeeded, as he has done in most of the feats that he has attempted. But *Prince Otto* is even less like his other productions than his other productions are like each other.

The part of life that he cares for most is youth, and the direct expression of the love of youth is the beginning and the end of his message. His appreciation of this delightful period amounts to a passion, and a passion, in the age in which we live, strikes us on the whole as a sufficient philosophy. It ought to satisfy Mr Archer, and there are writers who press harder than Mr Stevenson, on whose behalf no such moral motive can be alleged. Mingled with this almost equal love of a literary surface, it represents a real originality. This combination is the keynote of Mr Stevenson's faculty and the explanation of his perversities. The feelings of one's teens, and even of an earlier period (for the delights of crawling, and almost of the rattle, are embodied in *A Child's Garden of Verses*), and the feeling for happy turns — these, in the last analysis (and his sense of a happy turn is of the subtlest), are the corresponding halves of his character. If *Prince Otto* and *Doctor Jekyll* left me a clearer field for the assertion, I would say that everything he has written is a direct apology for boyhood; or rather (for it must be confessed that Mr Stevenson's tone is seldom apologetic), a direct rhapsody on the age of heterogeneous pockets. Even members of the very numerous class who have held their breath over *Treasure Island* may shrug their shoulders at this account of the author's religion; but it is none the less a great pleasure — the highest reward of observation — to put one's hand on a rare illustration, and Mr Stevenson is certainly rare. What makes him so is the singular maturity of the expression that he has given to young sentiments: he judges them, measures them, sees them from the outside, as well as entertains them. He describes credulity with all the resources of experience, and represents a crude stage with infinite ripeness. In a word, he is an artist accomplished even to sophistication, whose constant theme is the unsophisticated. Sometimes, as in *Kidnapped*, the art is so ripe that it lifts even the subject into the general air: the execution is so serious that the idea (the idea of a boy's romantic adventures) becomes a matter of universal relations. What he prizes most in the boy's ideal is the imaginative side of it, the capacity for successful make-believe. The general freshness in which this is a part of the gloss seems to him the divinest thing in life; considerably more divine, for instance, than the passion usually regarded as the supremely tender one. The idea of making believe appeals to him much more than the idea of making love. That delightful little book of rhymes, the *Child's Garden* commemorates, from beginning to end the picturing, personifying, dramatising faculty of infancy — the view of life from the level of the nursery-fender. The volume is a wonder for the extraordinary vividness with which it reproduces early impressions: a child might have written it if a child could see childhood from the outside, for it would seem that only a child is really near enough to the nursery floor. And what is peculiar to Mr Stevenson is that it is his own childhood he appears to delight in, and not the personal presence of little darlings. Oddly enough, there is no strong implication that he is fond of babies; he doesn't speak as a parent, or an uncle, or an educator — he speaks as a contemporary absorbed in his own game. That game is almost always a vision of dangers and triumphs, and if emotion, with him, infallibly resolves itself into memory, so memory is an evocation of throbs and thrills and suspense. He has given to the world the romance of boyhood, as others have produced that of the peerage and the police and the medical profession.

This amounts to saying that what he is most curious of in life is heroism — personal gallantry, if need be with a manner, or a banner, though he is also abundantly capable of enjoying it when it is artless. The delightful exploits of Jim Hawkins, in *Treasure Island*, are unaffectedly performed; but none the less 'the finest action is the better for a piece of purple,' as the author remarks in the paper on 'The English Admirals', in *Virginibus Puerisque* — a paper of which the moral is, largely, that 'we learn to desire a grand air in our heroes; and such a knowledge of the human stage as shall make them put the dots on their own i's, and leave us in no suspense as to when they mean to be heroic.' The love of brave words as well as brave deeds — which is simply Mr Stevenson's essential love of style — is recorded in this little paper with a charming, slightly sophistical ingenuity. 'They served their guns

merrily when it came to fighting, and they had the readiest ear
for a bold, honourable sentiment of any class of men the world
ever produced.' The author goes on to say that most men of high
destinies have even high-sounding names. Alan Breck, in *Kidnapped*, is a wonderful picture of the union of courage and swagger;
the little Jacobite adventurer, a figure worthy of Scott at his best,
and representing the highest point that Mr Stevenson's talent has
reached, shows us that a marked taste for tawdry finery — tar-
nished and tattered, some of it indeed, by ticklish occasions — is
quite compatible with a perfectly high mettle. Alan Breck is at
bottom a study of the love of glory, carried out with extreme
psychological truth. When the love of glory is of an inferior
order the reputation is cultivated rather than the opportunity;
but when it is a pure passion the opportunity is cultivated for the
sake of the reputation. Mr Stevenson's kindness for adventurers
extends even to the humblest of all, the mountebank and the stroll-
ing player, or even the pedlar whom he declares that in his foreign
travels he is habitually taken for, as we see in the whimsical apology for vagabonds which winds up *An Inland Voyage*. The
hungry conjurer, the gymnast whose *maillot* is loose, have something of the glamour of the hero, inasmuch as they too pay with
their person.

To be even one of the outskirters of art leaves a fine stamp on a man's
countenance. . . . That is the kind of thing that reconciles me to life; a
ragged, tippling, incompetent old rogue, with the manners of a gentleman and the vanity of an artist, to keep up his self-respect!

What reconciles Mr Stevenson to life is the idea that in the first
place it offers the widest field that we know of for odd doings, and
that in the second these odd doings are the best of pegs to hang a
sketch in three lines or a paradox in three pages.

As it is not odd, but extremely usual, to marry, he deprecates
that course in *Virginibus Puerisque*, the collection of short essays
which is most a record of his opinions — that is, largely, of his
likes and dislikes. It all comes back to his sympathy with the
juvenile and that feeling about life which leads him to regard
women as so many superfluous girls in a boy's game. They are

almost wholly absent from his pages (the main exception is *Prince Otto*, though there is a Clara apiece in *The Rajah's Diamond* and *The Pavilion on the Links*), for they don't like ships and pistols and fights, they encumber the decks and require separate apartments, and, almost worst of all, have not the highest literary standard. Why should a person marry when he might be swinging a cutlass or looking for a buried treasure? Why should he waste at the nuptial altar precious hours in which he might be polishing periods? It is one of those curious and to my sense fascinating inconsistencies that we encounter in Mr Stevenson's mind, that though he takes such an interest in the childish life, he takes no interest in the fireside. He has an indulgent glance for it in the verses of the *Garden*, but to his view the normal child is the child who absents himself from the family-circle, in fact when he can, in imagination when he cannot, in the disguise of a buccaneer. Girls don't do this, and women are only grown-up girls, unless it be the delightful maiden, fit daughter of an imperial race, whom he commemorates in *An Inland Voyage*.

A girl at school, in France, began to describe one of our regiments on parade to her French school-mates; and as she went on, she told me the recollection grew so vivid, she became so proud to be the countrywoman of such soldiers, and so sorry to be in another country, that her voice failed her, and she burst into tears. I have never forgotten that girl, and I think she very nearly deserves a statue. To call her a young lady, with all its niminy associations, would be to offer her an insult. She may rest assured of one thing; although she never should marry a heroic general, never see any great or immediate result of her life, she will not have lived in vain for her native land.

There is something of that in Mr Stevenson; when he begins to describe a British regiment on parade (or something of that sort), he too almost breaks down for emotion: which is why I have been careful to traverse the insinuation that he is primarily a chiseller of prose. If things had gone differently with him (I must permit myself this allusion to his personal situation, and I shall venture to follow it with two or three others), he might have been an historian of famous campaigns — a great painter of battle-pieces. Of course, however, in this capacity it would not have done for him to break down for emotion.

Although he remarks that marriage 'is a field of battle, and not a bed of roses,' he points out repeatedly that it is a terrible renunciation and somehow, in strictness, incompatible even with honour — the sort of roving, trumpeting honour that appeals most to his sympathy. After that step,

there are no more by-path meadows where you may innocently linger, but the road lies long and straight and dusty to the grave. . . . You may think you had a conscience and believed in God; but what is a conscience to a wife? . . . To marry is to domesticate the Recording Angel. Once you are married, there is nothing left for you, not even suicide, but to be good. . . . How, then, in such an atmosphere of compromise, to keep honour bright and abstain from base capitulations? . . . The proper qualities of each sex are, indeed, eternally surprising to the other. Between the Latin and the Teuton races there are similar divergences, not to be bridged by the most liberal sympathy. . . . It is better to face the fact and know, when you marry, that you take into your life a creature of equal if unlike frailties; whose weak, human heart beats no more tunefully than yours.

If there is a grimness in that it is as near as Mr Stevenson ever comes to being grim, and we have only to turn the page to find the corrective — something delicately genial, at least, if not very much less sad:

'The blind bow-boy' who smiles upon us from the end of terraces in old Dutch gardens laughingly hurls his bird-bolts among a fleeting generation. But for as fast as ever he shoots, the game dissolves and disappears into eternity from under his falling arrows; this one is gone ere he is struck; the other has but time to make one gesture and give one passionate cry; and they are all the things of a moment.

That is an admission that though it is soon over, the great sentimental surrender is inevitable. And there is geniality too, still over the page (in regard to quite another matter), geniality, at least, for the profession of letters, in the declaration that there is

one thing you can never make Philistine natures understand; one thing which yet lies on the surface, remains as unseizable to their wit as a high flight of metaphysics — namely, that the business of life is mainly carried on by the difficult art of literature, and according to a man's proficiency in that art shall be the freedom and fullness of his intercourse with other men.

Yet it is difficult not to believe that the ideal in which our author's spirit might most gratefully have rested would have been the character of the paterfamilias, when the eye falls on such a charming piece of observation as these lines about children, in the admirable paper on 'Child's Play':

If it were not for this perpetual imitation we should be tempted to fancy they despised us outright, or only considered us in the light of creatures brutally strong and brutally silly, among whom they condescended to dwell in obedience, like a philosopher at a barbarous court.

We know very little about a talent till we know where it grew up, and it would halt terribly at the start any account of the author of *Kidnapped* which should omit to insist promptly that he is a Scot of the Scots. Two facts, to my perception, go a great way to explain his composition: the first of which is that his boyhood was passed in the shadow of Edinburgh Castle, and the second that he came of a family that had set up great lights on the coast. His grandfather, his uncle, were famous constructors of lighthouses, and the name of the race is associated above all with the beautiful and beneficent tower of Skerryvore. We may exaggerate the way in which, in an imaginative youth, the sense of the 'story' of things would feed upon the impressions of Edinburgh — though I suspect it would be difficult really to do so. The streets are so full of history and poetry, of picture and song, of associations springing from strong passions and strange characters, that, for our own part, we find ourselves thinking of an urchin going and coming there as we used to think (wonderingly, enviously), of the small boys who figured as supernumeraries, pages or imps, in showy scenes at the theatre: the place seems the background, the complicated 'set' of a drama, and the children the mysterious little beings who are made free of the magic world. How must it not have beckoned on the imagination to pass and repass, on the way to school, under the Castle rock, conscious, acutely yet familiarly, of the grey citadel on the summit, lighted up with the tartans and bagpipes of Highland regiments? Mr Stevenson's mind, from an early age, was furnished with the concrete Highlander, who must have had much of the effect that we nowadays call decorative. We have encountered somewhere a fanciful paper of our author's,[1] in which there is a reflection of half-holiday afternoons and, unless our own fancy plays us a trick, of lights red, in the winter dusk, in the high-placed windows of the old town — a delightful rhapsody on the penny sheets of figures for the puppet-shows of infancy, in life-like position, and awaiting the impatient yet careful scissors. 'If landscapes were sold,' he says in *Travels with a Donkey*, 'like the sheets of characters of my boyhood, one penny plain and twopence coloured, I should go the length of twopence every day of my life.'

Indeed the colour of Scotland has entered into him altogether, and though, oddly enough, he has written but little about his native country, his happiest work shows, I think, that she has the best of his ability. *Kidnapped* (whose inadequate title I may deplore in passing) breathes in every line the feeling of moor and loch, and is the finest of his longer stories, and 'Thrawn Janet', a masterpiece in thirteen pages (lately republished in the volume of *The Merry Men*), is, among the shorter, the strongest in execution. The latter consists of a gruesome anecdote of the supernatural, related in the Scotch dialect, and the genuineness which this medium (at the sight of which, in general, the face of the reader grows long) wears in Mr Stevenson's hands is a proof of how living the question of form always is to him, and what a variety of answers he has for it. It would never have occurred to us that the style of *Travels with a Donkey* or *Virginibus Puerisque* and the idiom of the parish of Balweary could be a conception of the same mind. If it be a good fortune for a genius to have had such a country as Scotland for its primary stuff, this is doubly the case when there has been a certain process of detachment, of extreme secularization. Mr Stevenson has been emancipated: he is, as we may say, a Scotchman of the world. None other, I think, could have drawn with such a mixture of sympathetic and ironical observation the character of the canny young Lowlander

[1] 'A Penny Plain and Twopence Coloured', republished, since the above was written, in *Memories and Portraits*, 1887.

David Balfour, a good boy but an exasperating. *Treasure Island, The New Arabian Nights, Prince Otto, Doctor Jekyll and Mr Hyde,* are not very directly founded on observation; but that quality comes in with extreme fineness as soon as the subject involves consideration of race.

I have been wondering whether there is something more than this that our author's pages would tell us about him, or whether that particular something is in the mind of an admirer, because he happens to have had other lights on it. It has been possible for so acute a critic as Mr William Archer to read pure high spirits and the gospel of the young man rejoicing in his strength and his matutinal cold bath between the lines of Mr Stevenson's prose. And it is a fact that the note of a morbid sensibility is so absent from his pages, they contain so little reference to infirmity and suffering, that we feel a trick has really been played upon us on discovering by accident the actual state of the case with the writer who has indulged in the most enthusiastic allusion to the joy of existence. We must permit ourselves another mention of his personal situation, for it adds immensely to the interest of volumes through which there draws so strong a current of life, to know that they are not only the work of an invalid, but that have largely been written in bed, in dreary 'health resorts,' in the intervals of sharp attacks. There is almost nothing in them to lead us to guess this; the direct evidence indeed is almost all contained in the limited compass of *The Silverado Squatters.* In such a case, however, it is the indirect that is the most eloquent, and I know not where to look for that, unless in the paper called 'Ordered South,' and its companion 'Æs Triplex', in *Virginibus Puerisque.* It is impossible to read 'Ordered South' attentively without feeling that it is personal: the reflections it contains are from experience, not from fancy. The places and climates to which the invalid is carried to recover or to die are mainly beautiful, but

In his heart of hearts he has to confess that [they are] not beautiful for him. . . . He is like an enthusiast leading about with him a stolid, indifferent tourist. There is some one by who is out of sympathy with the scene, and is not moved up to the measure of the occasion; and that some one is himself. . . . He seems to himself to touch things with muffled hands and to see them through a veil. . . . Many a white town that sits far out on the promontory, many a comely fold of wood on the mountain-side, beckons and allures his imagination day after day, and is yet as inaccessible to his feet as the clefts and gorges of the clouds. The sense of distance grows upon him wonderfully; and after some feverish efforts and the fretful uneasiness of the first few days he falls contentedly in with the restrictions of his weakness. . . . He feels, if he is to be thus tenderly weaned from the passion of life, thus gradually inducted into the slumber of death, that when at last the end comes it will come quietly and fitly. . . . He will pray for Medea: when she comes, let her rejuvenate or slay.

The second of the short essays I have mentioned has a taste of mortality only because the purpose of it is to insist that the only sane behaviour is to leave death and the accidents that lead to it out of our calculations. Life 'is a honeymoon with us all through, and none of the longest. Small blame to us if we give our whole hearts to this glowing bride of ours;' the person who does so 'makes a very different acquaintance with the world, keeps all his pulses going true and fast, and gathers impetus as he runs, until if he be running towards anything better than wildfire, he may shoot up and become a constellation in the end'. Nothing can be more deplorable than to 'forego all the issues of living in a parlour with a regulated temperature'. Mr Stevenson adds that as for those whom the gods love dying young, a man dies too young at whatever age he parts with life. The testimony of 'Æs Triplex' to the author's own disabilities is after all very indirect. It consists mainly in the general protest not so much against the fact of extinction as against the theory of it. The reader only asks himself why the hero of *Travels with a Donkey*, the historian of Alan Breck, should think of these things. His appreciation of the active side of life has such a note of its own that we are surprised to find that it proceeds in a considerable measure from an intimate acquaintance with the passive. It seems too anomalous that the writer who has most cherished the idea of a certain free exposure should also be the one who has been reduced most to looking for it within, and that the figures of adventurers who, at least in our literature of today, are the most vivid, should be the most vicarious. The truth is, of course, that, as the *Travels with a Donkey* and *An Inland Voyage* abundantly show, the author has a fund of reminiscences. He did not spend his younger years 'in a parlour with a regulated temperature.' A reader who happens to be aware of how much it has been his later fate to do so may be excused for finding an added source of interest — something indeed deeply and constantly touching — in this association of peculiarly restrictive conditions with the vision of high spirits and romantic accidents, of a kind of honourably picturesque career. Mr Stevenson is, however, distinctly, in spite of his occasional practice of the gruesome, a frank optimist — an observer who not only loves life, but does not shrink from the responsibility of recommending it. There is a systematic brightness in him which testifies to this and which is after all but one of the innumerable ingenuities of patience. What is remarkable in his case is that his productions should constitute an exquisite expression, a sort of whimsical gospel, of enjoyment. The only difference between *An Inland Voyage*, or *Travels with a Donkey* and *The New Arabian Nights*, or *Treasure Island*, or *Kidnapped*, is that in the later books the enjoyment is reflective (though it stimulates spontaneity with singular art), whereas in the first two it is natural and, as it were, historical.

These little histories — the first volumes, if I mistake not, that introduced Mr Stevenson to lovers of good writing — abound in charming illustrations of his disposition to look at the world as a not exactly refined, but glorified, pacified Bohemia. They narrate the quest of personal adventure, on one occasion in a canoe on the Sambre and the Oise, and on another at a donkey's tail over the hills and valleys of the Cévennes. I well remember that when I read them, in their novelty, upward of ten years ago, I seemed to see the author, unknown as yet to fame, jump before my eyes into a style. His steps in literature presumably had not been many; yet he had mastered his form — it had in these cases perhaps more substance than his matter — and a singular air of literary experience. It partly, though not completely, explains the pheno-

menon, that he had already been able to write the exquisite little
story of 'Will of the Mill', published previously to *An Inland
Voyage*, and republished today in the volume of *The Merry Men*;
for in 'Will of the Mill' there is something exceedingly rare, poet-
ical, and unexpected, with that most fascinating quality a work of
imagination can have — a dash of alternative mystery as to its
meaning, an air (the air of life itself) of half inviting, half defying
you to interpret. This brief but finished composition stood in the
same relation to the usual 'magazine story' that a glass of Johan-
nisberg occupies to a draught of table d'hôte *vin ordinaire*.

One evening he asked the miller where the river went. . . . 'It goes out
into the lowlands, and waters the great corn country, and runs through
a sight of fine cities (so they say) where kings live all alone in great
palaces, with a sentry walking up and down before the door. And it
goes under bridges, with stone men upon them, looking down and
smiling so curious at the water, and living folks leaning their elbows on
the wall and looking over too. And then it goes on and on, and down
through marshes and sands, until at last it falls into the sea, where the
ships are that bring tobacco and parrots from the Indies.'

It is impossible not to open one's eyes at such a paragraph as that,
especially if one has taken a common texture for granted. Will of
the Mill spends his life in the valley through which the river runs,
and through which, year after year, post-chaises and wagons, and
pedestrians, and once an army, 'horse and foot, cannon and timb-
rel, drum and standard,' take their way, in spite of the dreams he
has once had of seeing the mysterious world, and it is not till
death comes that he goes on his travels. He ends by keeping an inn
where he converses with many more initiated spirits, and though
he is an amiable man, he dies a bachelor, having broken off with
more plainness than he would have used had he been less un-
travelled (of course he remains sadly provincial), his engagement
to the parson's daughter. The story is in the happiest key, and
suggests all kinds of things: but what does it in particular represent? The advantage of waiting, perhaps — the valuable truth,
that, one by one, we tide over our impatiences. There are sagacious people who hold that if one does not answer a letter it ends by
answering itself. So the sub-title of Mr Stevenson's tale might be

'The Beauty of Procrastination.' If you do not indulge your curiosities your slackness itself makes at last a kind of rich element, and it comes to very much the same thing in the end. When it came to the point, poor Will had not even the curiosity to marry; and the author leaves us in stimulating doubt as to whether he judges him too selfish or only too philosophic.

I find myself speaking of Mr Stevenson's last volume (at the moment I write), before I have spoken, in any detail, of its predecessors: which I must let pass as a sign that I lack space for a full enumeration. I may mention two more of his productions as completing the list of those that have a personal reference. *The Silverado Squatters* describes a picnicking episode, undertaken on grounds of health, on a mountain-top in California; but this free sketch, which contains a hundred humorous touches, and in the figure of Irvine Lovelands one of Mr Stevenson's most veracious portraits, is perhaps less vivid, as it is certainly less painful, than those other pages in which, some years ago, he commemorated the twelvemonth he spent in America — the history of a journey from New York to San Francisco in an emigrant-train, performed as the sequel to a voyage across the Atlantic in the same severe conditions. He has never made his points better than in this half-humorous, half-tragical recital, nor given a more striking instance of his talent for reproducing the feeling of queer situations and contacts. It is much to be regretted that this little masterpiece had not been brought to light a second time, as also that he has not given the world (as I believe he came very near doing), his observations in the steerage of an Atlantic liner. If, as I say, our author has a taste for the impressions of Bohemia, he has been very consistent, and has not shrunk from going far afield in search of them. And as I have already been indiscreet, I may add that if it has been his fate to be converted in fact from the sardonic view of matrimony, this occurred under an influence which should have the particular sympathy of American readers. He went to California for his wife, and Mrs Stevenson, as appears moreover by the title-page of his work, has had a hand — evidently a light and practised one — in *The Dynamiter*, the second series, characterised by a rich extravagance, of *The New Arabian Nights*. *The Silverado Squatters* is the history of a honeymoon, prosperous it would seem, putting Irvine Lovelands aside, save for the death of dog Chuchu 'in his teens, after a life so shadowed and troubled, continually shaken with alarm, and the tear of elegant sentiment permanently in his eye.'

Mr Stevenson has a theory of composition in regard to the novel, on which he is to be congratulated, as any positive and genuine conviction of this kind is vivifying so long as it is not narrow. The breath of the novelist's being is his liberty, and the incomparable virtue of the form he uses is that it lends itself to views innumerable and diverse, to every variety of illustration. There is certainly no other mould of so large a capacity. The doctrine of M. Zola himself, so jejune if literally taken, is fruitful, inasmuch as in practice he romantically departs from it. Mr Stevenson does not need to depart, his individual taste being as much to pursue the romantic as his principle is to defend it. Fortunately, in England today, it is not much attacked. The triumphs that are to be won in the portrayal of the strange, the improbable, the heroic, especially as these things shine from afar in the credulous eye of youth, are his strongest, most constant incentive. On one happy occasion, in relating the history of *Doctor Jekyll*, he has seen them as they present themselves to a maturer vision. *Doctor Jekyll* is not a 'boys' book', nor yet is *Prince Otto*; the latter, however, is not, like the former, an experiment in mystification — it is, I think, more than anything else, an experiment in style, conceived one summer's day, when the author had given the reins to his high appreciation of Mr George Meredith. It is perhaps the most literary of his works, but it is not the most natural. It is one of those coquetries, as we may call them for want of a better word, which may be observed in Mr Stevenson's activity — a kind of artful inconsequence. It is easy to believe that if his strength permitted him to be a more abundant writer he would still more frequently play this eminently literary trick — that of dodging off in a new direction — upon those who might have fancied they knew all about him. I made the reflection, in speaking of 'Will of the Mill', that there is a kind of anticipatory malice in the subject of that fine story: as if the writer had intended to say to his reader 'You will never guess, from the unction with which I describe the life of a man who never stirred five miles from home, that I am destined to make my greatest hits in treating of the rovers of the deep.' Even here, however, the author's characteristic irony would have come in; for — the rare chances of life being what he most keeps his eye on — the uncommon belongs as much to the way the inquiring Will sticks to his door-sill as to the incident, say, of John Silver and his men, when they are dragging Jim Hawkins to his doom, hearing, in the still woods of Treasure Island, the strange hoot of the maroon.

The novelist who leaves the extraordinary out of his account is liable to awkward confrontations, as we are compelled to reflect in this age of newspapers and of universal publicity. The next report of the next divorce case (to give an instance) shall offer us a picture of astounding combinations of circumstance and behaviour, and the annals of any energetic race are rich in curious anecdote and startling example. That interesting compilation, *Vicissitudes of Families* is but a superficial record of strange accidents; the family (taken of course in the long piece), is as a general thing a catalogue of odd specimens and tangled situations, and we must remember that the most singular products are those which are not exhibited. Mr Stevenson leaves so wide a margin for the wonderful — it impinges with easy assurance upon the text — that he escapes the danger of being brought up by cases he has not allowed for. When he allows for Mr Hyde he allows for everything, and one feels moreover that even if he did not wave so gallantly the flag of the imaginative and contend that the improbable is what has most character, he would still insist that we ought to make believe. He would say we ought to make believe that the extraordinary is the best part of life even if it were not, and to do so because the finest feelings — suspense, daring, decision, passion, curiosity, gallantry, eloquence, friendship — are involved in it, and it is of infinite importance that the tradition of these precious things should not perish. He would prefer, in a word, any day in the week, Alexandre Dumas to Honoré de Balzac, and it is indeed my impression that he prefers the author of *The Three Musketeers* to any novelist except Mr George Meredith. I should go so far as to suspect that his ideal of the delightful work of fiction would be the adventures of Monte Cristo related by the author of *Richard Feverel*. There is some magnanimity in his esteem for Alexandre Dumas, inasmuch as in *Kidnapped* he has put into a fable worthy of that inventor a closeness of notation with which Dumas never had anything to do. He makes us say, Let the tradition live, by all means, since it was delightful; but at the same time he is the cause of our perceiving afresh that a tradition is kept alive only by something being added to it. In this particular case — in *Doctor Jekyll* and *Kidnapped* — Mr Stevenson has added psychology.

The New Arabian Nights offers us, as the title indicates, the wonderful in the frankest, most delectable form. Partly extravagant, and partly very specious, they are the result of a very happy idea, that of placing a series of adventures which are pure adventures in the setting of contemporary English life, and relating them in the placidly ingenuous tone of Scheherezade. This device is carried to perfection in *The Dynamiter*, where the manner takes on more of a kind of high-flown serenity in proportion as the incidents are more 'steep'. In this line *The Suicide Club* is Mr Stevenson's greatest success, and the first two pages of it, not to mention others, live in the memory. For reasons which I am conscious of not being able to represent as sufficient, I find something ineffaceably impressive — something really haunting — in the incident of Prince Florizel and Colonel Geraldine, who, one evening in March, are 'driven by a sharp fall of sleet into an Oyster Bar in the immediate neighbourhood of Leicester Square', and there have occasion to observe the entrance of a young man followed by a couple of commissionaires, each of whom carries a large dish of cream-tarts under a cover — a young man who 'pressed these confections on every one's acceptance with exaggerated courtesy'. There is no effort at a picture here, but the imagination makes one of the lighted interior, the London sleet outside, the company that we guess, given the locality, and the strange politeness of the young man, leading on to circumstances stranger still. This is what may be called putting one in the mood for a story. But Mr Stevenson's most brilliant stroke of that kind is the opening episode of *Treasure Island*, the arrival of the brown old seaman, with the sabre-cut, at the 'Admiral Benbow,' and the advent, not long after, of the blind sailor, with a green shade over his eyes, who comes tapping down the road, in quest of him, with his stick. *Treasure Island* is a 'boy's book', in the sense that it embodies a boy's vision of the extraordinary, but it is unique in this, and calculated to fascinate the weary mind of experience, that what we see in it is not only the ideal fable but, as part and parcel of that, as it were, the young reader himself and his state of mind: we seem to read it over his shoulder, with an arm around his neck. It is all as perfect as a well-played boy's game, and nothing can exceed the spirit and skill, the humour and the open-air feeling with which the thing is kept at the palpitating pitch. It is not only a record of queer chances, but a study of young feelings: there is a moral side in it, and the figures are not puppets with vague faces. If Jim Hawkins illustrates successful daring, he does so with a delightful rosy good-boyishness and a conscious, modest liability to error. His luck is tremendous, but it does not make him proud, and his manner is refreshingly provincial and human. So is that, even more, of the admirable John Silver, one of the most picturesque and indeed in every way most genially presented villains in the whole literature of romance. He has a singularly distinct and expressive countenance, which of course turns out to be a grimacing mask. Never was a mask more knowingly, vividly painted. *Treasure Island* will surely become — it must already have become and will remain — in its way a classic: thanks to this indescribable mixture of the prodigious and the human, of surprising coincidences and familiar feelings. The language in which Mr Stevenson has chosen to tell his story is an admirable vehicle for these feelings: with its humorous braveries and quaintnesses, its echoes of old ballads and yarns, it touches all kinds of sympathetic chords.

Is *Doctor Jekyll and Mr Hyde* a work of high philosophic intention, or simply the most ingenious and irresponsible of fictions? It has the stamp of a really imaginative production, that we may take it in different ways; but I suppose it would be called the most serious of the author's tales. It deals with the relation of the baser parts of man to his nobler, of the capacity for evil that exists in the most generous natures; and it expresses these things in a fable which is a wonderfully happy invention. The subject is endlessly interesting, and rich in all sorts of provocation, and Mr Stevenson is to be congratulated on having touched the core of it. I may do him injustice, but it is, however, here, not the profundity of the idea which strikes me so much as the art of the presentation — the extremely successful form. There is a genuine feeling for the perpetual moral question, a fresh sense of the difficulty of being good and the brutishness of being bad; but what there is above all is a singular ability in holding the interest. I confess that that, to my sense, is the most edifying thing in the short, rapid, concentrated story, which is really a masterpiece of concision. There is something almost impertinent in the way, as I have noticed, in which Mr Stevenson achieves his best effects without the aid of the ladies, and *Doctor Jekyll* is a capital example of his heartless independence. It is usually supposed that a truly poignant impression cannot be made without them, but in the drama of Mr Hyde's fatal ascendency they remain altogether in the wing. It is very obvious — I do not say it cynically — that they must have played an important part in his development. The gruesome tone of the tale is, no doubt, deepened by their absence: it is like the late afternoon light of a foggy winter Sunday, when even inanimate objects have a kind of wicked look. I remember few situations in the pages of mystifying fiction more to the purpose than the episode of Mr Utterson's going to Dr Jekyll's to confer with the butler when the Doctor is locked up in his laboratory, and the old servant, whose sagacity has hitherto encountered successfully the problems of the sideboard and the pantry, confesses that this time he is utterly baffled. The way the two men, at the door of the laboratory, discuss the identity of the mysterious

personage inside, who has revealed himself in two or three inhuman glimpses to Poole, has those touches of which irresistible
shudders are made. The butler's theory is that his master has been
murdered, and that the murderer is in the room, personating him
with a sort of clumsy diabolism. 'Well, when that masked thing
like a monkey jumped from among the chemicals and whipped
into the cabinet, it went down my spine like ice.' That is the effect
upon the reader of most of the story. I say of most rather than of
all, because the ice rather melts in the sequel, and I have some
difficulty in accepting the business of the powders, which seems
to me too explicit and explanatory. The powders constitute the
machinery of the transformation, and it will probably have struck
many readers that this uncanny process would be more conceivable (so far as one may speak of the conceivable in such a case), if
the author had not made it so definite.

I have left Mr Stevenson's best book to the last, as it is also the
last he has given (at the present speaking) to the public — the
tales comprising *The Merry Men* having already appeared; but I
find that on the way I have anticipated some of the remarks that
I had intended to make about it. That which is most to the point
is that there are parts of it so fine as to suggest that the author's
talent has taken a fresh start, various as have been the impulses in
which it had already indulged, and serious the hindrances among
which it is condemned to exert itself. There would have been a
kind of perverse humility in his keeping up the fiction that a production so literary as *Kidnapped* is addressed to immature minds,
and though it was originally given to the world, I believe, in a
'boy's paper', the story embraces every occasion that it meets to
satisfy the higher criticism. It has two weak spots, which need
simply to be mentioned. The cruel and miserly uncle, in the first
chapters, is rather in the tone of superseded tradition, and the
tricks he plays upon his ingenuous nephew are a little like those
of country conjurers. In these pages we feel that Mr Stevenson is
thinking too much of what a 'boy's paper' is expected to contain.
Then the history stops without ending, as it were; but I think I
may add that this accident speaks for itself. Mr Stevenson has

often to lay down his pen for reasons that have nothing to do with the failure of inspiration, and the last page of David Balfour's adventures is an honourable plea for indulgence. The remaining five-sixths of the book deserve to stand by *Henry Esmond*, as a fictive autobiography in archaic form. The author's sense of the English idiom of the last century, and still more of the Scotch, have enabled him to give a gallant companion to Thackeray's *tour de force*. The life, the humour, the colour of the central portions of *Kidnapped* have a singular pictorial virtue: these passages read like a series of inspired foot-notes on some historic page. The charm of the most romantic episode in the world, though perhaps it would be hard to say why it is the most romantic, when it was intermingled with so much stupidity, is over the whole business, and the forlorn hope of the Stuarts is revived for us without evoking satiety. There could be no better instance of the author's talent for seeing the familiar in the heroic, and reducing the extravagant to plausible detail, than the description of Alan Breck's defence in the cabin of the ship and the really magnificent chapters of 'The Flight in the Heather.' Mr Stevenson has in a high degree (and doubtless for good reasons of his own) what may be called the imagination of physical states, and this has enabled him to arrive at a wonderfully exact translation of the miseries of his panting Lowland hero, dragged for days and nights over hill and dale, through bog and thicket, without meat or drink or rest, at the tail of an Homeric Highlander. The great superiority of the book resides to my mind, however, in the fact that it puts two characters on their feet with admirable rectitude. I have paid my tribute to Alan Breck, and I can only repeat that he is a masterpiece. It is interesting to observe that though the man is extravagant, the author's touch exaggerates nothing: it is throughout of the most truthful, genial, ironical kind, full of penetration, but with none of the grossness of moralising satire. The figure is a genuine study, and nothing can be more charming than the way Mr Stevenson both sees through it and admires it. Shall I say that he sees through David Balfour? This would be perhaps to underestimate the density of that medium. Beautiful, at any rate, is the expression which this unfortunate though circumspect youth gives to those qualities which combine to excite our respect and our objurgation in the Scottish character. Such a scene as the episode of the quarrel of the two men on the mountain-side is a real stroke of genius, and has the very logic and rhythm of life; a quarrel which we feel to be inevitable, though it is about nothing, or almost nothing, and which springs from exasperated nerves and the simple shock of temperaments. The author's vision of it has a profundity which goes deeper, I think, than *Doctor Jekyll*. I know of few better examples of the way genius has ever a surprise in its pocket — keeps an ace, as it were, up its sleeve. And in this case it endears itself to us by making us reflect that such a passage as the one I speak of is in fact a signal proof of what the novel can do at its best, and what nothing else can do so well. In the presence of this sort of success we perceive its immense value. It is capable of a rare transparency — it can illustrate human affairs in cases so delicate and complicated that any other vehicle would be clumsy. To those who love the art that Mr Stevenson practises he will appear, in pointing this incidental moral, not only to have won a particular triumph, but to have given a delightful pledge.

GUY DE MAUPASSANT

1888

THE first artists, in any line, are doubtless not those whose general ideas about their art are most often on their lips — those who most abound in precept, apology, and formula and can best tell us the reasons and the philosophy of things. We know the first usually by their energetic practice, the constancy with which they apply their principles, and the serenity with which they leave us to hunt for their secret in the illustration, the concrete example. None the less it often happens that a valid artist utters his mystery, flashes upon us for a moment the light by which he works, shows us the rule by which he holds it just that he should be measured. This accident is happiest, I think, when it is soonest over; the shortest explanations of the products of genius are the best, and there is many a creator of living figures whose friends, however full of faith in his inspiration, will do well to pray for him when he sallies forth into the dim wilderness of theory. The doctrine is apt to be so much less inspired than the work, the work is often so much more intelligent than the doctrine. M. Guy de Maupassant has lately traversed with a firm and rapid step a literary crisis of this kind; he has clambered safely up the bank at the further end of the morass. If he has relieved himself in the preface to *Pierre et Jean*, the last-published of his tales, he has also rendered a service to his friends; he has not only come home in a recognisable plight, escaping gross disaster with a success which even his extreme good sense was far from making in advance a matter of course, but he has expressed in intelligible terms (that by itself is a ground of felicitation) his most general idea, his own sense of his direction. He has arranged, as it were, the light in which he wishes to sit. If it is a question of attempting, under however many disadvantages, a sketch of him, the critic's business therefore is simplified: there will be no difficulty in placing him, for he himself has chosen the spot, he has made the chalk mark on the floor.

I may as well say at once that in dissertation M. de Maupassant does not write with his best pen; the philosopher in his composition is perceptibly inferior to the storyteller. I would rather have written half a page of *Boule de Suif* than the whole of the introduction to Flaubert's *Letters to Madame Sand*; and his little disquisition on the novel in general, attached to that particular example of it which he has just put forth,[1] is considerably less to the point than the masterpiece which it ushers in. In short, as a commentator M. de Maupassant is slightly common, while as an artist he is wonderfully rare. Of course we must, in judging a writer, take one thing with another, and if I could make up my mind that M. de Maupassant is weak in theory, it would almost make me like him better, render him more approachable, give him the touch of softness that he lacks, and show us a human flaw. The most general quality of the author of *La Maison Tellier* and *Bel-Ami*, the impression that remains last, after the others have been accounted for, is an essential hardness — hardness of form, hardness of nature; and it would put us more at ease to find that if the fact with him (the fact of execution) is so extraordinarily definite and adequate, his explanations, after it, were a little vague and sentimental. But I am not sure that he must even be held foolish to have noticed the race of critics: he is at any rate so much less foolish than several of that fraternity. He has said his say concisely and as if he were saying it once for all. In fine, his readers must be grateful to him for such a passage as that in which he remarks that whereas the public at large very legitimately says to a writer, 'Console me, amuse me, terrify me, make me cry, make me dream, or make me think,' what the sincere critic says is, 'Make me something fine in the form that shall suit you best, according to your temperament.' This seems to me to put into a nutshell the whole question of the different classes of fiction, concerning which there has recently been so much discourse. There

---

[1] *Pierre et Jean*, Ollendorff, Paris, 1888.

are simply as many different kinds as there are persons practising the art, for if a picture, a tale, or a novel be a direct impression of life (and that surely constitutes its interest and value), the impression will vary according to the plate that takes it, the particular structure and mixture of the recipient.

I am not sure that I know what M. de Maupassant means when he says, 'The critic shall appreciate the result only according to the nature of the effort; he has no right to concern himself with tendencies.' The second clause of that observation strikes me as rather in the air, thanks to the vagueness of the last word. But our author adds to the definiteness of his contention when he goes on to say that any form of the novel is simply a vision of the world from the standpoint of a person constituted after a certain fashion, and that it is therefore absurd to say that there is, for the novelist's use, only one reality of things. This seems to me commendable, not as a flight of metaphysics, hovering over bottomless gulfs of controversy, but, on the contrary, as a just indication of the vanity of certain dogmatisms. The particular way we see the world is our particular illusion about it, says M. de Maupassant, and this illusion fits itself to our organs and senses; our receptive vessel becomes the furniture of *our* little plot of the universal consciousness.

How childish, moreover, to believe in reality, since we each carry our own in our thought and in our organs. Our eyes, our ears, our sense of smell, of taste, differing from one person to another, create as many truths as there are men upon earth. And our minds, taking instruction from these organs, so diversely impressed, understand, analyse, judge, as if each of us belonged to a different race. Each one of us, therefore, forms for himself an illusion of the world, which is the illusion poetic, or sentimental, or joyous, or melancholy, or unclean, or dismal, according to his nature. And the writer has no other mission than to reproduce faithfully this illusion, with all the contrivances of art that he has learned and has at his command. The illusion of beauty, which is a human convention! The illusion of ugliness, which is a changing opinion! The illusion of truth, which is never immutable! The illusion of the ignoble, which attracts so many! The great artists are those who make humanity accept their particular illusion. Let us, therefore, not get angry with any one theory, since every theory is the generalised expression of a temperament asking itself questions.

What is interesting in this is not that M. de Maupassant happens to hold that we have no universal measure of the truth, but that it is the last word on a question of art from a writer who is rich in experience and has had success in a very rare degree. It is of secondary importance that our impression should be called, or not called, an illusion; what is excellent is that our author has stated more neatly than we have lately seen it done that the value of the artist resides in the clearness with which he gives forth that impression. His particular organism constitutes a *case*, and the critic is intelligent in proportion as he apprehends and enters into that case. To quarrel with it because it is not another, which it could not possibly have been without a wholly different outfit, appears to M. de Maupassant a deplorable waste of time. If this appeal to our disinterestedness may strike some readers as chilling (through their inability to conceive of any other form than the one they like — a limitation excellent for a reader but poor for a judge), the occasion happens to be none of the best for saying so, for M. de Maupassant himself precisely presents all the symptoms of a 'case' in the most striking way, and shows us how far the consideration of them may take us. Embracing such an opportunity as this, and giving ourselves to it freely, seems to me indeed to be a course more fruitful in valid conclusions, as well as in entertainment by the way, than the more common method of establishing one's own premises. To make clear to ourselves those of the author of *Pierre et Jean* — those to which he is committed by the very nature of his mind — is an attempt that will both stimulate and repay curiosity. There is no way of looking at his work less dry, less academic, for as we proceed from one of his peculiarities to another, the whole horizon widens, yet without our leaving firm ground, and we see ourselves landed, step by step, in the most general questions — those explanations of things which reside in the race, in the society. Of course there are cases and cases, and it is the salient ones that the disinterested critic is delighted to meet.

What makes M. de Maupassant salient is two facts: the first of which is that his gifts are remarkably strong and definite, and the second that he writes directly *from* them, as it were: holds the fullest, the most uninterrupted — I scarcely know what to call it — the boldest communication with them. A case is poor when the cluster of the artist's sensibilities is small, or they themselves are wanting in keenness, or else when the personage fails to admit them — either through ignorance, or diffidence, or stupidity, or the error of a false ideal — to what may be called a legitimate share in his attempt. It is, I think, among English and American writers that this latter accident is most liable to occur; more than the French we are apt to be misled by some convention or other as to the sort of feeler we *ought* to put forth, forgetting that the best one will be the one that nature happens to have given us. We have doubtless often enough the courage of our opinions (when it befalls that we have opinions), but we have not so constantly that of our perceptions. There is a whole side of our perceptive apparatus that we in fact neglect, and there are probably many among us who would erect this tendency into a duty. M. de Maupassant neglects nothing that he possesses; he cultivates his garden with admirable energy; and if there is a flower you miss from the rich parterre, you may be sure that it could not possibly have been raised, his mind not containing the soil for it. He is plainly of the opinion that the first duty of the artist, and the thing that makes him most useful to his fellow-men, is to master his instrument, whatever it may happen to be.

His own is that of the senses, and it is through them alone, or almost alone, that life appeals to him; it is almost alone by their help that he describes it, that he produces brilliant works. They render him this great assistance because they are evidently, in his constitution, extraordinarily alive; there is scarcely a page in all his twenty volumes that does not testify to their vivacity. Nothing could be further from his thought than to disavow them and to minimise their importance. He accepts them frankly, gratefully, works them, rejoices in them. If he were told that there are many English writers who would be sorry to go with him in this, he would, I imagine, staring, say that that is about what was to have been expected of the Anglo-Saxon race, or even that many of them probably could not go with him if they would. Then he would ask how our authors can be so foolish as to sacrifice such a *moyen*, how they can afford to, and exclaim, 'They must be pretty works, those they produce, and give a fine, true, complete account of life, with such omissions, such lacunæ!' M. de Maupassant's productions teach us, for instance, that his sense of smell is exceptionally acute — as acute as that of those animals of the field and forest whose subsistence and security depend upon it. It might be thought that he would, as a student of the human race, have found an abnormal development of this faculty embarrassing, scarcely knowing what to do with it, where to place it. But such an apprehension betrays an imperfect conception of his directness and resolution, as well as of his constant economy of means. Nothing whatever prevents him from representing the relations of men and women as largely governed by the scent of the parties. Human life in his pages (would this not be the most general description he would give of it?) appears for the most part as a sort of concert of odours, and his people are perpetually engaged, or he is engaged on their behalf, in sniffing up and distinguishing them, in some pleasant or painful exercise of the nostril. 'If everything in life speaks to the nostril, why on earth shouldn't we say so?' I suppose him to inquire; 'and what a proof of the empire of poor conventions and hypocrisies, *chez vous autres*, that you should pretend to describe and characterise, and yet take no note (or so little that it comes to the same thing) of that essential sign!'

Not less powerful is his visual sense, the quick, direct discrimination of his eye, which explains the singularly vivid concision of his descriptions. These are never prolonged nor analytic, have nothing of enumeration, of the quality of the observer, who counts the items to be sure he has made up the sum. His eye *selects* unerringly, unscrupulously, almost impudently — catches the particular thing in which the character of the object or the scene resides, and, by expressing it with the artful brevity of a master, leaves a convincing, original picture. If he is inveterately synthetic, he is never more so than in the way he brings this hard, short, intelligent gaze to bear. His vision of the world is for the most part a vision of ugliness, and even when it is not, there is in his easy power to generalise a certain absence of love, a sort of bird's-eye-view contempt. He has none of the superstitions of observation, none of our English indulgences, our tender and often imaginative superficialities. If he glances into a railway carriage bearing its freight into the Parisian suburbs of a summer Sunday, a dozen dreary lives map themselves out in a flash.

There were stout ladies in farcical clothes, those middle-class good-wives of the *banlieue* who replace the distinction they don't possess by an irrelevant dignity; gentlemen weary of the office, with sallow faces and twisted bodies, and one of their shoulders a little forced up by perpetual bending at work over a table. Their anxious, joyless faces spoke moreover of domestic worries, incessant needs for money, old hopes finally shattered; for they all belonged to the army of poor threadbare devils who vegetate frugally in a mean little plaster house, with a flower-bed for a garden.

Even in a brighter picture, such as the admirable vignette of the drive of Mme Tellier and her companions, the whole thing is an impression, as painters say nowadays, in which the figures are cheap. The six women at the station clamber into a country cart and go jolting through the Norman landscape to the village.

But presently the jerky trot of the nag shook the vehicle so terribly that the chairs began to dance, tossing up the travelers to right, to left, with movements like puppets, scared grimaces, cries of dismay suddenly interrupted by a more violent bump. They clutched the sides of the trap, their bonnets turned over on to their backs, or upon the nose or the shoulder; and the white horse continued to go, thrusting out his head and straightening the little tail, hairless like that of a rat, with which from time to time he whisked his buttocks. Joseph Rivet, with one foot stretched upon the shaft, the other leg bent under him, and his elbows very high, held the reins and emitted from his throat every moment a kind of cluck which caused the animal to prick up his ears and quicken his pace. On either side of the road the green country stretched away. The colza, in flower, produced in spots a great carpet of undulating yellow, from which there rose a strong, wholesome smell, a smell penetrating and pleasant, carried very far by the breeze. In the tall rye the cornflowers held up their little azure heads, which the women wished to pluck; but M. Rivet refused to stop. Then, in some place, a whole field looked as if it were sprinkled with blood, it was so crowded with poppies. And in the midst of the great level, taking colour in this fashion from the flowers of the soil, the trap passed on with the jog of the white horse, seeming itself to carry a nosegay of richer hues; it disappeared behind the big trees of a farm, to come out again where the foliage stopped and parade afresh through the green and yellow crops, pricked with red or blue, its blazing cartload of women, which receded in the sunshine.

As regards the other sense, the sense *par excellence*, the sense which we scarcely mention in English fiction, and which I am not very sure I shall be allowed to mention in an English periodical, M. de Maupassant speaks for that, and of it, with extraordinary distinctness and authority. To say that it occupies the first place in his picture is to say too little; it covers in truth the whole canvas, and his work is little else but a report of its innumerable manifestations. These manifestations are not, for him, so many incidents of life; they are life itself, they represent the standing answer to any question that we may ask about it. He describes them in detail, with a familiarity and a frankness which leave nothing to be added; I should say with singular truth, if I did not consider that in regard to this article he may be taxed with a certain exaggeration. M. de Maupassant would doubtless affirm that where the empire of the sexual sense is concerned, no exaggeration is possible: nevertheless it may be said that whatever depths may be discovered by those who dig for them, the impression of the human spectacle for him who takes it as it comes has less analogy with that of the monkeys' cage than this admirable writer's account of it. I speak of the human spectacle as we Anglo-Saxons see it — as we Anglo-Saxons pretend we see it, M. de Maupassant would possibly say.

At any rate, I have perhaps touched upon this peculiarity sufficiently to explain my remark that his point of view is almost solely that of the senses. If he is a very interesting case, this makes him also an embarrassing one, embarrassing and mystifying for the moralist. I may as well admit that no writer of the day strikes me as equally so. To find M. de Maupassant a lion in the path — that may seem to some people a singular proof of want of courage; but I think the obstacle will not be made light of by those who have really taken the measure of the animal. We are accustomed to

think, we of the English faith, that a cynic is a living advertise-
ment of his errors, especially in proportion as he is a thorough-
going one; and M. de Maupassant's cynicism, unrelieved as it is,
will not be disposed of off-hand by a critic of a competent literary
sense. Such a critic is not slow to perceive, to his no small confusion, that though, judging from usual premises, the author of *Bel-
Ami* ought to be a warning, he somehow is not. His baseness, as it
pervades him, ought to be written all over him; yet somehow there
are there certain aspects — and those commanding, as the house
agents say — in which it is not in the least to be perceived. It is
easy to exclaim that if he judges life only from the point of view
of the senses, many are the noble and exquisite things that he
must leave out. What he leaves out has no claim to get itself considered till after we have done justice to what he takes in. It is this
positive side of M. de Maupassant that is most remarkable — the
fact that his literary character is so complete and edifying. 'Auteur
à peu près irréprochable dans un genre qui ne l'est pas,' as that
excellent critic M. Jules Lemaître says of him, he disturbs us by
associating a conscience and a high standard with a temper long
synonymous, in our eyes, with an absence of scruples. The situation would be simpler certainly if he were a bad writer; but none
the less it is possible, I think, on the whole, to circumvent him,
even without attempting to prove that after all he is one.

The latter part of his introduction to *Pierre et Jean* is less felicitous than the beginning, but we learn from it — and this is
interesting — that he regards the analytic fashion of telling a
story, which has lately begotten in his own country some such
remarkable experiments (few votaries as it has attracted among
ourselves), as very much less profitable than the simple epic
manner which 'avoids with care all complicated explanations, all
dissertations upon motives, and confines itself to making persons
and events pass before our eyes.' M. de Maupassant adds that in
his view 'psychology should be hidden in a book, as it is hidden
in reality under the facts of existence. The novel conceived in this
manner gains interest, movement, colour, the bustle of life'. When
it is a question of an artistic process, we must always mistrust very

sharp distinctions, for there is surely in every method a little of every other method. It is as difficult to describe an action without glancing at its motive, its moral history, as it is to describe a motive without glancing at its practical consequence. Our history and our fiction are what we do; but it surely is not more easy to determine where what we do begins than to determine where it ends — notoriously a hopeless task. Therefore it would take a very subtle sense to draw a hard and fast line on the borderland of explanation and illustration. If psychology be hidden in life, as, according to M. de Maupassant, it should be in a book, the question immediately comes up, 'From whom is it hidden?' From some people, no doubt, but very much less from others; and all depends upon the observer, the nature of one's observation, and one's curiosity. For some people motives, reasons, relations, explanations, are a part of the very surface of the drama, with the footlights beating full upon them. For me an act, an incident, an attitude, may be a sharp, detached, isolated thing, of which I give a full account in saying that in such and such a way it came off. For you it may be hung about with implications, with relations, and conditions as necessary to help you to recognise it as the clothes of your friends are to help you know them in the street. You feel that they would seem strange to you without petticoats and trousers.

M. de Maupassant would probably urge that the right thing is to know, or to guess, how events come to pass, but to say as little about it as possible. There are matters in regard to which he feels the importance of being explicit, but that is not one of them. The contention to which I allude strikes me as rather arbitrary, so difficult is it to put one's finger upon the reason why, for instance, there should be so little mystery about what happened to Christiane Andermatt, in *Mont-Oriol*, when she went to walk on the hills with Paul Brétigny, and so much, say, about the forces that formed her for that gentleman's convenience, or those lying behind any other odd collapse that our author may have related. The rule misleads, and the best rule certainly is the tact of the individual writer, which will adapt itself to the material as the material comes to him. The cause we plead is ever pretty sure to be the cause of our idiosyncrasies, and if M. de Maupassant thinks meanly of 'explanations', it is, I suspect, that they come to him in no great affluence. His view of the conduct of man is so simple as scarcely to require them; and indeed so far as they are needed he *is*, virtually, explanatory. He deprecates reference to motives, but there is one, covering an immense ground in his horizon, as I have already hinted, to which he perpetually refers. If the sexual impulse be not a moral antecedent, it is none the less the wire that moves almost all M. de Maupassant's puppets, and as he has not hidden it, I cannot see that he has eliminated analysis or made a sacrifice to discretion. His pages are studded with that particular analysis; he is constantly peeping behind the curtain, telling us what he discovers there. The truth is that the admirable system of simplification which makes his tales so rapid and so concise (especially his shorter ones, for his novels in some degree, I think, suffer from it) strikes us as not in the least a conscious intellectual effort, a selective, comparative process. He tells us all he knows, all he suspects, and if these things take no account of the moral nature of man, it is because he has no window looking in that direction, and not because artistic scruples have compelled him to close it up. The very compact mansion in which he dwells presents on that side a perfectly dead wall.

This is why, if his axiom that you produce the effect of truth better by painting people from the outside than from the inside has a large utility, his example is convincing in a much higher degree. A writer is fortunate when his theory and his limitations so exactly correspond, when his curiosities may be appeased with such precision and promptitude. M. de Maupassant contends that the most that the analytic novelist can do is to put himself — his own peculiarities — into the costume of the figure analysed. This may be true, but if it applies to one manner of representing people who are not ourselves, it applies also to any other manner. It is the limitation, the difficulty of the novelist, to whatever clan or camp he may belong. M. de Maupassant is remarkably objective and impersonal, but he would go too far if he were to entertain the belief that he has kept himself out of his books. They speak of him eloquently, even if it only be to tell us how easy — how easy, given his talent of course — he has found this impersonality. Let us hasten to add that in the case of describing a character it is doubtless more difficult to convey the impression of something that is not one's self (the constant effort, however delusive at bottom, of the novelist) than in the case of describing some object more immediately visible. The operation is more delicate, but that circumstance only increases the beauty of the problem.

On the question of style our author has some excellent remarks; we may be grateful indeed for every one of them, save an odd reflection about the way to 'become original' if we happen not to be so. The recipe for this transformation, it would appear, is to sit down in front of a blazing fire, or a tree in a plain, or any object we encounter in the regular way of business, and remain there until the tree, or the fire, or the object, whatever it be, become different for us from all other specimens of the same class. I doubt whether this system would always answer, for surely the resemblance is what we wish to discover, quite as much as the difference, and the best way to preserve it is not to look for something opposed to it. Is not this indication of the road to take to become, as a writer, original touched with the same fallacy as the recommendation about eschewing analysis? It is the only *naïveté* I have encountered in M. de Maupassant's many volumes. The best originality is the most unconscious, and the best way to describe a tree is the way in which it has struck us. 'Ah, but we don't always know how it has struck us', the answer to that may be, 'and it takes some time and ingenuity — much fasting and prayer — to find out.' If we do not know, it probably has not struck us very much: so little indeed that our inquiry had better be relegated to that closed chamber of an artist's meditations, that sacred back kitchen, which no *a priori* rule can light up. The best thing the artist's adviser can do in such a case is to trust him and turn away, to let him fight the matter out with his conscience. And be this said with a full appreciation of the degree in which M. de Maupassant's observations on the whole question of a writer's style, at the point we have come to today, bear the stamp of intelligence and experience. His own style is of so excellent a tradition that the presumption is altogether in favour of what he may have to say.

He feels oppressively, discouragingly, as many another of his countrymen must have felt — for the French have worked their language as no other people have done — the penalty of coming at the end of three centuries of literature, the difficulty of dealing with an instrument of expression so worn by friction, of drawing new sounds from the old familiar pipe. 'When we read, so saturated with French writing as we are that our whole body gives us the impression of being a paste made of words, do we ever find a line, a thought, which is not familiar to us, and of which we have not had at least a confused presentiment?' And he adds that the matter is simple enough for the writer who only seeks to amuse the public by means already known; he attempts little, and he produces 'with confidence, in the candour of his mediocrity' works which answer no question and leave no trace. It is he who wants to do more than this that has less and less an easy time of it. Everything seems to him to have been done, every effect produced, every combination already made. If he be a man of genius, his trouble is lightened, for mysterious ways are revealed to him, and new combinations spring up for him even after novelty is dead. It is to the simple man of taste and talent, who has only a conscience and a will, that the situation may sometimes well appear desperate; he judges himself as he goes, and he can only go step by step over ground where every step is already a footprint.

If it be a miracle whenever there is a fresh tone, the miracle has been wrought for M. de Maupassant. Or is he simply a man of genius to whom short cuts have been disclosed in the watches of the night? At any rate he has had faith — religion has come to his aid; I mean the religion of his mother tongue, which he has loved well enough to be patient for her sake. He has arrived at the peace which passeth understanding, at a kind of conservative piety. He has taken his stand on simplicity, on a studied sobriety, being persuaded that the deepest science lies in that direction rather than in the multiplication of new terms, and on this subject he delivers himself with superlative wisdom.

There is no need of the queer, complicated, numerous, and Chinese vocabulary which is imposed on us today under the name of artistic writing, to fix all the shades of thought; the right way is to distinguish with an extreme clearness all those modifications of the value of a word which come from the place it occupies. Let us have fewer nouns, verbs and adjectives of an almost imperceptible sense, and more different phrases variously constructed, ingeniously cast, full of the science of sound and rhythm. Let us have an excellent general form rather than be collectors of rare terms.

M. de Maupassant's practice does not fall below his exhortation (though I must confess that in the foregoing passage he makes use of the detestable expression 'stylist', which I have not reproduced). Nothing can exceed the masculine firmness, the quiet force of his own style, in which every phrase is a close sequence, every epithet a paying piece, and the ground is completely cleared of the vague, the ready-made and the second-best. Less than any one today does he beat the air; more than any one does he hit out from the shoulder.

He has produced a hundred short tales and only four regular novels; but if the tales deserve the first place in any candid appreciation of his talent it is not simply because they are so much the more numerous: they are also more characteristic; they represent him best in his originality, and their brevity, extreme in some cases, does not prevent them from being a collection of masterpieces. (They are very unequal, and I speak of the best.) The little story is but scantily relished in England, where readers take their fiction rather by the volume than by the page, and the novelist's idea is apt to resemble one of those old-fashioned carriages which require a wide court to turn round. In America, where it is associated pre-eminently with Hawthorne's name, with Edgar Poe's, and with that of Mr Bret Harte, the short tale has had a better fortune. France, however, has been the land of its great prosperity, and M. de Maupassant had from the first the advantage of addressing a public accustomed to catch on, as the modern phrase is,

quickly. In some respects, it may be said, he encountered pre-
judices too friendly, for he found a tradition of indecency ready
made to his hand. I say indecency with plainness, though my
indication would perhaps please better with another word, for we
suffer in English from a lack of roundabout names for the *conte
leste* — that element for which the French, with their *grivois*, their
gaillard, their *égrillard*, their *gaudriole*, have so many convenient
synonyms. It is an honoured tradition in France that the little
story, in verse or in prose, should be liable to be more or less
obscene (I can think only of that alternative epithet), though I
hasten to add that among literary forms it does not monopolise
the privilege. Our uncleanness is less producible — at any rate it
is less produced.

For the last ten years our author has brought forth with regularity these condensed compositions, of which, probably, to an
English reader, at a first glance, the most universal sign will be
their licentiousness. They really partake of this quality, however,
in a very differing degree, and a second glance shows that they
may be divided into numerous groups. It is not fair, I think, even
to say that what they have most in common is their being extremely *lestes*. What they have most in common is their being
extremely strong, and after that their being extremely brutal. A
story may be obscene without being brutal, and *vice versa*, and
M. de Maupassant's contempt for those interdictions which are
supposed to be made in the interest of good morals is but an incident — a very large one indeed — of his general contempt. A
pessimism so great that its alliance with the love of good work, or
even with the calculation of the sort of work that pays best in a
country of style, is, as I have intimated, the most puzzling of
anomalies (for it would seem in the light of such sentiments that
nothing is worth anything); this cynical strain is the sign of such
gems of narration as *La Maison Tellier, L'Histoire d'une fille de
Ferme, L'Ane, Le Chien, Mademoiselle Fifi, Monsieur Parent,
L'Héritage, En Famille, Le Baptême, Le Père Amable.* The
author fixes a hard eye on some small spot of human life, usually
some ugly, dreary, shabby, sordid one, takes up the particle, and

squeezes it either till it grimaces or till it bleeds. Sometimes the grimace is very droll, sometimes the wound is very horrible; but in either case the whole thing is real, observed, noted, and represented, not an invention or a castle in the air. M. de Maupassant sees human life as a terribly ugly business relieved by the comical, but even the comedy is for the most part the comedy of misery, of avidity, of ignorance, helplessness, and grossness. When his laugh is not for these things, it is for the little *saletés* (to use one of his own favourite words) of luxurious life, which are intended to be prettier, but which can scarcely be said to brighten the picture. I like *La Bête à Maître Belhomme, La Ficelle, Le Petit Fût, Le Cas de Madame Luneau, Tribuneaux Rustiques*, and many others of this category much better than his anecdotes of the mutual confidences of his little *marquises* and *baronnes*.

Not counting his novels for the moment, his tales may be divided into the three groups of those which deal with the Norman peasantry, those which deal with the *petit employé* and small shopkeeper, usually in Paris, and the miscellaneous, in which the upper walks of life are represented, and the fantastic, the whimsical, the weird, and even the supernatural, figure as well as the unexpurgated. These last things range from *Le Horla* (which is not a specimen of the author's best vein — the only occasion on which he has the weakness of imitation is when he strikes us as emulating Edgar Poe) to *Miss Harriet*, and from *Boule de Suif* (a triumph) to that almost inconceivable little growl of Anglophobia, *Découverte* — inconceivable I mean in its irresponsibility and ill-nature on the part of a man of M. de Maupassant's distinction; passing by such little perfections as *Petit Soldat, L'Abandonné, Le Collier* (the list is too long for complete enumeration), and such gross imperfections (for it once in a while befalls our author to go woefully astray) as *La Femme de Paul, Châli, Les Sœurs Rondoli*. To these might almost be added as a special category the various forms in which M. de Maupassant relates adventures in railway carriages. Numerous, to his imagination, are the pretexts for enlivening fiction afforded by first, second, and third class compartments; the accidents (which have nothing to do with the conduct of the train) that occur there constitute no inconsiderable part of our earthly transit.

It is surely by his Norman peasant that his tales will live; he knows this worthy as if he had made him, understands him down to the ground, puts him on his feet with a few of the freest, most plastic touches. M. de Maupassant does not admire him, and he is such a master of the subject that it would ill become an outsider to suggest a revision of judgment. He is a part of the contemptible furniture of the world, but on the whole, it would appear, the most grotesque part of it. His caution, his canniness, his natural astuteness, his stinginess, his general grinding sordidness, are as unmistakable as that quaint and brutish dialect in which he expresses himself, and on which our author plays like a virtuoso. It would be impossible to demonstrate with a finer sense of the humour of the thing the fatuities and densities of his ignorance, the bewilderments of his opposed appetites, the overreachings of his caution. His existence has a gay side, but it is apt to be the barbarous gaiety commemorated in *Farce Normande*, an anecdote which, like many of M. de Maupassant's anecdotes, it is easier to refer the reader to than to repeat. If it is most convenient to place *La Maison Tellier* among the tales of the peasantry, there is no doubt that it stands at the head of the list. It is absolutely unadapted to the perusal of ladies and young persons, but it shares this peculiarity with most of its fellows, so that to ignore it on that account would be to imply that we must forswear M. de Maupassant altogether, which is an incongruous and insupportable conclusion. Every good story is of course both a picture and an idea, and the more they are interfused the better the problem is solved. In *La Maison Tellier* they fit each other to perfection; the capacity for sudden innocent delights latent in natures which have lost their innocence is vividly illustrated by the singular scenes to which our acquaintance with Madame and her staff (little as it may be a thing to boast of) successively introduces us. The breadth, the freedom, and brightness of all this give the measure of the author's talent, and of that large, keen way of looking at life which sees the pathetic and the droll, the stuff of which the whole piece is made, in the queerest and humblest patterns. The tone of *La Maison Tellier* and the few compositions which closely resemble it, expresses M. de Maupassant's nearest approach to geniality. Even here, however, it is the geniality of the showman exhilarated by the success with which he feels that he makes his mannikins (and especially his womankins) caper and squeak, and who after the performance tosses them into their box with the irreverence of a practised hand. If the pages of the author of *Bel-Ami* may be searched almost in vain for a manifestation of the sentiment of respect, it is naturally not by Mme Tellier and her charges that we must look most to see it called forth; but they are among the things that please him most.

Sometimes there is a sorrow, a misery, or even a little heroism, that he handles with a certain tenderness (*Une Vie* is the capital example of this), without insisting on the poor, the ridiculous, or, as he is fond of saying, the bestial side of it. Such an attempt, admirable in its sobriety and delicacy, is the sketch, in *L'Abandonné*, of the old lady and gentleman, Mme de Cadour and M. d'Apreval, who, staying with the husband of the former at a little watering-place on the Normandy coast, take a long, hot walk on a summer's day, on a straight, white road, into the interior, to catch a clandestine glimpse of a young farmer, their illegitimate son. He has been pensioned, he is ignorant of his origin, and is a commonplace and unconciliatory rustic. They look at him, in his dirty farmyard, and no sign passes between them; then they turn away and crawl back, in melancholy silence, along the dull French road. The manner in which this dreary little occurrence is related makes it as large as a chapter of history. There is tenderness in *Miss Harriet*, which sets forth how an English old maid, fantastic, hideous, sentimental, and tract-distributing, with a smell of india rubber, fell in love with an irresistible French painter, and drowned herself in the well because she saw him kissing the maidservant; but the figure of the lady grazes the farcical. Is it because we know Miss Harriet (if we are not mistaken in the type the author has had in his eye) that we suspect the good spinster was not so weird and desperate, addicted though her class may be, as he says, to

'haunting all the *tables d'hôte* in Europe, to spoiling Italy, poison-
ing Switzerland, making the charming towns of the Mediter-
ranean uninhabitable, carrying everywhere their queer little
manias, their *mœurs de vestales pétrifiées*, their indescribable garments, and that odour of india rubber which makes one think that
at night they must be slipped into a case'? What would Miss
Harriet have said to M. de Maupassant's friend, the hero of the
Découverte, who, having married a little Anglaise because he
thought she was charming when she spoke broken French, finds
she is very flat as she becomes more fluent, and has nothing more
urgent than to denounce her to a gentleman he meets on the steam-
boat, and to relieve his wrath in ejaculations of 'Sales Anglais'?

M. de Maupassant evidently knows a great deal about the army
of clerks who work under government, but it is a terrible tale that
he has to tell of them and of the *petit bourgeois* in general. It is
true that he has treated the *petit bourgeois* in *Pierre et Jean* without holding him up to our derision, and the effort has been so
fruitful, that we owe to it the work for which, on the whole, in the
long list of his successes, we are most thankful. But of *Pierre et
Jean*, a production neither comic nor cynical (in the degree, that is,
of its predecessors), but serious and fresh, I will speak anon. In
*Monsieur Parent, L'Héritage, En Famille, Une Partie de Cam-
pagne, Promenade,* and many other pitiless little pieces, the author
opens the window wide to his perception of everything mean,
narrow, and sordid. The subject is ever the struggle for existence
in hard conditions, lighted up simply by more or less *polisson-
nerie*. Nothing is more striking to an Anglo-Saxon reader than
the omission of all the other lights, those with which our imagination, and I think it ought to be said our observation, is familiar, and which our own works of fiction at any rate do not permit us to forget: those of which the most general description is that
they spring from a certain mixture of good humour and piety —
piety, I mean, in the civil and domestic sense quite as much as in
the religious. The love of sport, the sense of decorum, the necessity for action, the habit of respect, the absence of irony, the
pervasiveness of childhood, the expansive tendency of the race,

are a few of the qualities (the analysis might, I think, be pushed much further) which ease us off, mitigate our tension and irritation, rescue us from the nervous exasperation which is almost the commonest element of life as depicted by M. de Maupassant. No doubt there is in our literature an immense amount of conventional blinking, and it may be questioned whether pessimistic representation in M. de Maupassant's manner does not follow his particular original more closely than our perpetual quest of pleasantness (does not Mr Rider Haggard make even his African carnage pleasant?) adheres to the lines of the world we ourselves know.

Fierce indeed is the struggle for existence among even our pious and good-humoured millions, and it is attended with incidents as to which after all little testimony is to be extracted from our literature of fiction. It must never be forgotten that the optimism of that literature is partly the optimism of women and of spinsters; in other words the optimism of ignorance as well as of delicacy. It might be supposed that the French, with their mastery of the *arts d'agrément*, would have more consolations than we, but such is not the account of the matter given by the new generation of painters. To the French we seem superficial, and we are certainly open to the reproach; but none the less even to the infinite majority of readers of good faith there will be a wonderful want of correspondence between the general picture of *Bel-Ami*, of *Mont-Oriol*, of *Une Vie*, *Yvette* and *En Famille*, and our own vision of reality. It is an old impression of course that the satire of the French has a very different tone from ours; but few English readers will admit that the feeling of life is less in ours than in theirs. The feeling of life is evidently, *de part et d'autre*, a very different thing. If in ours, as the novel illustrates it, there are superficialities, there are also qualities which are far from being negatives and omissions: a large imagination and (is it fatuous to say?) a large experience of the positive kind. Even those of our novelists whose manner is most ironic pity life more and hate it less than M. de Maupassant and his great initiator Flaubert. It comes back I suppose to our good humour (which may apparently also be an artistic force); at any rate, we have reserves about our shames and our sorrows, indulgences and tolerances about our Philistinism, forbearances about our blows, and a general friendliness of conception about our possibilities, which take the cruelty from our self-derision and operate in the last resort as a sort of tribute to our freedom. There is a horrible, admirable scene in *Monsieur Parent*, which is a capital example of triumphant ugliness. The harmless gentleman who gives his name to the tale has an abominable wife, one of whose offensive attributes is a lover (unsuspected by her husband), only less impudent than herself. M. Parent comes in from a walk with his little boy, at dinner time, to encounter suddenly in his abused, dishonoured, deserted home, convincing proof of her misbehaviour. He waits and waits dinner for her, giving her the benefit of every doubt; but when at last she enters, late in the evening, accompanied by the partner of her guilt, there is a tremendous domestic concussion. It is to the peculiar vividness of this scene that I allude, the way we hear it and see it, and its most repulsive details are evoked for us: the sordid confusion, the vulgar noise, the disordered table and ruined dinner, the shrill insolence of the wife, her brazen mendacity, the scared inferiority of the lover, the mere momentary heroics of the weak husband, the scuffle and somersault, the eminently unpoetic justice with which it all ends.

When Thackeray relates how Arthur Pendennis goes home to take pot luck with the insolvent Newcomes at Boulogne, and how the dreadful Mrs Mackenzie receives him, and how she makes a scene, when the frugal repast is served, over the diminished mutton bone, we feel that the notation of that order of misery goes about as far as we can bear it. But this is child's play to the history of M. and Mme Caravan and their attempt, after the death (or supposed death) of the husband's mother, to transfer to their apartment before the arrival of the other heirs certain miserable little articles of furniture belonging to the deceased, together with the frustration of the manœuvre not only by the grim resurrection of the old woman (which is a sufficiently fantastic item), but by the shock of battle when a married daughter and her husband

appear. No one gives us like M. de Maupassant the odious words
exchanged on such an occasion as that: no one depicts with so just
a hand the feelings of small people about small things. These feelings are very apt to be 'fury'; that word is of strikingly frequent
occurrence in his pages. *L'Héritage* is a drama of private life in
the little world of the Ministère de la Marine — a world, according
to M. de Maupassant, of dreadful little jealousies and ineptitudes.
Readers of a robust complexion should learn how the wretched
M. Lesable was handled by his wife and her father on his failing
to satisfy their just expectations, and how he comported himself
in the singular situation thus prepared for him. The story is a
model of narration, but it leaves our poor average humanity dang-
ling like a beaten rag.

Where does M. de Maupassant find the great multitude of his
detestable women? or where at least does he find the courage to
represent them in such colours? Jeanne de Lamare, in *Une Vie*,
receives the outrages of fate with a passive fortitude; and there is
something touching in Mme Roland's *âme tendre de caissière*, as
exhibited in *Pierre et Jean*. But for the most part M. de Maupassant's heroines are a mixture of extreme sensuality and extreme
mendacity. They are a large element in that general disfigurement, that *illusion de l'ignoble, qui attire tant d'êtres,* which makes
the perverse or the stupid side of things the one which strikes him
first, which leads him, if he glances at a group of nurses and children sunning themselves in a Parisian square, to notice primarily
the *yeux de brute* of the nurses; or if he speaks of the longing for a
taste of the country which haunts the shopkeeper fenced in behind
his counter, to identify it as the *amour bête de la nature*; or if he
has occasion to put the boulevards before us on a summer's evening, to seek his effect in these terms: 'The city, as hot as a stew,
seemed to sweat in the suffocating night. The drains puffed their
pestilential breath from their mouths of granite, and the under-
ground kitchens poured into the streets, through their low windows, the infamous miasmas of their dishwater and old sauces.' I
do not contest the truth of such indications, I only note the particular selection and their seeming to the writer the most *apropos*.

Is it because of the inadequacy of these indications when applied to the long stretch that M. de Maupassant's novels strike us as less complete, in proportion to the talent expended upon them, than his *contes* and *nouvelles?* I make this invidious distinction in spite of the fact that *Une Vie* (the first of the novels in the order of time) is a remarkably interesting experiment, and that *Pierre et Jean* is, so far as my judgment goes, a faultless production. *Bel-Ami* is full of the bustle and the crudity of life (its energy and expressiveness almost bribe one to like it), but it has the great defect that the physiological explanation of things here too visibly contracts the problem in order to meet it. The world represented is too special, too little inevitable, too much to take or to leave as we like — a world in which every man is a cad and every woman a harlot. M. de Maupassant traces the career of a finished blackguard who succeeds in life through women, and he represents him primarily as succeeding in the profession of journalism. His colleagues and his mistresses are as depraved as himself, greatly to the injury of the ironic idea, for the real force of satire would have come from seeing him engaged and victorious with natures better than his own. It may be remarked that this was the case with the nature of Mme Walter; but the reply to that is — hardly! Moreover the author's whole treatment of the episode of Mme Walter is the thing on which his admirers have least to congratulate him. The taste of it is so atrocious, that it is difficult to do justice to the way it is made to stand out. Such an instance as this pleads with irresistible eloquence, as it seems to me, the cause of that salutary diffidence or practical generosity which I mentioned on a preceding page. I know not the English or American novelist who could have written this portion of the history of *Bel-Ami* if he would. But I also find it impossible to conceive of a member of that fraternity who would have written it if he could. The subject of *Mont-Oriol* is full of queerness to the English mind. Here again the picture has much more importance than the idea, which is simply that a gentleman, if he happen to be a low animal, is liable to love a lady very much less if she presents him with a pledge of their affection. It need scarcely be said that the lady and

gentleman who in M. de Maupassant's pages exemplify this interesting truth are not united in wedlock — that is with each other.

M. de Maupassant tells us that he has imbibed many of his principles from Gustave Flaubert, from the study of his works as well
as, formerly, the enjoyment of his words. It is in *Une Vie* that
Flaubert's influence is most directly traceable, for the thing has a
marked analogy with *L'Éducation Sentimentale.* That is, it is the
presentation of a simple piece of a life (in this case a long piece), a
series of observations upon an episode *quelconque*, as the French
say, with the minimum of arrangement of the given objects. It is
an excellent example of the way the impression of truth may be
conveyed by that form, but it would have been a still better one if
in his search for the effect of dreariness (the effect of dreariness
may be said to be the subject of *Une Vie*, so far as the subject is
reducible) the author had not eliminated excessively. He has arranged, as I say, as little as possible; the necessity of a 'plot' has in
no degree imposed itself upon him, and his effort has been to give
the uncomposed, unrounded look of life, with its accidents, its
broken rhythm, its queer resemblance to the famous description
of 'Bradshaw' — a compound of trains that start but don't arrive,
and trains that arrive but don't start. It is almost an arrangement
of the history of poor Mme de Lamare to have left so many things
out of it, for after all she is described in very few of the relations
of life. The principal ones are there certainly; we see her as a
daughter, a wife, and a mother, but there is a certain accumulation
of secondary experience that marks any passage from youth to
old age which is a wholly absent element in M. de Maupassant's
narrative, and the suppression of which gives the thing a tinge of
the arbitrary. It is in the power of this secondary experience to
make a great difference, but nothing makes any difference for
Jeanne de Lamare as M. de Maupassant puts her before us. Had
she no other points of contact than those he describes? — no
friends, no phases, no episodes, no chances, none of the miscellaneous *remplissage* of life? No doubt M. de Maupassant would
say that he has had to select, that the most comprehensive enumeration is only a condensation, and that, in accordance with the

very just principles enunciated in that preface to which I have perhaps too repeatedly referred, he has sacrificed what is uncharacteristic to what is characteristic. It characterizes the career of this French country lady of fifty years ago that its long grey expanse should be seen as peopled with but five or six figures. The essence of the matter is that she was deceived in almost every affection, and that essence is given if the persons who deceived her are given.

The reply is doubtless adequate, and I have only intended my criticism to suggest the degree of my interest. What it really amounts to is that if the subject of this artistic experiment had been the existence of an English lady, even a very dull one, the air of verisimilitude would have demanded that she should have been placed in a denser medium. *Une Vie* may after all be only a testimony to the fact of the melancholy void of the coast of Normandy, even within a moderate drive of a great seaport, under the Restoration and Louis Philippe. It is especially to be recommended to those who are interested in the question of what constitutes a 'story', offering as it does the most definite sequences at the same time that it has nothing that corresponds to the usual idea of a plot, and closing with an implication that finds us prepared. The picture again in this case is much more dominant than the idea, unless it be an idea that loneliness and grief are terrible. The picture, at any rate, is full of truthful touches, and the work has the merit and the charm that it is the most delicate of the author's productions and the least hard. In none other has he occupied himself so continuously with so innocent a figure as his soft, bruised heroine; in none other has he paid our poor blind human history the compliment (and this is remarkable, considering the flatness of so much of the particular subject) of finding it so little *bête*. He may think it, here, but comparatively he does not say it. He almost betrays a sense of moral things. Jeanne is absolutely passive, she has no moral spring, no active moral life, none of the edifying attributes of character (it costs her apparently as little as may be in the way of a shock, a complication of feeling, to discover, by letters, after her mother's death, that this lady has

not been the virtuous woman she has supposed); but her chron-
icler has had to handle the immaterial forces of patience and renunciation, and this has given the book a certain purity, in spite
of two or three 'physiological' passages that come in with violence
— a violence the greater as we feel it to be a result of selection. It
is very much a mark of M. de Maupassant that on the most
striking occasion, with a single exception, on which his picture is
not a picture of libertinage it is a picture of unmitigated suffering.
Would he suggest that these are the only alternatives?

The exception that I here allude to is for *Pierre et Jean*, which I
have left myself small space to speak of. Is it because in this
masterly little novel there is a show of those immaterial forces
which I just mentioned, and because Pierre Roland is one of the
few instances of operative character that can be recalled from so
many volumes, that many readers will place M. de Maupassant's
latest production altogether at the head of his longer ones? I am
not sure, inasmuch as after all the character in question is not
extraordinarily distinguished, and the moral problem not presented in much complexity. The case is only relative. Perhaps it is
not of importance to fix the reasons of preference in respect to a
piece of writing so essentially a work of art and of talent. *Pierre et
Jean* is the best of M. de Maupassant's novels mainly because M.
de Maupassant has never before been so clever. It is a pleasure to
see a mature talent able to renew itself, strike another note, and
appear still young. This story suggests the growth of a perception
that everything has not been said about the actors on the world's
stage when they are represented either as helpless victims or as
mere bundles of appetites. There is an air of responsibility about
Pierre Roland, the person on whose behalf the tale is mainly told,
which almost constitutes a pledge. An inquisitive critic may ask
why in this particular case M. de Maupassant should have stuck to
the *petit bourgeois*, the circumstances not being such as to typify
that class more than another. There are reasons indeed which on
reflection are perceptible; it was necessary that his people should
be poor, and necessary even that to attenuate Mme Roland's misbehaviour she should have had the excuse of the contracted life of

a shopwoman in the Rue Montmartre. Were the inquisitive critic slightly malicious as well, he might suspect the author of a fear that he should seem to give way to the *illusion du beau* if in addition to representing the little group in *Pierre et Jean* as persons of about the normal conscience he had also represented them as of the cultivated class. If they belong to the humble life this belittles and — I am still quoting the supposedly malicious critic — M. de Maupassant *must*, in one way or the other, belittle. To the English reader it will appear, I think, that Pierre and Jean are rather more of the cultivated class than two young Englishmen in the same social position. It belongs to the drama that the struggle of the elder brother — educated, proud, and acute — should be partly with the pettiness of his opportunities. The author's choice of a *milieu*, moreover, will serve to English readers as an example of how much more democratic contemporary French fiction is than that of his own country. The greater part of it — almost all the work of Zola and of Daudet, the best of Flaubert's novels, and the best of those of the brothers De Goncourt — treat of that vast, dim section of society which, lying between those luxurious walks on whose behalf there are easy presuppositions and that darkness of misery which, in addition to being picturesque, brings philanthropy also to the writer's aid, constitutes really, in extent and expressiveness, the substance of any nation. In England, where the fashion of fiction still sets mainly to the country house and the hunting-field, and yet more novels are published than anywhere else in the world, that thick twilight of mediocrity of condition has been little explored. May it yield triumphs in the years to come!

It may seem that I have claimed little for M. de Maupassant, so far as English readers are concerned with him, in saying that after publishing twenty improper volumes he has at last published a twenty-first, which is neither indecent nor cynical. It is not this circumstance that has led me to dedicate so many pages to him, but the circumstance that in producing all the others he yet remained, for those who are interested in these matters, a writer with whom it was impossible not to reckon. This is why I called him, to begin with, so many ineffectual names: a rarity, a 'case', an embarrassment, a lion in the path. He is still in the path as I conclude these observations, but I think that in making them we have discovered a legitimate way round. If he is a master of his art and it is discouraging to find what low views are compatible with mastery, there is satisfaction, on the other hand, in learning on what particular condition he holds his strange success. This condition, it seems to me, is that of having totally omitted one of the items of the problem, an omission which has made the problem so much easier that it may almost be described as a short cut to a solution. The question is whether it be a fair cut. M. de Maupassant has simply skipped the whole reflective part of his men and women — that reflective part which governs conduct and produces character. He may say that he does not see it, does not know it; to which the answer is, 'So much the better for you, if you wish to describe life without it. The strings you pull are by so much the less numerous, and you can therefore pull those that remain with greater promptitude, consequently with greater firmness, with a greater air of knowledge.' Pierre Roland, I repeat, shows a capacity for reflection, but I cannot think who else does, among the thousand figures who compete with him — I mean for reflection addressed to anything higher than the gratification of an instinct. We have an impression that M. d'Apreval and Mme de Cadour reflect, as they trudge back from their mournful excursion, but that indication is not pushed very far. An aptitude for this exercise is a part of disciplined manhood, and disciplined manhood M. de Maupassant has simply not attempted to represent. I can remember no instance in which he sketches any considerable capacity for conduct, and his women betray that capacity as little as his men. I am much mistaken if he has once painted a gentleman, in the English sense of the term. His gentlemen, like Paul Brétigny and Gontran de Ravenel, are guilty of the most extraordinary deflections. For those who are conscious of this element in life, look for it and like it, the gap will appear to be immense. It will lead them to say, 'No wonder you have a contempt if that is the way you limit the field. No wonder you judge people roughly if that is the way you see them. Your work, on your premisses, remains the admirable thing it is, but is your 'case' not adequately explained?'

The erotic element in M. de Maupassant, about which much more might have been said, seems to me to be explained by the same limitation, and explicable in a similar way wherever else its literature occurs in excess. The carnal side of man appears the most characteristic if you look at it a great deal; and you look at it a great deal if you do not look at the other, at the side by which he reacts against his weaknesses, his defeats. The more you look at the other, the less the whole business to which French novelists have ever appeared to English readers to give a disproportionate place — the business, as I may say, of the senses — will strike you as the only typical one. Is not this the most useful reflection to make in regard to the famous question of the morality, the decency, of the novel? It is the only one, it seems to me, that will meet the case as we find the case today. Hard and fast rules, *a priori* restrictions, mere interdictions (you shall not speak of this, you shall not look at that) have surely served their time, and will in the nature of the case never strike an energetic talent as anything but arbitrary. A healthy, living and growing art, full of curiosity and fond of exercise, has an indefeasible mistrust of rigid prohibitions. Let us then leave this magnificent art of the novelist to itself and to its perfect freedom, in the faith that one example is as good as another, and that our fiction will always be decent enough if it be sufficiently general. Let us not be alarmed at this prodigy (though prodigies are alarming) of M. de Maupassant, who is at once so licentious and so impeccable, but gird ourselves up with the conviction that another point of view will yield another perfection.

TURGENEV AND TOLSTOY

1897

THERE is perhaps no novelist of alien race who more naturally than Ivan Turgenev inherits a niche in a Library for English readers; and this not because of any advance or concession that in his peculiar artistic independence he ever made, or could dream of making, such readers, but because it was one of the effects of his peculiar genius to give him, even in his lifetime, a special place in the regard of foreign publics. His position is in this respect singular; for it is his Russian savour that as much as anything has helped generally to domesticate him.

Born in 1818, at Orel in the heart of Russia, and dying in 1883, at Bougival near Paris, he had spent in Germany and France the latter half of his life; and had incurred in his own country in some degree the reprobation that is apt to attach to the absent — the penalty they pay for such extension or such beguilement as they may have happened to find over the border. He belonged to the class of large rural proprietors of land and of serfs; and with his ample patrimony, offered one of the few examples of literary labour achieved in high independence of the question of gain — a character that he shares with his illustrious contemporary Tolstoy, who is of a type in other respects so different. It may give us an idea of his primary situation to imagine some large Virginian or Carolinian slave-holder, during the first half of the century, inclining to 'Northern' views; and becoming (though not predominantly under pressure of these, but rather by the operation of an exquisite genius) the great American novelist — one of the great novelists of the world. Born under a social and political order sternly repressive, all Turgenev's deep instincts, all his moral passion, placed him on the liberal side; with the consequence that early in life, after a period spent at a German university, he found himself, through the accident of a trifling public utterance, under such suspicion in high places as to be sentenced to a term of tempered exile — confinement to his own estate. It was partly under these circumstances perhaps that he gathered material for the work from the appearance of which his reputation dates — *A Sportsman's Sketches*, published in two volumes in 1852. This admirable collection of impressions of homely country life, as the old state of servitude had made it, is often spoken of as having borne to the great decree of Alexander II the relation borne by Mrs Beecher Stowe's famous novel to the emancipation of the Southern slaves. Incontestably, at any rate, Turgenev's rustic studies sounded, like *Uncle Tom's Cabin*, a particular hour: with the difference, however, of not having at the time produced an agitation — of having rather presented the case with an art too insidious for instant recognition, an art that stirred the depths more than the surface.

The author was designated promptly enough, at any rate, for such influence as might best be exercised at a distance: he travelled, he lived abroad; early in the sixties he was settled in Germany; he acquired property at Baden-Baden, and spent there the last years of the prosperous period — in the history of the place — of which the Franco-Prussian War was to mark the violent term. He cast in his lot after that event mainly with the victims of the lost cause; setting up a fresh home in Paris — near which city he had, on the Seine, a charming alternate residence — and passing in it, and in the country, save for brief revisitations, the remainder of his days. His friendships, his attachments, in the world of art and of letters, were numerous and distinguished; he never married; he produced, as the years went on, without precipitation or frequency; and these were the years during which his reputation gradually established itself as, according to the phrase, European — a phrase denoting in this case, perhaps, a public more alert in the United States even than elsewhere.

Tolstoy, his junior by ten years, had meanwhile come to fruition; though, as in fact happened, it was not till after Turgenev's death that the greater fame of *War and Peace* and of *Anna Karé-*

nina began to be blown about the world. One of the last acts of the elder writer, performed on his deathbed, was to address to the other (from whom for a considerable term he had been estranged by circumstances needless to reproduce) an appeal to return to the exercise of the genius that Tolstoy had already so lamentably, so monstrously forsworn.

I am on my death-bed; there is no possibility of my recovery. I write you expressly to tell you how happy I have been to be your contemporary, and to utter my last, my urgent prayer. Come back, my friend, to your literary labours. That gift came to you from the source from which all comes to us. Ah, how happy I should be could I think you would listen to my entreaty! My friend, great writer of our Russian land, respond to it, obey it!

These words, among the most touching surely ever addressed by one great spirit to another, throw an indirect light — perhaps I may even say a direct one — upon the nature and quality of Turgenev's artistic temperament; so much so that I regret being without opportunity, in this place, to gather such aid for a portrait of him as might be supplied by following out the unlikeness between the pair. It would be too easy to say that Tolstoy was, from the Russian point of view, for home consumption, and Turgenev for foreign: *War and Peace* has probably had more readers in Europe and America than *A House of Gentlefolk* or *On the Eve* or *Smoke*,—a circumstance less detrimental than it may appear to my claim of our having, in the Western world, supremely adopted the author of the latter works. Turgenev is in a peculiar degree what I may call the novelists' novelist — an artistic influence extraordinarily valuable and ineradicably established. The perusal of Tolstoy — a wonderful mass of life — is an immense event, a kind of splendid accident, for each of us: his name represents nevertheless no such eternal spell of method, no such quiet irresistibility of presentation, as shines, close to us and lighting our possible steps, in that of his precursor. Tolstoy is a reflector as vast as a natural lake; a monster harnessed to his great subject — all human life! — as an elephant might be harnessed, for purposes of traction, not to a carriage, but to a coach-house.

His own case is prodigious, but his example for others dire: disciples not elephantine he can only mislead and betray.

One by one, for thirty years, with a firm, deliberate hand, with intervals and patiences and waits, Turgenev pricked in his sharp outlines. His great external mark is probably his concision: an ideal he never threw over — it shines most perhaps even when he is least brief — and that he often applied with a rare felicity. He has masterpieces of a few pages; his perfect things are sometimes his least prolonged. He abounds in short tales, episodes clipped as by the scissors of Atropos; but for a direct translation of the whole we have still to wait — depending meanwhile upon the French and German versions, which have been, instead of the original text (thanks to the paucity among us of readers of Russian), the source of several published in English. For the novels and *A Sportsman's Sketches* we depend upon the nine volumes (1897) of Mrs Garnett. We touch here upon the remarkable side, to our vision, of the writer's fortune — the anomaly of his having constrained to intimacy even those who are shut out from the enjoyment of his medium, for whom that question is positively prevented from existing. Putting aside extrinsic intimations, it is impossible to read him without the conviction of his being, in the vividness of his own tongue, of the strong type of those made to bring home to us the happy truth of the unity, in a generous talent, of material and form — of their being inevitable faces of the same medal; the type of those, in a word, whose example deals death to the perpetual clumsy assumption that subject and style are — æsthetically speaking, or in the living work — different and separable things. We are conscious, reading him in a language not his own, of not being reached by his personal tone, his individual accent.

It is a testimony therefore to the intensity of his presence, that so much of his particular charm does reach us; that the mask turned to us has, even without his expression, still so much beauty. It is the beauty (since we must try to formulate) of the finest presentation of the familiar. His vision is of the world of character and feeling, the world of the relations life throws up at every hour and on every spot; he deals little, on the whole, in the miracles of chance, — the hours and spots over the edge of time and space; his air is that of the great central region of passion and motive, of the usual, the inevitable, the intimate — the intimate for weal or woe. No theme that he ever chooses but strikes us as full; yet with all have we the sense that their animation comes from within, and is not pinned to their backs like the pricking objects used of old in the horse races of the Roman carnival, to make the animals run. Without a patch of 'plot' to draw blood, the story he mainly tells us, the situation he mainly gives, runs as if for dear life. His first book was practically full evidence of what, if we have to specify, is finest in him — the effect, for the commonest truth, of an exquisite envelope of poetry. In this medium of feeling — full, as it were, of all the echoes and shocks of the universal danger and need — everything in him goes on; the sense of fate and folly and pity and wonder and beauty. The tenderness, the humour, the variety of *A Sportsman's Sketches* revealed on the spot an observer with a rare imagination. These faculties had attached themselves, together, to small things and to great: to the misery, the simplicity, the piety, the patience, of the unemancipated peasant; to all the natural wonderful life of earth and air and winter and summer and field and forest; to queer apparitions of country neighbours, of strange local eccentrics; to old-world practices and superstitions; to secrets gathered and types disinterred and impressions absorbed in the long, close contacts with man and nature involved in the passionate pursuit of game. Magnificent in stature and original vigour, Turgenev, with his love of the chase, or rather perhaps of the inspiration he found in it, would have been the model of the mighty hunter, had not such an image been a little at variance with his natural mildness, the softness that often accompanies the sense of an extraordinary reach of limb and play of muscle. He was in person the model rather of the strong man at rest: massive and towering, with the voice of innocence and the smile almost of childhood. What seemed still more of a contradiction to so much of him, however, was that his work was all delicacy and fancy, penetration and compression.

If I add, in their order of succession, *Rudin, Fathers and Children, Spring Floods,* and *Virgin Soil,* to the three novels I have (also in their relation of time) named above, I shall have indicated the larger blocks of the compact monument, with a base resting deep and interstices well filled, into which that work disposes itself. The list of his minor productions is too long to draw out: I can only mention, as a few of the most striking — 'A Correspondence', 'The Wayside Inn', 'The Brigadier', 'The Dog', 'The Jew', 'Visions', 'Mumu', 'Three Meetings', 'A First Love', 'The Forsaken', 'Assia', 'The Journal of a Superfluous Man', 'The Story of Lieutenant Yergunov', 'A King Lear of the Steppe'. The first place among his novels would be difficult to assign: general opinion probably hesitates between *A House of Gentlefolk* and *Fathers and Children.* My own predilection is great for the exquisite *On the Eve;* though I admit that in such a company it draws no supremacy from being exquisite. What is less contestable is that *Virgin Soil* — published shortly before his death, and the longest of his fictions — has, although full of beauty, a minor perfection.

Character, character expressed and exposed, is in all these things what we inveterately find. Turgenev's sense of it was the great light that artistically guided him; the simplest account of him is to say that the mere play of it constitutes in every case his sufficient drama. No one has had a closer vision, or a hand at once more ironic and more tender, for the individual figure. He sees it with its minutest signs and tricks — all its heredity of idiosyncrasies, all its particulars of weakness and strength, of ugliness and beauty, of oddity and charm; and yet it is of his essence that he sees it in the general flood of life, steeped in its relations and contacts, struggling or submerged, a hurried particle in the stream. This gives him, with his quiet method, his extraordinary breadth; dissociates his rare power to particularize from dryness or hardness, from any peril of caricature. He understands so much that we almost wonder he can express anything; and his expression is indeed wholly in absolute projection, in illustration, in giving of everything the unexplained and irresponsible specimen. He is of a spirit so human that we almost wonder at his control of his matter; of a pity so deep and so general that we almost wonder at his curiosity. The element of poetry in him is constant, and yet reality stares through it without the loss of a wrinkle. No one has more of that sign of the born novelist which resides in a respect unconditioned for the freedom and vitality, the absoluteness when summoned, of the creatures he invokes; or is more superior to the strange and second-rate policy of explaining or presenting them by reprobation or apology,—of taking the short cuts and anticipating the emotions and judgments about them that should be left, at the best, to the perhaps not most intelligent reader. And yet his system, as it may summarily be called, of the mere particularized report, has a lucidity beyond the virtue of the cruder moralist.

If character, as I say, is what he gives us at every turn, I should speedily add that he offers it not in the least as a synonym, in our Western sense, of resolution and prosperity. It wears the form of the almost helpless detachment of the short-sighted individual soul; and the perfection of his exhibition of it is in truth too often but the intensity of what, for success, it just does not produce. What works in him most is the question of the will; and the most constant induction he suggests, bears upon the sad figure that principle seems mainly to make among his countrymen. He had seen — he suggests to us — its collapse in a thousand quarters; and the most general tragedy, to his view, is that of its desperate adventures and disasters, its inevitable abdication and defeat. But if the men, for the most part, let it go, it takes refuge in the other sex; many of the representatives of which, in his pages, are supremely strong — in wonderful addition, in various cases, to being otherwise admirable. This is true of such a number — the younger women, the girls, the 'heroines' in especial — that they form in themselves, on the ground of moral beauty, of the finest distinction of soul, one of the most striking groups the modern novel has given us. They are heroines to the letter, and of a heroism obscure and undecorated: it is almost they alone who have the energy to determine and to act. Elena, Lisa, Tatyana, Gemma,

Marianna — we can write their names and call up their images, but I lack space to take them in turn. It is by a succession of the finest and tenderest touches that they live; and this, in all Turgenev's work, is the process by which he persuades and succeeds.

It was his own view of his main danger that he sacrificed too much to detail; was wanting in composition, in the gift that conduces to unity of impression. But no novelist is closer and more cumulative; in none does distinction spring from a quality of truth more independent of everything but the subject, but the idea itself. This idea, this subject, moreover — a spark kindled by the innermost friction of things,— is always as interesting as an unopened telegram. The genial freedom — with its exquisite delicacy — of his approach to the 'innermost' world, the world of our finer consciousness, has in short a side that I can only describe and commemorate as nobly disinterested; a side that makes too many of his rivals appear to hold us in comparison by violent means, and introduce us in comparison to vulgar things.

NATHANIEL HAWTHORNE

1897[1]

IT is perhaps an advantage in writing of Nathaniel Hawthorne's work that his life offers little opportunity to the biographer. The record of it makes so few exactions that in a critical account of him — even as brief as this — the work may easily take most of the place. He was one of those happy men of letters in whose course the great milestones are simply those of his ideas that found successful form. Born at Salem, Massachusetts, on 4 July, 1804, of established local Puritan — and in a conspicuous degree, sturdy seafaring — stock, he was educated at his birthplace and at Bowdoin College, Maine, where H. W. Longfellow was one of his fellow students. Another was Franklin Pierce, who was to be elected President of the United States in 1852, and with whom Hawthorne formed relations that became an influence in his life. On leaving college in 1825 he returned to Salem to live, and in 1828 published in Boston a short romance called *Fanshawe*, of which the scene, in spite of its being a 'love-story', is laid, but for a change of name, at Bowdoin, with professors and undergraduates for its male characters. The experiment was inevitably faint, but the author's beautiful touch had begun to feel its way. In 1837, after a dozen years spent in special solitude, as he later testified, at Salem, he collected as the first series of *Twice-Told Tales* various more or less unremunerated contributions to the magazines and annuals of the day. In 1845 appeared the second series, and in 1851 the two volumes were, with a preface peculiarly graceful and touching, reissued together; he is in general never more graceful than when prefatory. In 1851 and 1854 respectively came

---

[1] This essay first appeared in vol. XII of an anthology, *Library of the World's Best Literature*, edited by Charles Dudley Warner, New York, 1897, and was never reprinted by James.

to light *The Snow Image* and *Mosses from an Old Manse*, which form, with the previous double sheaf, his three main gatherings-in of the shorter fiction. I neglect, for brevity and as addressed to children, *Grandfather's Chair* and *The Wonder Book* (1851), as well as *Tanglewood Tales* (1852). Of the other groups, some preceded, some followed, the appearance in 1850 of his second novel, *The Scarlet Letter*.

These things — the experiments in the shorter fiction — had sounded, with their rare felicity, from the very first the note that was to be Hawthorne's distinguished mark — that feeling for the latent romance of New England, which in summary form is the most final name to be given, I think, to his inspiration. This element, which is what at its best his genius most expresses, was far from obvious — it had to be looked for; and Hawthorne found it, as he wandered and mused, in the secret play of the Puritan faith: the secret, I say particularly, because the direct and ostensible, face to face with common tasks and small conditions (as I may call them without prejudice to their general grimness), arrived at forms of which the tender imagination could make little. It could make a great deal, on the other hand, of the spiritual contortions, the darkened outlook, of the ingrained sense of sin, of evil, and of responsibility. There had been other complications in the history of the community surrounding him — savages from behind, soldiers from before, a cruel climate from every quarter, and a pecuniary remittance from none. But the great complication was the pressing moral anxiety, the restless individual conscience. These things were developed at the cost of so many others that there were almost no others left to help them to make a picture for the artist. The artist's imagination had to deck out the subject, to work it up, as we nowadays say; and Hawthorne's was — on intensely chastened lines, indeed — equal to the task. In that manner it came into exercise from the first, through the necessity of taking for granted, on the part of the society about him, a life of the spirit more complex than anything that met the mere eye of sense. It was a question of looking behind and beneath for the suggestive idea, the artistic motive; the effect of all of which was an invaluable training for the faculty that evokes and enhances. This ingenuity grew alert and irrepressible as it manœuvred for the back view and turned up the under side of common aspects — the laws secretly broken, the impulses secretly felt, the hidden passions, the double lives, the dark corners, the closed rooms, the skeletons in the cupboard and at the feast. It made, in short, and cherished, for fancy's sake, a mystery and a glamour where there were otherwise none very ready to its hand; so that it ended by living in a world of things symbolic and allegoric, a presentation of objects casting, in every case, far behind them a shadow more curious and more amusing than the apparent figure. Any figure therefore easily became with him an emblem, any story a parable, any appearance a cover: things with which his concern is — gently, indulgently, skilfully, with the lightest hand in the world — to pivot them round and show the odd little stamp or sign that gives them their value for the collector.

The specimens he collected, as we may call them, are divisible into groups, but with the mark in common that they are all early products of the dry New England air. Some are myths and mysteries of old Massachusetts — charming ghostly passages of colonial history. Such are 'The Grey Champion', 'The Maypole of Merry Mount', the four beautiful 'Legends of the Province House'. Others, like 'Roger Malvin's Burial', 'Rappaccini's Daughter', 'Young Goodman Brown', are 'moralities' without the moral, as it were; small cold apologues, frosty and exquisite, occasionally gathered from beyond the sea. Then there are the chapters of the fanciful all for fancy's sake, of the pure whimsical, and of observation merely amused and beguiled; pages, many of them, of friendly humorous reflections on what, in Salem or in Boston, a dreamer might meet in his walks. What Hawthorne encountered he instinctively embroidered, working it over with a fine, slow needle, and with flowers pale, rosy, or dusky, as the case might suggest. We have a handful of these in 'The Great Carbuncle' and 'The Great Stone Face', 'The Seven Vagabonds', 'The Threefold Destiny', 'The Village Uncle', 'The Toll Gatherer's Day', 'A Rill from the Town Pump', and 'Chippings with a

Chisel'. The inequalities in his work are not, to my sense, great; and in specifying, we take and leave with hesitation.

The Scarlet Letter, in 1850, brought him immediate distinction, and has probably kept its place not only as the most original of his novels, but as the most distinguished piece of prose fiction that was to spring from American soil. He had received in 1839 an appointment to a small place in the Boston custom-house, where his labours were sordid and sterile, and he had given it up in permissible weariness. He had spent in 1841 near Roxbury, Massachusetts, a few months in the co-operative community of Brook Farm, a short-lived socialistic experiment. He had married in the following year and gone to live at the old Manse at Concord, where he remained till 1846, when, with a fresh fiscal engagement, he returned to his native town. It was in the intervals of his occupation at the Salem custom-house that *The Scarlet Letter* was written. The book has achieved the fortune of the small supreme group of novels: it has hung an ineffaceable image in the portrait gallery, the reserved inner cabinet, of literature. Hester Prynne is not one of those characters of fiction whom we use as a term of comparison for a character of fact: she is almost more than that — she decorates the museum in a way that seems to forbid us such a freedom. Hawthorne availed himself, for her history, of the most striking anecdote the early Puritan chronicle could give him — give him in the manner set forth by the long, lazy Prologue or Introduction, an exquisite commemoration of the happy dullness of his term of service at the custom-house, where it is his fancy to pretend to have discovered in a box of old papers the faded relic and the musty documents which suggested to him his title and his theme.

It is the story as old as the custom of marriage — the story of the husband, the wife, and the lover; but bathed in a misty, moonshiny light, and completely neglecting the usual sources of emotion. The wife, with the charming child of her guilt, had stood under the stern inquisitorial law in the public pillory of the adulteress; while the lover, a saintly young minister, undetected and unbetrayed, has in an anguish of pusillanimity suffered her to pay the whole fine. The husband, an ancient scholar, a man of abstruse and profane learning, finds his revenge years after the wrong, in making himself insidiously the intimate of the young minister, and feeding secretly on the remorse, the inward torments, which he does everything to quicken but pretends to have no ground for suspecting. The march of the drama lies almost wholly in the malignant pressure exercised in this manner by Chillingworth upon Dimmesdale; an influence that at last reaches its climax in the extraordinary penance of the subject, who in the darkness, in the sleeping town, mounts, himself, upon the scaffold on which, years before, the partner of his guilt has undergone irrevocable anguish. In this situation he calls to him Hester Prynne and her child, who, belated in the course of the merciful ministrations to which Hester has now given herself up, pass, among the shadows, within sight of him; and they in response to his appeal ascend for a second time to the place of atonement, and stand there with him under cover of night. The scene is not complete, of course, till Chillingworth arrives to enjoy the spectacle and his triumph. It has inevitably gained great praise, and no page of Hawthorne's shows more intensity of imagination; yet the main achievement of the book is not what is principally its subject — the picture of the relation of the two men. They are too faintly — the husband in particular — though so fancifully figured. *The Scarlet Letter* lives, in spite of too many cold *concetti* — Hawthorne's general danger — by something noble and truthful in the image of the branded mother and the beautiful child. Strangely enough, this pair are almost wholly outside the action; yet they preserve and vivify the work.

The House of the Seven Gables, written during a residence of two years at Lenox, Massachusetts, was published in 1851. If there are probably no four books of any author among which, for a favourite, readers hesitate longer than between Hawthorne's four longest stories, there are at any rate many for whom this remains distinctly his largest and fullest production. Suffused as it is with a pleasant autumnal haze, it yet brushes more closely than its companions the surface of American life, comes a trifle nearer to being a novel of manners. The manners it shows us indeed are all interfused with the author's special tone, seen in a slanting afternoon light; but detail and illustration are sufficiently copious; and I am tempted for my own part to pronounce the book, taking subject and treatment together, and in spite of the position as a more concentrated classic enjoyed by *The Scarlet Letter*, the closest approach we are likely to have to the great work of fiction, so often called for, that is to do us nationally most honour and most good. The subject reduced to its essence, indeed, accounts not quite altogether for all that there is in the picture. What there is besides is an extraordinary charm of expression, of sensibility, of humour, of touch. The question is that of the mortal shrinkage of a family once uplifted, the last spasm of their starved gentility and flicker of their slow extinction. In the haunted world of Hawthorne's imagination the old Pyncheon house, under its elm in the Salem by-street, is the place where the ghosts are most at home. Ghostly even are its actual tenants, the ancient virgin Hepzibah, with her turban, her scowl, her creaking joints, and her map of the great territory to the eastward belonging to her family — reduced, in these dignities, to selling profitless pennyworths over a counter; and the bewildered bachelor Clifford, released, like some blinking and noble *déterré* of the old Bastile, from twenty years of wrongful imprisonment. We meet at every turn, with Hawthorne, his favourite fancy of communicated sorrows and inevitable atonements. Life is an experience in which we expiate the sins of others in the intervals of expiating our own. The heaviest visitation of the blighted Pyncheons is the responsibility they have incurred through the misdeeds of a hard-hearted witch-burning ancestor. This ancestor has an effective return to life in the person of the one actually robust and successful representative of the race — a bland, hard, showy, shallow 'ornament of the bench', a massive hypocrite and sensualist, who at last, though indeed too late, pays the penalty and removes the curse. The idea of the story is at once perhaps a trifle thin and a trifle obvious — the idea that races and individuals may die of mere dignity and heredity, and that they need for refreshment and cleansing to be, from without, breathed upon like dull mirrors. But the art of the thing is exquisite, its charm irresistible, its distinction complete. *The House of the Seven Gables*, I may add, contains in the rich portrait of Judge Pyncheon a character more solidly suggested than — with the possible exception of the Zenobia of *The Blithedale Romance* — any other figure in the author's list.

Weary of Lenox, Hawthorne spent several months of 1852 at West Newton near Boston, where *The Blithedale Romance* was brought forth. He made the most, for the food of fancy, of what came under his hand — happy in an appetite that could often find a feast in meagre materials. The third of his novels is an echo, delightfully poetized, of his residence at Brook Farm. 'Transcendentalism' was in those days in New England much in the air; and the most comprehensive account of the partakers of this quaint experiment appears to have been held to be that they were Transcendentalists. More simply stated, they were young, candid radicals, reformers, philanthropists. The fact that it sprang — all irresponsibly indeed — from the observation of a known episode, gives *The Blithedale Romance* also a certain value as a picture of manners; the place portrayed, however, opens quickly enough into the pleasantest and idlest dream-world. Hawthorne, we gather, dreamed there more than he worked; he has traced his attitude delightfully in that of the fitful and ironical Coverdale, as to whom we wonder why he chose to rub shoulders quite so much. We think of him as drowsing on a hillside with his hat pulled over his eyes, and the neighbouring hum of reform turning in his ears, to a refrain as vague as an old song. One thing is certain: that if he failed his companions as a labourer in the field, it was only that he might associate them with another sort of success.

We feel, however, that he lets them off easily, when we think of some of the queer figures and queer nostrums then abroad in the land, and which his mild satire — incurring none the less some mild reproach — fails to grind in its mill. The idea that he most tangibly presents is that of the unconscious way in which the search for the common good may cover a hundred interested impulses and personal motives; the suggestion that such a company could only be bound together more by its delusions, its mutual suspicions and frictions, than by any successful surrender of self. The book contains two images of large and admirable intention: that of Hollingsworth, the heavy-handed radical, selfish and sincere, with no sense for jokes, for forms, or for shades; and that of Zenobia, the woman of 'sympathies', the passionate patroness of 'causes', who plays as it were with revolution, and only encounters embarrassment. Zenobia is the most graceful of all portraits of the strong-minded of her sex; borrowing something of her grace, moreover, from the fate that was not to allow her to grow old and shrill, and not least touching from the air we attribute to her of looking, with her fine imagination, for adventures that were hardly, under the circumstances, to be met. We fill out the figure, perhaps, and even lend to the vision something more than Hawthorne intended. Zenobia was, like Coverdale himself, a subject of dreams that were not to find form at Roxbury; but Coverdale had other resources, while she had none but her final failure. Hawthorne indicates no more interesting aspect of the matter than her baffled effort to make a hero of Hollingsworth, who proves, to her misfortune, so much too inelastic for the part. All this, as we read it today, has a soft, shy glamour, a touch of the poetry of far-off things. Nothing of the author's is a happier expression of what I have called his sense of the romance of New England.

In 1853 Franklin Pierce, then President, appointed him consul at Liverpool, which was the beginning of a residence of some seven years in England and in Italy, the period to which we owe *The Marble Faun* and *Our Old Home*. The material for the latter of these was the first to be gathered; but the appearance of *The Marble Faun*, begun in Rome in 1858 and finished during a second stay in England, preceded that of its companion. This is his only long drama on a foreign stage. Drawn from his own air, however, are much of its inspiration and its character. Hawthorne took with him to Italy, as he had done to England, more of the old Puritan consciousness than he left behind. The book has been consecrated as a kind of manual of Roman sights and impressions, brought together indeed in the light of a sympathy always detached and often withheld; and its value is not diminished by its constant reference to an order of things of which, at present, the yearning pilgrim — before a board for the most part swept bare — can only pick up the crumbs. The mystical, the mythical, are in *The Marble Faun* more than ever at hide-and-seek with the real. The author's fancy for freakish correspondences has its way, with Donatello's points of resemblance to the delightful statue in the Capitol. What he offers us is the history of a character blissfully immature, awakening to manhood through the accidental, the almost unconscious, commission of a crime. For the happy youth before his act — the first complete act of his life — there have been no unanswered questions; but after it he finds himself confronted with all the weary questions of the world. This act consists of his ridding of an obscure tormentor — the obscurity is rather a mistake — a woman whom he loves, and who is older, cleverer, and more acquainted with life than himself. The humanizing, the moralizing of the faun is again an ingenious conceit; but it has had for result to have made the subject of the process — and the case is unique in Hawthorne's work — one of those creations of the story-teller who give us a name for a type. There is a kind of young man whom we have now only to call a Donatello, to feel that we sufficiently classify him. It is a part of the scheme of the story to extend to still another nature than his the same sad initiation. A young woman from across the Atlantic, a gentle copyist in Roman galleries of still gentler Guidos and Guercinos, happens to have caught a glimpse, at the critical moment, of the dismal secret that unites Donatello and Miriam. This, for her, is the tree of bitter knowledge, the taste of which sickens and saddens her. The burden is more than she can bear, and one of the most charming passages in the book describes how at last, at a summer's end, in sultry solitude, she stops at St Peter's before a confessional, and Protestant and Puritan as she is, yields to the necessity of kneeling there and ridding herself of her obsession. Hawthorne's young women are exquisite; Hilda is a happy sister to the Phœbe of *The House of the Seven Gables* and the Priscilla of *The Blithedale Romance.*

The drama in *The Marble Faun* none the less, I think, is of an effect less complete than that of the almost larger element that I can only call the landscape and the spirit. Nothing is more striking than the awkward grace with which the author utters, without consenting to it — for he is full of half-amiable, half-angry protest and prejudice — the message, the mystery of the medium in which his actors move. Miriam and her muffled bandit have faded away, and we have our doubts and even our fears about Kenyon and his American statuary; but the breath of old Rome, the sense of old Italy, still meet us as we turn the page, and the book will long, on the great sentimental journey, continue to peep out of most pockets.

He returned to America in 1860, settled once more at Concord, and died at Plymouth, New Hampshire, in the arms of Franklin Pierce, in 1864. At home, with the aid of many memories and of the copious diaries ultimately published by his wife and children, he brought forth, one by one, the chapters eventually collected under the title of *Our Old Home.* The American *Note Books,* the English, and the French and Italian, were given to the world after his death — in 1868, 1870, and 1871 respectively; and if I add to these the small 'campaign' *Life of Franklin Pierce* (1852), two posthumous fragments, *Septimius Felton* and *The Dolliver Romance,* and those scraps and shreds of which his table drawers were still more exhaustively emptied, his literary catalogue — none of the longest — becomes complete.

The important item in this remainder is the close, ripe cluster, the series presented by himself, of his impressions of England. These admirable papers, with much of the same fascination, have something of the same uncomforted note with which he had surrendered himself to the charm of Italy: the mixture of sensibility and reluctance, of response and dissent, the strife between his sense of beauty and his sense of banishment. He came to the Old World late in life — though after dabbling for years, indeed, in the fancied phenomena of time, and with inevitable reserves, mistrusts, and antagonisms. The striking thing to my sense, however, is not what he missed but what he so ingeniously and vividly made out. If he had been, imaginatively, rather old in his youth, he was youthful in his age; and when all is said, we owe him, as a contribution to the immemorial process of lively repartee between the motherland and the daughter, the only pages of the business that can be said to belong to pure literature. He was capable of writing *The Marble Faun*, and yet of declaring, in a letter from Rome, that he bitterly detested the place and should rejoice to bid it farewell forever. Just so he was capable of drawing from English aspects a delight that they had yielded not even to Washington Irving, and yet of insisting, with a perversity that both smiled and frowned, that they rubbed him mainly all the wrong way. At home he had fingered the musty, but abroad he seemed to pine for freshness. In truth, for many persons his great, his most touching sign will have been his aloofness wherever he is. He is outside of everything, and an alien everywhere. He is an æsthetic solitary. His beautiful, light imagination is the wing that on the autumn evening just brushes the dusky window. It was a faculty that gave him much more a terrible sense of human abysses than a desire rashly to sound them and rise to the surface with his report. On the surface — the surface of the soul and the edge of the tragedy — he preferred to remain. He lingered, to weave his web, in the thin exterior air. This is a partial expression of his characteristic habit of dipping, of diving just for sport, into the moral world without being in the least a moralist. He had none of the heat nor of the dogmatism of that character; none of the impertinence, as we feel he would almost have held it, of an intermeddling. He never intermeddled; he was divertedly and discreetly contemplative, pausing oftenest wherever, amid prosaic aspects, there seemed most of an appeal to a sense for subtleties. But of all cynics he was the brightest and kindest, and the subtleties he spun are mere silken threads for stringing polished beads. His collection of moral mysteries is the cabinet of a dilettante.

GUSTAVE FLAUBERT

1902

THE first thing I find today and on my very threshold to say about Gustave Flaubert is that he has been reported on by M. Emile Faguet in the series of Les Grands Écrivains Français with such lucidity as may almost be taken to warn off a later critic. I desire to pay at the outset my tribute to M. Faguet's exhaustive study, which is really in its kind a model and a monument. Never can a critic have got closer to a subject of this order; never can the results of the approach have been more copious or more interesting; never in short can the master of a complex art have been more mastered in his turn, nor his art more penetrated, by the application of an earnest curiosity. That remark I have it at heart to make, so pre-eminently has the little volume I refer to not left the subject where it found it. It abounds in contributive light, and yet, I feel on reflection that it scarce wholly dazzles another contributor away. One reason of this is that, though I enter into everything M. Faguet has said, there are things — things perhaps especially of the province of the artist, the fellow-craftsman of Flaubert — that I am conscious of his not having said; another is that inevitably there are particular possibilities of reaction in our English-speaking consciousness that hold up a light of their own. Therefore I venture to follow even on a field so laboured, only paying this toll to the latest and best work because the author has made it impossible to do less.

Flaubert's life is so almost exclusively the story of his literary application that to speak of his five or six fictions is pretty well to account for it all. He died in 1880 after a career of fifty-nine years singularly iittle marked by changes of scene, of fortune, of attitude, of occupation, of character, and above all, as may be said, of mind. He would be interesting to the race of novelists if only because, quite apart from the value of his work, he so personally gives us the example and the image, so presents the intellectual case. He was born a novelist, grew up, lived, died a novelist, breathing, feeling, thinking, speaking, performing every operation of life, only as that votary; and this though his production was to be small in amount and though it constituted all his diligence. It was not indeed perhaps primarily so much that he was born and lived a novelist as that he was born and lived literary, and that to be literary represented for him an almost overwhelming situation. No life was long enough, no courage great enough, no fortune kind enough to support a man under the burden of this character when once such a doom had been laid on him. His case was a doom because he felt of his vocation almost nothing but the difficulty. He had many strange sides, but this was the strangest, that if we argued from his difficulty to his work, the difficulty being registered for us in his letters and elsewhere, we should expect from the result but the smallest things. We should be prepared to find in it well-nigh a complete absence of the signs of a gift. We should regret that the unhappy man had not addressed himself to something he might have found at least comparatively easy. We should singularly miss the consecration supposedly given to a work of art by its having been conceived in joy. That is Flaubert's remarkable, his so far as I know unmatched distinction, that he has left works of an extraordinary art even the conception of which failed to help him to think in serenity. The chapter of execution, from the moment execution gets really into the shafts, is of course always and everywhere a troubled one — about which moreover too much has of late been written; but we frequently find Flaubert cursing his subjects themselves, wishing he had not chosen them, holding himself up to derision for having done so, and hating them in the very act of sitting down to them. He cared immensely for the medium, the task and the triumph involved, but was himself the last to be able to say why. He is sustained only by the rage and the habit of effort; the mere *love* of letters, let alone the love of life, appears at an early age to have deserted him. Certain passages in his correspondence make us even wonder if it be not hate that sustains him most. So, successively, his several supremely finished and crowned compositions came into the world, and we may feel sure that none others of the kind, none that were to have an equal fortune, had sprung from such adversity.

I insist upon this because his at once excited and baffled passion gives the key of his life and determines its outline. I must speak of him at least as I feel him and as in his very latest years I had the fortune occasionally to see him. I said just now, practically, that he is for many of our tribe at large *the* novelist, intent and typical, and so, gathered together and foreshortened, simplified and fixed, the lapse of time seems to show him. It has made him in his prolonged posture extraordinarily objective, made him even resemble one of his own productions, constituted him as a subject, determined him as a figure; the limit of his range, and above all of his reach, is after this fashion, no doubt, sufficiently indicated, and yet perhaps in the event without injury to his name. If our consideration of him cultivates a certain tenderness on the double ground that he suffered supremely in the cause and that there is endlessly much to be learned from him, we remember at the same time that, indirectly, the world at large possesses him not less than the *confrère*. He has fed and fertilized, has filtered through others, and so arrived at contact with that public from whom it was his theory that he was separated by a deep and impassable trench, the labour of his own spade. He is none the less more interesting, I repeat, as a failure however qualified than as a success however explained, and it is as so viewed that the unity of his career attaches and admonishes. Save in some degree by a condition of health (a liability to epileptic fits at times frequent, but never so frequent as to have been generally suspected), he was not outwardly hampered as the tribe of men of letters goes — an anxious brotherhood at the best; yet the fewest possible things appear to have ever succeeded in happening to him. The only son of an eminent provincial physician, he inherited a modest ease and no other incumbrance than, as was the case for Balzac, an overattentive, an importunate mother; but freedom spoke to him from behind a veil, and when we have mentioned the few apparent facts of experience that make up his landmarks over and beyond his interspaced publications we shall have completed his biography. Tall, strong, striking, he caused his friends to admire in him the elder, the florid Norman type, and he seems himself, as a man of imagination, to have found some transmission of race in his stature and presence, his light-coloured salient eyes and long tawny moustache.

The central event of his life was his journey to the East in 1849 with M. Maxime Du Camp, of which the latter has left in his *Impressions littéraires* a singularly interesting and, as we may perhaps say, slightly treacherous report, and which prepared for Flaubert a state of nostalgia that was not only never to leave him, but that was to work in him as a motive. He had during that year, and just in sufficient quantity, his revelation, the particular appropriate disclosure to which the gods at some moment treat the artist unless they happen too perversely to conspire against him: he tasted of the knowledge by which he was subsequently to measure everything, appeal from everything, find everything flat. Never probably was an impression so assimilated, so positively transmuted to a function; he lived on it to the end and we may say that in *Salammbô* and *La Tentation de Saint-Antoine* he almost died of it. He made afterwards no other journey of the least importance save a disgusted excursion to the Rigi-Kaltbad shortly before his death. The Franco-German War was of course to him for the time as the valley of the shadow itself; but this was an ordeal, unlike most of his other ordeals, shared after all with millions. He never married — he declared, toward the end, to the most comprehending of his confidants, that he had been from the first 'afraid of life'; and the friendliest element of his later time was, we judge, that admirable comfortable commerce, in her fullest maturity, with Mme George Sand, the confidant I just referred to; which has been preserved for us in the published correspondence of each. He had in Ivan Turgenev a friend almost as valued; he spent each year a few months in Paris, where (to mention everything) he had his natural place, so far as he cared to take it, at the small literary court of the Princess Mathilde; and, lastly, he lost toward the close of his life, by no fault of his own, a considerable part of his modest fortune. It is, however, in the long security, the almost unbroken solitude of Croisset, near Rouen, that he mainly figures for us, gouging out his successive books in the wide old room, of many windows, that, with an intervening terrace, over-looked the broad Seine and the passing boats. This was virtually a monastic cell, closed to echoes and accidents; with its stillness for long periods scarce broken save by the creak of the towing-chain of the tugs across the water. When I have added that his published letters offer a view, not very refreshing, of his youthful entangle-ment with Mme Louise Colet — whom we name because, appar-ently not a shrinking person, she long ago practically named herself — I shall have catalogued his personal vicissitudes. And I may add further that the connection with Mme Colet, such as it was, rears its head for us in something like a desert of immunity from such complications.

His complications were of the spirit, of the literary vision, and though he was thoroughly profane he was yet essentially anchor-etic. I perhaps miss a point, however, in not finally subjoining that he was liberally accessible to his friends during the months he regularly spent in Paris. Sensitive, passionate, perverse, not less than *immediately* sociable — for if he detested his collective con-temporaries this dropped, thanks to his humanizing shyness, be-fore the individual encounter — he was in particular and super-excellently not *banal*, and he attached men perhaps more than women, inspiring a marked, a by no means colourless shade of respect; a respect not founded, as the air of it is apt to be, on the vague presumption, but addressed almost in especial to his dis-parities and oddities and thereby, no doubt, none too different from affection. His friends at all events were a rich and eager *cénacle*, among whom he was on occasion, by his picturesque personality, a natural and overtopping centre; partly perhaps be-cause he was so much and so familiarly at home. He wore, up to any hour of the afternoon, that long, colloquial dressing-gown, with trousers to match, which one has always associated with

literature in France — the uniform really of freedom of talk. Freedom of talk abounded by his winter fire, for the *cénacle* was made
up almost wholly of the more finely distinguished among his
contemporaries; of philosophers, men of letters and men of affairs
belonging to his own generation and the next. He had at the time
I have in mind a small perch, far aloft, at the distant, the then
almost suburban, end of the Faubourg Saint-Honoré, where on
Sunday afternoons, at the very top of an endless flight of stairs,
were to be encountered in a cloud of conversation and smoke
most of the novelists of the general Balzac tradition. Others of a
different birth and complexion were markedly not of the number,
were not even conceivable as present; none of those, unless I mis-
remember, whose fictions were at that time 'serialised' in the
Revue des Deux Mondes. In spite of Renan and Taine and two or
three more, the contributor to the *Revue* would indeed at no time
have found in the circle in question his foot on his native heath.
One could recall if one would two or three vivid allusions to him,
not of the most quotable, on the lips of the most famous of 'naturalists' — allusions to him as represented for instance by M. Victor
Cherbuliez and M. Octave Feuillet. The author of these pages re-
calls a concise qualification of this last of his fellows on the lips of
Émile Zola, which that absorbed auditor had too directly, too
rashly asked for; but which is alas not reproducible here. There
was little else but the talk, which had extreme intensity and variety; almost nothing, as I remember, but a painted and gilded idol,
of considerable size, a relic and a memento, on the chimney-piece.
Flaubert was huge and diffident, but florid too and resonant, and
my main remembrance is of a conception of courtesy in him, an
accessibility to the human relation, that only wanted to be sure of
the way taken or to take. The uncertainties of the French for the
determination of intercourse have often struck me as quite match-
ing the sharpness of their certainties, as we for the most part feel
these latter, which sometimes in fact throw the indeterminate into
almost touching relief. I have thought of them at such times as the
people in the world one may have to go more of the way to meet
than to meet any other, and this, as it were, through their being

seated and embedded, provided for at home, in a manner that is all their own and that has bred them to the positive preacceptance of interest on their behalf. We at least of the Anglo-American race, more abroad in the world, perching everywhere, so far as grounds of intercourse are concerned, more vaguely and superficially, as well as less intelligently, are the more ready by that fact with inexpensive accommodations, rather conscious that these themselves forbear from the claim to fascinate, and advancing with the good nature that is the mantle of our obtuseness to any point whatever where entertainment may be offered us. My recollection is at any rate simplified by the fact of the presence almost always, in the little high room of the Faubourg's end, of other persons and other voices. Flaubert's own voice is clearest to me from the uneffaced sense of a winter week-day afternoon when I found him by exception alone and when something led to his reading me aloud, in support of some judgment he had thrown off, a poem of Théophile Gautier's. He cited it as an example of verse intensely and distinctively French, and French in its melancholy, which neither Goethe nor Heine nor Leopardi, neither Pushkin nor Tennyson nor, as he said, Byron, could at all have matched in *kind*. He converted me at the moment to this perception, alike by the sense of the thing and by his large utterance of it; after which it is dreadful to have to confess not only that the poem was then new to me, but that, hunt as I will in every volume of its author, I am never able to recover it. This is perhaps after all happy, causing Flaubert's own full tone, which was the note of the occasion, to linger the more unquenched. But for the rhyme in fact I could have believed him to be spouting to me something strange and sonorous of his own. The thing really rare would have been to hear him do that — hear him *gueuler*, as he liked to call it. Verse, I felt, we had always with us, and almost any idiot of goodwill could give it a value. The value of so many a passage of *Salammbô* and of *L'Éducation* was on the other hand exactly such as gained when he allowed himself, as had by the legend ever been frequent *dans l'intimité*, to 'bellow' it to its fullest effect.

One of the things that make him most exhibitional and most describable, so that if we had invented him as an illustration or a character we would exactly so have arranged him, is that he was formed intellectually of two quite distinct compartments, a sense of the real and a sense of the romantic, and that his production, for our present cognizance, thus neatly and vividly divides itself. The divisions are as marked as the sections on the back of a scarab, though their distinctness is undoubtedly but the final expression of much inward strife. M. Faguet indeed, who is admirable on this question of our author's duality, gives an account of the romanticism that found its way for him into the real and of the reality that found its way into the romantic; but he none the less strikes us as a curious splendid insect sustained on wings of a different colouration, the right a vivid red, say, and the left as frank a yellow. This duality has in its sharp operation placed *Madame Bovary* and *L'Éducation* on one side together and placed together on the other *Salammbô* and *La Tentation*. *Bouvard et Pécuchet* it can scarce be spoken of, I think, as having placed anywhere or anyhow. If it was Flaubert's way to find his subject impossible there was none he saw so much in that light as this last-named, but also none that he appears to have held so important for that very reason to pursue to the bitter end. Posterity agrees with him about the impossibility, but rather takes upon itself to break with the rest of the logic. We may perhaps, however, for symmetry, let *Bouvard et Pécuchet* figure as the tail — if scarabs ever have tails — of our analogous insect. Only in that case we should also append as the very tip the small volume of the *Trois Contes*, preponderantly of the deepest imaginative hue.

His imagination was great and splendid; in spite of which, strangely enough, his masterpiece is not his most imaginative work. *Madame Bovary*, beyond question, holds that first place, and *Madame Bovary* is concerned with the career of a country doctor's wife in a petty Norman town. The elements of the picture are of the fewest, the situation of the heroine almost of the meanest, the material for interest, considering the interest yielded, of the most unpromising; but these facts only throw into relief one of those incalculable incidents that attend the proceedings of genius. *Madame Bovary* was doomed by circumstances and causes — the freshness of comparative youth and good faith on the author's part being perhaps the chief — definitely to take its position, even though its subject was fundamentally a negation of the remote, the splendid and the strange, the stuff of his fondest and most cultivated dreams. It would have seemed very nearly to exclude the free play of the imagination, and the way this faculty on the author's part nevertheless presides is one of those accidents, manœuvres, inspirations, we hardly know what to call them, by which masterpieces grow. He of course knew more or less what he was doing for his book in making Emma Bovary a victim of the imaginative habit, but he must have been far from designing or measuring the total effect which renders the work so general, so complete an expression of himself. His separate idiosyncrasies, his irritated sensibility to the life about him, with the power to catch it in the fact and hold it hard, and his hunger for style and history and poetry, for the rich and the rare, great reverberations, great adumbrations, are here represented together as they are not in his later writings. There is nothing of the near, of the directly observed, though there may be much of the directly perceived and the minutely detailed, either in *Salammbô* or in *Saint-Antoine*, and little enough of the extravagance of illusion in that indefinable last word of restrained evocation and cold execution *L'Éducation sentimentale*. M. Faguet has of course excellently noted this — that the fortune and felicity of the book were assured by the stroke that made the central figure an embodiment of helpless romanticism. Flaubert himself but narrowly escaped being such an embodiment after all, and he is thus able to express the romantic mind with extraordinary truth. As to the rest of the matter he had the luck of having been in possession from the first, having begun so early to nurse and work up his plan that, familiarity and the native air, the native soil, aiding, he had finally made out to the last lurking shade the small sordid sunny dusty village picture, its emptiness constituted and peopled. It is in the background and the accessories that the real, the real of his theme, abides: and the romantic, the romantic of his theme, accordingly occupies the front. Emma Bovary's poor adventures are a tragedy for the very reason that in a world unsuspecting, unassisting, unconsoling, she has herself to distill the rich and the rare. Ignorant, unguided, undiverted, ridden by the very nature and mixture of her consciousness, she makes of the business an inordinate failure, a failure which in its turn makes for Flaubert the most pointed, the most *told* of anecdotes.

There are many things to say about *Madame Bovary*, but an old admirer of the book would be but half-hearted — so far as they represent reserves or puzzlements — were he not to note first of all the circumstances by which it is most endeared to him. To remember it from far back is to have been present all along at a process of singular interest to a literary mind, a case indeed full of comfort and cheer. The finest of Flaubert's novels is today, on the French shelf of fiction, one of the first of the classics; it has attained that position, slowly but steadily, before our eyes; and we seem so to follow the evolution of the fate of a classic. We see how the thing takes place; which we rarely can, for we mostly miss either the beginning or the end, especially in the case of a consecration as complete as this. The consecrations of the past are too far behind and those of the future too far in front. That the production before us *should* have come in for the heavenly crown may be a fact to offer English and American readers a mystifying side; but it is exactly our ground and a part moreover of the total interest. The author of these remarks remembers, as with a sense of the way such things happen, that when a very young person in Paris he took up from the parental table the latest number of the periodical in which Flaubert's then duly unrecognized masterpiece was in course of publication. The moment is not historic, but it was to become in the light of history, as may be said, so unforgettable that every small feature of it yet again lives for him: it rests there like the backward end of the span. The cover of the old *Revue de Paris* was yellow, if I mistake not, like that of the new, and *Madame Bovary: Mœurs de Province*, on the inside of it, was already, on the spot, as a title, mysteriously arresting, inscrutably charged. I was ignorant of what had preceded and was not to know till much later what followed; but present to me still is the act of standing there before the fire, my back against the low be-plushed and begarnished French chimney-piece and taking in what I might of that instalment, taking it in with so surprised an interest, and perhaps as well such a stir of faint foreknowledge, that the sunny little salon, the autumn day, the window ajar and the cheerful outside clatter of the Rue Montaigne are all now for me more or less in the story and the story more or less in them. The story, however, was at that moment having a difficult life; its fortune was all to make; its merit was so far from suspected that, as Maxime Du Camp — though verily with no excess of contri-tion — relates, its cloth of gold barely escaped the editorial shears. This, with much more, contributes for us to the course of things to come. The book, on its appearance as a volume, proved a shock to the high propriety of the guardians of public morals under the second Empire, and Flaubert was prosecuted as author of a work indecent to scandal. The prosecution in the event fell to the ground, but I should perhaps have mentioned this agitation as one of the very few, of any public order, in his short list. *Le Candidat* fell at the Vaudeville Theatre, several years later, with a violence indicated by its withdrawal after a performance of but two nights, the first of these marked by a deafening uproar; only if the comedy was not to recover from this accident the misprised lustre of the novel was entirely to reassert itself. It is strange enough at present — so far have we travelled since then — that *Madame Bovary* should in so comparatively recent a past have been to that extent a cause of reprobation; and suggestive above all, in such connec-tions, as to the large unconsciousness of superior minds. The desire of the superior mind of the day — that is the governmental, official, legal — to distinguish a book with such a destiny before it is a case conceivable, but conception breaks down before its design of making the distinction purely invidious. We can ima-gine its knowing so little, however face to face with the object, what it had got hold of; but for it to have been so urged on by a blind inward spring to publish to posterity the extent of its ignorance, that would have been beyond imagination, beyond everything but pity.

And yet it is not after all that the place the book has taken is so overwhelmingly explained by its inherent dignity; for here comes in the curiosity of the matter. Here comes in especially its fund of admonition for alien readers. The dignity of its substance is the dignity of Mme Bovary herself as a vessel of experience — a question as to which, unmistakably, I judge, we can only depart from the consensus of French critical opinion. M. Faguet for example commends the character of the heroine as one of the most living and discriminated figures of women in all literature, praises it as a field for the display of the romantic spirit that leaves nothing to be desired. Subject to an observation I shall presently make and that bears heavily in general, I think, on Flaubert as a painter of life, subject to this restriction he is right; which is a proof that a work of art may be markedly open to objection and at the same time be rare in its kind, and that when it is perfect to this point nothing else particularly matters. *Madame Bovary* has a perfection that not only stamps it, but that makes it stand almost alone; it holds itself with such a supreme unapproachable assurance as both excites and defies judgment. For it deals not in the least, as to unapproachability, with things exalted or refined; it only confers on its sufficiently vulgar elements of exhibition a final unsurpassable form. The form is in *itself* as interesting, as active, as much of the essence of the subject as the idea, and yet so close is its fit and so inseparable its life that we catch it at no moment on any errand of its own. That verily is to *be* interesting — all round; that is to be genuine and whole. The work is a classic because the thing, such as it is, is ideally *done*, and because it shows that in such doing eternal beauty may dwell. A pretty young woman who lives, socially and morally speaking, in a hole, and who is ignorant, foolish, flimsy, unhappy, takes a pair of lovers by whom she is successively deserted; in the midst of the bewilderment of which, giving up her husband and her child, letting everything go, she sinks deeper into duplicity, debt, despair, and arrives on the spot, on the small scene itself of her poor depravities, at a pitiful tragic

end. In especial she does these things while remaining absorbed in
romantic intention and vision, and she remains absorbed in romantic intention and vision while fairly rolling in the dust. That is
the triumph of the book as the triumph stands, that Emma interests us by the nature of her consciousness and the play of her
mind, thanks to the reality and beauty with which those sources
are invested. It is not only that they represent *her* state; they are
so true, so observed and felt, and especially so shown, that they
represent the state, actual or potential, of all persons like her,
persons romantically determined. Then her setting, the medium
in which she struggles, becomes in its way as important, becomes
eminent with the eminence of art; the tiny world in which she revolves, the contracted cage in which she flutters, is hung out in
space for her, and her companions in captivity there are as true as
herself.

I have said enough to show what I mean by Flaubert's having
in this picture expressed something of his intimate self, given his
heroine something of his own imagination: a point precisely that
brings me back to the restriction at which I just now hinted, in
which M. Faguet fails to indulge and yet which is immediate for
the alien reader. Our complaint is that Emma Bovary, in spite of
the nature of her consciousness and in spite of her reflecting so
much that of her creator, is really too small an affair. This, critically speaking, is in view both of the value and the fortune of her
history, a wonderful circumstance. She associates herself with
Frédéric Moreau in *L'Éducation* to suggest for us a question that
can be answered, I hold, only to Flaubert's detriment. Emma
taken alone would possibly not so directly press it, but in her
company the hero of our author's second study of the 'real' drives
it home. Why did Flaubert choose, as special conduits of the life
he proposed to depict, such inferior and in the case of Frédéric
such abject human specimens? I insist only in respect to the latter,
the perfection of Mme Bovary scarce leaving one much warrant
for wishing anything other. Even here, however, the general scale
and size of Emma, who is small even of her sort, should be a
warning to hyperbole. If I say that in the matter of Frédéric at all

events the answer is inevitably detrimental I mean that it weighs heavily on our author's general credit. He wished in each case to make a picture of experience — middling experience, it is true — and of the world close to him; but if he imagined nothing better for his purpose than such a heroine and such a hero, both such limited reflectors and registers, we are forced to believe it to have been by a defect of his mind. And that sign of weakness remains even if it be objected that the images in question were addressed to his purpose better than others would have been: the purpose itself then shows as inferior. *L'Éducation sentimentale* is a strange, an indescribable work, about which there would be many more things to say than I have space for, and all of them of the deepest interest. It is moreover, to simplify my statement, very much less satisfying a thing, less pleasing whether in its unity or its variety, than its specific predecessor. But take it as we will, for a success or a failure — M. Faguet indeed ranks it, by the measure of its quantity of intention, a failure, and I on the whole agree with him — the personage offered us as bearing the weight of the drama, and in whom we are invited to that extent to interest ourselves, leaves us mainly wondering what our entertainer could have been thinking of. He takes Frédéric Moreau on the threshold of life and conducts him to the extreme of maturity without apparently suspecting for a moment either our wonder or our protest — 'Why, why *him?*' Frédéric is positively too poor for his part, too scant for his charge; and we feel with a kind of embarrassment, certainly with a kind of compassion, that it is somehow the business of a protagonist to prevent in his designer an excessive waste of faith. When I speak of the faith in Emma Bovary as proportionately wasted I reflect on M. Faguet's judgment that she is from the point of view of deep interest richly or at least roundedly representative. Representative of what? he makes us ask even while granting all the grounds of misery and tragedy involved. The plea for her is the plea made for all the figures that live without evaporation under the painter's hand — that they are not only particular persons but types of their kind, and as valid in one light as in the other. It is Emma's 'kind' that I question for this responsibility, even if it be inquired of me why I then fail to question that of Charles Bovary, in its perfection, or that of the inimitable, the immortal Homais. If we express Emma's deficiency as the poverty of her consciousness for the typical function, it is certainly not, one must admit, that she is surpassed in this respect either by her platitudinous husband or by his friend the pretentious apothecary. The difference is none the less somehow in the fact that they are respectively studies but of their character and office, which function in each expresses adequately *all* they are. It may be, I concede, because Emma is the only woman in the book that she is taken by M. Faguet as *femininely* typical, typical in the larger illustrative way, whereas the others pass with him for images specifically conditioned. Emma is this same for myself, I plead; she is conditioned to such an excess of the specific, and the specific in her case leaves out so many even of the commoner elements of conceivable life in a woman when we are invited to see that life as pathetic, as dramatic agitation, that we challenge both the author's and the critic's scale of importances. The book is a picture of the middling as much as they like, but does Emma attain even to *that?* Hers is a narrow middling even for a little imaginative person whose 'social' significance is small. It is greater on the whole than her capacity of consciousness, taking this all round; and so, in a word, we feel her less illustrational than she might have been not only if the world had offered her more points of contact, but if she had had more of these to give it.

We meet Frédéric first, we remain with him long, as a *moyen*, a provincial bourgeois of the mid-century, educated and not without fortune, thereby with freedom, in whom the life of his day reflects itself. Yet the life of his day, on Flaubert's showing, hangs together with the poverty of Frédéric's own inward or for that matter outward life; so that, the whole thing being, for scale, intention and extension, a sort of epic of the usual (with the Revolution of 1848 introduced indeed as an episode), it affects us as an epic without air, without wings to lift it; reminds us in fact more than anything else of a huge balloon, all of silk pieces strongly sewn together and patiently blown up, but that absolutely refuses to leave the ground. The discrimination I here make as against our author is, however, the only one inevitable in a series of remarks so brief. What it really represents — and nothing could be more curious — is that Frédéric enjoys his position not only without the aid of a single 'sympathetic' character of consequence, but even without the aid of one with whom we can directly communicate. Can we communicate with the central personage? or would we really if we could? A hundred times no, and if he himself can communicate with the people shown us as surrounding him this only proves him of their kind. Flaubert on his 'real' side was in truth an ironic painter, and ironic to a tune that makes his final accepted state, his present literary dignity and 'classic' peace, superficially anomalous. There is an explanation to which I shall immediately come; but I find myself feeling for a moment longer in presence of *L'Éducation* how much more interesting a writer may be on occasion by the given failure than by the given success. Successes pure and simple disconnect and dismiss him; failures — though I admit they must be a bit qualified — keep him in touch and in relation. Thus it is that as the work of a 'grand écrivain' *L'Éducation*, large, laboured, immensely 'written', with beautiful passages and a general emptiness, with a kind of leak in its stored sadness, moreover, by which its moral dignity escapes — thus it is that Flaubert's ill-starred novel is a curiosity for a literary museum. Thus it is also that it suggests a hundred reflections, and suggests perhaps most of them directly to the intending labourer in the same field. If in short, as I have said, Flaubert is the novelist's novelist, this performance does more than any other toward making him so.

I have to add in the same connection that I had not lost sight of Mme Arnoux, the main ornament of *L'Éducation*, in pronouncing just above on its deficiency in the sympathetic. Mme Arnoux is exactly the author's one marked attempt, here or elsewhere, to represent beauty otherwise than for the senses, beauty of character and life; and what becomes of the attempt is a matter highly significant. M. Faguet praises with justice his conception of the figure and of the relation, the relation that never bears fruit, that keeps Frédéric adoring her, through hindrance and change, from the beginning of life to the end; that keeps her, by the same constraint, forever immaculately 'good', from youth to age, though deeply moved and cruelly tempted and sorely tried. Her contacts with her adorer are not even frequent, in proportion to the field of time; her conditions of fortune, of association and occupation are almost sordid, and we see them with the march of the drama, such as it is, become more and more so; besides which — I again remember that M. Faguet excellently notes it — nothing in the nature of 'parts' is attributed to her; not only is she not presented as clever, she is scarce invested with a character at all. Almost nothing that she says is repeated, almost nothing that she does is shown. She is an image none the less beautiful and vague, an image of passion cherished and abjured, renouncing all sustenance and yet persisting in life. Only she has for real distinction the extreme drawback that she is offered us quite preponderantly through Frédéric's vision of her, that we see her practically in no other light. Now Flaubert unfortunately has not been able not so to discredit Frédéric's vision in general, his vision of everyone and everything, and in particular of his own life, that it makes a medium good enough to convey adequately a noble impression. Mme Arnoux is of course ever so much the best thing in his life — which is saying little; but his life is made up of such queer material that we find ourselves displeased at her being 'in' it on whatever terms; all the more that she seems scarcely to affect, improve or determine it. Her creator in short never had a more awkward idea than this attempt to give us the benefit of such a conception in such a way; and even though I have still something else to say about that I may as well speak of it at once as a mistake that gravely counts against him. It is but one of three, no doubt, in all his work; but I shall not, I trust, pass for extravagant if I call it the most indicative. What makes it so is its being the least superficial; the two others are, so to speak, intellectual, while this is somehow moral. It was a mistake, as I have already hinted, to propose to register in so mean a consciousness as that of such a hero so large and so mixed a quantity of life as *L'Éducation* clearly intends; and it was a mistake of the tragic sort that is a theme mainly for silence to have embarked on *Bouvard et Pécuchet* at all, not to have given it up sooner than be given up by it. But these were at the worst not wholly compromising blunders. What *was* compromising — and the great point is that it remained so, that nothing has an equal weight against it — is the unconsciousness of error in respect to the opportunity that would have counted as his finest. We feel not so much that Flaubert misses it, for that we could bear; but that he doesn't *know* he misses it is what stamps the blunder. We do not pretend to say how he might have shown us Mme Arnoux better — that was his own affair. What is ours is that he really thought he was showing her as well as he could, or as she might be shown; at which we veil our face. For once that he had a conception quite apart, apart I mean from the array of his other conceptions and more delicate than any, he 'went', as we say, and spoiled it. Let me add in all tenderness, and to make up for possibly too much insistence, that it is the only stain on his shield; let me even confess that I should not wonder if, when all is said, it is a blemish no one has ever noticed.

Perhaps no one has ever noticed either what was present to me just above as the partial makeweight there glanced at, the fact that in the midst of this general awkwardness, as I have called it, there is at the same time a danger so escaped as to entitle our author to full credit. I scarce know how to put it with little enough of the ungracious, but I think that even the true Flaubertist finds himself wondering a little that some flaw of taste, some small but unfortunate lapse by the way, *should* as a matter of fact not somehow or somewhere have waited on the demonstration of the platonic purity prevailing between this heroine and her hero — so far as we do find that image projected. It is alike difficult to indicate without offence or to ignore without unkindness a fond reader's apprehension here of a possibility of the wrong touch, the just perceptibly false note. I would not have staked my life on Flaubert's security of instinct in such a connection — as an absolutely fine and predetermined security; and yet in the event that felicity has settled, there is not so much as the lightest wrong breath (speaking of the matter in this light of tact and taste) or the shade of a crooked stroke. One exclaims at the end of the question 'Dear old Flaubert after all — !' and perhaps so risks seeming to patronise for fear of not making a point. The point made for what it is worth, at any rate, I am the more free to recover the benefit of what I mean by critical 'tenderness' in our general connection — expressing in it as I do our general respect, and my own particular, for our author's method and process and history, and my sense of the luxury of such a sentiment at such a vulgar literary time. It is a respect positive and settled and the thing that has most to do with consecrating for us that loyalty to him as the novelist of the novelist — unlike as it is even the best feeling inspired by any other member of the craft. He may stand for our operative conscience or our vicarious sacrifice; animated by a sense of literary honour, attached to an ideal of perfection, incapable of lapsing in fine from a self-respect, that enable us to sit at ease, to surrender to the age, to indulge in whatever comparative meannesses (and no meanness in art is so mean as the sneaking economic) we may find most comfortable or profitable. May it not in truth be said that we practice our industry, so many of us, at relatively little cost just *because* poor Flaubert, producing the most expensive fictions ever written, so handsomely paid for it? It is as if this put it in our power to produce cheap and thereby sell dear; as if, so expressing it, literary honour being by his example effectively secure for the firm at large and the general concern, on its whole æsthetic side, floated once for all, we find our individual attention free for literary and æsthetic indifference. All the while we thus lavish our indifference the spirit of the author of *Madame Bovary*, in the cross-light of the old room above the Seine, is trying to the last admiration for the thing itself. That production puts the matter into a nutshell: *Madame Bovary*, subject to whatever qualification, as absolutely the most literary of novels, so literary that it covers us with its mantle. It shows us once for all that there is no *intrinsic* call for a debasement of the type. The mantle I speak of is wrought with surpassing fineness, and we may always. under stress of whatever charge of illiteracy, frivolity, vulgarity, flaunt it as the flag of the guild. Let us therefore frankly concede that to surround Flaubert with our consideration is the least return we can make for such a privilege. The consideration moreover is idle unless it be real, unless it be intelligent enough to measure his effort and his success. Of the effort as mere effort I have already spoken, of the desperate difficulty involved for him in making his form square with his conception; and I by no means attach general importance to these secrets of the workshop, which are but as the contortions of the fastidious muse who is the servant of the oracle. They are really rather secrets of the kitchen and contortions of the priestess of *that* tripod — they are not an upstairs matter. It is of their specially distinctive importance I am now speaking, of the light shed on them by the results before us.

They all represent the pursuit of a style, of the ideally right one for its relations, and would still be interesting if the style had not been achieved. *Madame Bovary, Salammbô, Saint-Antoine, L'Éducation* are so written and so composed (though the last-named in a minor degree) that the more we look at them the more we find in them, under this head, a beauty of intention and of effect; the more they figure in the too often dreary desert of fictional prose a class by themselves and a little living oasis. So far as that desert is of the complexion of our own English speech it supplies with remarkable rarity this particular source of refreshment. So strikingly is that the case, so scant for the most part any dream of a scheme of beauty in these connections, that a critic betrayed at artless moments into a plea for composition may find himself as blankly met as if his plea were for trigonometry. He makes inevitably his reflections, which are numerous enough; one of them being that if we turn our back so squarely, so universally to this order of considerations it is because the novel is so preponderantly cultivated among us by women, in other words by a sex ever gracefully, comfortably, enviably unconscious (it would be too much to call them even suspicious) of the requirements of form. The case is at any rate sharply enough made for us, or against us, by the circumstance that women are held to have achieved on all our ground, in spite of this weakness and others, as great results as any. The judgment is undoubtedly founded: Jane Austen was instinctive and charming, and the other recognitions — even over the heads of the ladies, some of them, from Fielding to Pater — are obvious; without, however, in the least touching my contention. For signal examples of what composition, distribution, arrangement can do, of how they intensify the life of a work of art, we have to go elsewhere; and the value of Flaubert for us is that he admirably points the moral. This is the explanation of the 'classic' fortune of *Madame Bovary* in especial, though I may add that also of Hérodias and Saint-Julien l'Hospitalier in the *Trois Contes*, as well as an aspect of these works endlessly suggestive. I spoke just now of the small field of the picture in the longest of them, the small capacity, as I called it, of the vessel; yet the way the thing is done not only triumphs over the question of value but in respect to it fairly misleads and confounds us. Where else shall we find in anything proportionately so small such an air of dignity of size? Flaubert *made* things big — it was his way, his ambition and his necessity; and I say this while remembering that in *L'Éducation* (in proportion I mean again) the effect has not been produced. The subject of *L'Éducation* is in spite of Frédéric large, but an indefinable shrinkage has overtaken it in the execution. The exception so marked, however, is single; *Salammbô* and *Saint-Antoine* are both at once very 'heavy' conceptions and very consistently and splendidly high applications of a manner.

It is in this assured manner that the lesson sits aloft, that the spell for the critical reader resides; and if the conviction under which Flaubert labours is more and more grossly discredited among us his compact mass is but the greater. He regarded the work of art as *existing* but by its expression, and defied us to name any other measure of its life that is not a stultification. He held style to be accordingly an indefeasible part of it, and found beauty, interest and distinction as dependent on it for emergence as a letter committed to the post office is dependent on an addressed envelope. Strange enough it may well appear to us to have to apologize for such notions as eccentric. There are persons who consider that style comes of itself — we see and hear at present, I think, enough of them; and to whom he would doubtless have remarked that it goes, of itself, still faster. The thing naturally differs in fact with the nature of the imagination; the question is one of proprieties and affinities, sympathy and proportion. The sympathy of the author of *Salammbô* was all with the magnificent, his imagination for the phrase as variously noble or ignoble in itself, contributive or destructive, adapted and harmonious or casual and common. The worse among such possibilities have been multiplied by the infection of bad writing, and he denied that the better ever do anything so obliging as to come of themselves. They scarcely indeed for Flaubert 'came' at all; their arrival was determined only by fasting and prayer or by patience of pursuit, the arts of the chase, long waits and watches, figuratively speaking, among the peaks or by the waters. The production of a book was of course made inordinately slow by the fatigue of these measures; in illustration of which his letters often record that it has taken him three days[1] to arrive at one right sentence, tested by the pitch of his ideal of the right for the suggestion aimed at. His difficulties drew from the author, as I have mentioned, much resounding complaint; but those voices have ceased to trouble us and the final voice remains. No feature of the whole business is more edifying than the fact that he in the first place never misses style and in the second never appears to have beaten about for it. That betrayal is of course the worst betrayal of all, and I think the way he has escaped it the happiest form of the peace that has finally visited him. It was truly a wonderful success to be so the devotee of the phrase and yet never its victim. Fine as

[1] It was true, delightfully true, that, extravagance in this province of his life, though apparently in no other, being Flaubert's necessity and law, he deliberated and hung fire, wrestled, retreated and returned, indulged generally in a tragicomedy of waste; which I recall a charming expression of on the lips of Edmond de Goncourt, who quite recognized the heroic legend, but prettily qualified it: '*Il faut vous dire qu'il y avait là-dedans beaucoup de coucheries et d'école buissonière.*' And he related how on the occasion of a stay with his friend under the roof of the Princess Mathilde, the friend, missed during the middle hours of a fine afternoon, was found to have undressed himself and gone to bed to think!

he inveterately desired it should be he still never lost sight of the question Fine for what? It is always so related and associated, so properly part of something else that is in turn part of something other, part of a reference, a tone, a passage, a page, that the simple may enjoy it for its least bearing and the initiated for its greatest. That surely is to be a writer of the first order, to resemble when in the hand and however closely viewed a shapely crystal box, and yet to be seen when placed on the table and opened to contain innumerable compartments, springs and tricks. One is ornamental either way, but one is in the second way precious too.

The crystal box then figures the style of *Salammbô* and *Saint-Antoine* in a greater degree than that of *Bovary*, because, as the two former express the writer's romantic side, he had in them, while equally covering his tracks, still further to fare and still more to hunt. Beyond this allusion to their completing his duality I shall not attempt closely to characterize them; though I admit that in not insisting on them I press most lightly on the scale into which he had in his own view cast his greatest pressure. He lamented the doom that drove him so oddly, so ruefully, to choose his subjects, but he lamented it least when these subjects were most pompous and most exotic, feeling as he did that they had then after all most affinity with his special eloquence. In dealing with the near, the directly perceived, he had to keep down his tone, to make the eloquence small; though with the consequence, as we have seen, that in spite of such precautions the whole thing mostly insists on being ample. The familiar, that is, under his touch, took on character, importance, extension, one scarce knows what to call it, in order to carry the style or perhaps rather, as we may say, sit with proper ease in the vehicle, and there was accordingly a limit to its smallness; whereas in the romantic books, the preferred world of Flaubert's imagination, there was practically no need of compromise. The compromise gave him throughout endless trouble, and nothing would be more to the point than to show, had I space, why in particular it distressed him. It was obviously his strange predicament that the only spectacle open to him by experience and direct knowledge was the bourgeois, which

on that ground imposed on him successively his three so intensely
bourgeois themes. He was obliged to treat these themes, which
he hated, because his experience left him no alternative; his only
alternative was given by history, geography, philosophy, fancy,
the world of erudition and of imagination, the world especially of
this last. In the bourgeois sphere his ideal of expression laboured
under protest; in the other, the imagined, the projected, his need
for facts, for matter, and his pursuit of them, sat no less heavily.
But as his style all the while required a certain exercise of pride he
was on the whole more at home in the exotic than in the familiar;
he escaped above all in the former connection the associations,
the disparities he detested. He could be frankly noble in *Salammbô* and *Saint-Antoine*, whereas in *Bovary* and *L'Éducation* he
could be but circuitously and insidiously so. He could in the one
case cut his coat according to his cloth — if we mean by his cloth
his predetermined tone, while in the other he had to take it already
cut. Singular enough in his life the situation so constituted: the
comparatively meagre human consciousness — for we must come
back to that in him — struggling with the absolutely large artistic;
and the large artistic half wreaking itself on the meagre human
and half seeking a refuge from it, as well as a revenge against it, in
something quite different.

Flaubert had in fact command of two refuges which he worked
in turn. The first of these was the attitude of irony, so constant in
him that *L'Éducation* bristles and hardens with it and *Bouvard et
Pécuchet* — strangest of 'poetic' justices — is made as dry as sand
and as heavy as lead; the second only was, by processes, by
journeys the most expensive, to get away altogether. And we inevitably ask ourselves whether, eschewing the policy of flight, he
might not after all have fought out his case a little more on the
spot. Might he not have addressed himself to the human still
otherwise than in *L'Éducation* and in *Bouvard*? When one thinks
of the view of the life of his country, of the vast French community and its constituent creatures, offered in these productions, one
declines to believe it could make up the *whole* vision of a man of
his quality. Or when all was said and done was he absolutely and

exclusively condemned to irony? The second refuge I speak of, the getting away from the human, the congruously and measurably human, altogether, perhaps becomes in the light of this possibility but an irony the more. Carthage and the Thebaid, Salammbô, Spendius, Matho, Hannon, Saint Anthony, Hilarion, the Paternians, the Marcosians and the Carpocratians, what are all these, inviting because queer, but a confession of supreme impatience with the actual and the near, often queer enough too, no doubt, but not consolingly, not transcendently? Last remains the question whether, even if our author's immediate as distinguished from his remote view had had more reach, the particular gift we claim for him, the perfection of arrangement and form, would have had in certain directions the acquired flexibility. States of mind, states of soul, of the simpler kind, the kinds supposable in the Emma Bovarys, the Frédérics, the Bouvards and the Pécuchets, to say nothing of the Carthaginians and the Eremites — for Flaubert's eremites are eminently artless — these conditions represent, I think, his proved psychological range. And that throws us back remarkably, almost confoundingly, upon another face of the general anomaly. The 'gift' was of the greatest, a force in itself, in virtue of which he is a consummate writer; and yet there are whole sides of life to which it was never addressed and which it apparently quite failed to suspect as a field of exercise. If he never approached the complicated character in man or woman — Emma Bovary is not the least little bit complicated — or the really furnished, the finely civilized, was this because, surprisingly, he could not? *L'âme française* at all events shows in him but ill.

This undoubtedly marks a limit, but limits are for the critic familiar country, and he may mostly well feel the prospect wide enough when he finds something positively well enough done. By disposition or by obligation Flaubert selected, and though his selection was in some respects narrow he stops not too short to have left us three really 'cast' works and a fourth of several perfect parts, to say nothing of the element of perfection, of the superlative for the size, in his three *nouvelles*. What he attempted he attempted in a spirit that gives an extension to the idea of the achievable and the achieved in a literary thing, and it is by this that we contentedly gauge the matter. As success goes in this world of the approximate it may pass for success of the greatest. If I am unable to pursue the proof of my remark in *Salammbô* and *Saint-Antoine* it is because I have also had to select and have found the questions connected with their two companions more interesting. There are numerous judges, I hasten to mention, who, showing the opposite preference, lose themselves with rapture in the strange bristling archæological picture — yet all amazingly vivified and co-ordinated — of the Carthaginian mercenaries in revolt and the sacred veil of the great goddess profaned and stolen; as well in the still more peopled panorama of the ancient sects, superstitions and mythologies that swim in the desert before the fevered eyes of the Saint. One may be able, however, at once to breathe more freely in *Bovary* than in *Salammbô* and yet to hope that there is no intention of the latter that one has missed. The great intention certainly, and little as we may be sweetly beguiled, holds us fast; which is simply the author's indomitable purpose of fully pervading his field. There are countries beyond the sea in which tracts are allowed to settlers on condition that they will really, not nominally, cultivate them. Flaubert is on his romantic ground like one of these settlers; he makes good with all his might his title to his tract, and in a way that shows how it is not only for him a question of safety but a question of honour. Honour demands that he shall set up his home and his faith there in such a way that every inch of the surface be planted or paved. He would have been ashamed merely to encamp and, after the fashion of most other adventurers, knock up a log hut among charred stumps. This was not what would have been for him taking artistic possession, it was not what would have been for him even personal honour, let alone literary; and yet the general lapse from integrity was a thing that, wherever he looked, he saw not only condoned but acclaimed and rewarded. He lived, as he felt, in an age of mean production and cheap criticism, the practical upshot of which took on for him a name that was often on his lips. He called it the hatred of literature, a hatred in the midst of which, the most literary of men, he found himself appointed to suffer. I may not, however, follow him in that direction — which would take us far; and the less that he was for himself after all, in spite of groans and imprecations, a man of resources and remedies, and that there was always his possibility of building himself in.

This he did equally in all his books — built himself into literature by means of a material put together with extraordinary art; but it leads me again to the question of what such a stiff ideal imposed on him for the element of exactitude. This element, in the romantic, was his merciless law; it was perhaps even in the romantic that — if there could indeed be degrees for him in such matters — he most despised the loose and the more-or-less. To be intensely definite and perfectly positive, to know so well what he meant that he could at every point strikingly and conclusively verify it, was the first of his needs; and if in addition to being thus synthetically final he could be strange and sad and terrible, and leave the cause of these effects inscrutable, success then had for him its highest savour. We feel the inscrutability in those memorable few words that put before us Frédéric Moreau's start upon his vain course of travel, '*Il connût alors la mélancholie des paquebots*'; an image to the last degree comprehensive and embracing, but which haunts us, in its droll pathos, without our quite knowing why. But he was really never so pleased as when he could be both rare and precise about the dreadful. His own sense of all this, as I have already indicated, was that beauty comes with expression, that expression is creation, that it *makes* the reality, and only in the degree in which it *is*, exquisitely, expression; and that we move in literature through a world of different values and relations, a blest world in which we know nothing except by style, but in which also everything is saved by it, and in which the image is thus always superior to the thing itself. This quest and multiplication of the image, the image tested and warranted and consecrated for the occasion, was accordingly his high elegance, to which he too much sacrificed and to which *Salammbô* and partly *Saint-Antoine* are monstrous monuments. Old cruelties and perversities, old wonders and errors and terrors, endlessly appealed to him; they constitute the unhuman side of his work, and if we have not the bribe of curiosity, of a lively interest in method, or rather in evocation just *as* evocation, we tread our way among them, especially in *Salammbô*, with a reserve too dry for our pleasure. To my own view the curiosity and the literary interest are equal in dealing with the non-romantic books, and the world presented, the aspects and agents, are less deterrent and more amenable both to our own social and expressional terms. Style itself moreover, with all respect to Flaubert, never *totally* beguiles; since even when we are so queerly constituted as to be ninety-nine parts literary we are still a hundredth part something else. This hundredth part may, once we possess the book — or the book possesses us — make us imperfect as readers, and yet without it should we want or get the book at all? The curiosity at any rate, to repeat, is even greatest for me in *Madame Bovary*, say, for here I can measure, can more directly appreciate, the terms. The aspects and impressions being of an experience conceivable to me I am more touched by the beauty; my interest gets more of the benefit of the beauty even though this be not intrinsically greater. Which brings back our appreciation inevitably at last to the question of our author's lucidity.

I have sufficiently remarked that I speak from the point of view of his interest to a reader of his own craft, the point of view of his extraordinary technical wealth — though indeed when I think of the general power of *Madame Bovary* I find myself desiring not to narrow the ground of the lesson, not to connect the lesson, to its prejudice, with that idea of the 'technical', that question of the way a thing is done, so abhorrent, as a call upon attention, in whatever art, to the wondrous Anglo-Saxon mind. Without proposing Flaubert as the type of the newspaper novelist, or as an easy alternative to golf or the bicycle, we should do him less than justice in failing to insist that a masterpiece like *Madame Bovary* may benefit even with the simple-minded by the way it has been done. It derives from its firm roundness that sign of all rare works that there is something in it for every one. It may be read ever so attentively, ever so freely, without a suspicion of how it is written, to say nothing of put together; it may equally be read under the excitement of these perceptions alone, one of the greatest known to the reader who is fully open to them. Both readers will have been transported, which is all any can ask. Leaving the first of them, however that may be, to state the case for himself, I state it yet again for the second, if only on this final ground. The book and its companions represent for us a practical solution, Flaubert's own troubled but settled one, of the eternal dilemma of the painter of life. From the moment this rash adventurer deals with his mysterious matter at all directly his desire is not to deal with it stintedly. It at the same time remains true that from the moment he desires to produce forms in which it shall be preserved, he desires that these forms, things of *his* creation, shall not be, as testifying to his way with them, weak or ignoble. He must make them complete and beautiful, of satisfactory production, intrinsically interesting, under peril of disgrace with those who know. Those who don't know of course don't count for him, and it neither helps nor hinders him to say that every one knows about life. Every one does not — it is distinctly the case of the few; and if it were in fact the case of the many the knowledge still might exist, on the evidence around us, even in an age of unprecedented printing, without attesting itself by a multiplication of masterpieces. The question for the artist can only be of doing the artistic utmost, and thereby of *seeing* the general task. When it is seen with the intensity with which it presented itself to Flaubert a lifetime is none too much for fairly tackling it. It must either be left alone or be dealt with, and to leave it alone is a comparatively simple matter.

To deal with it is on the other hand to produce a certain number of finished works; there being no other known method; and the quantity of life depicted will depend on this array. What will this array, however, depend on, and what will condition the number of pieces of which it is composed? The 'finish', evidently, that the formula so glibly postulates and for which the novelist is thus so handsomely responsible. He has on the one side to feel his subject and on the other side to render it, and there are undoubtedly two ways in which his situation may be expressed, especially perhaps by himself. The more he feels his subject the more he *can* render it — that is the first way. The more he renders it the more he *can* feel it — that is the second way. This second way was unmistakably Flaubert's, and if the result of it for him was a bar to abundant production he could only accept such an incident as part of the game. He probably for that matter would have challenged any easy definition of 'abundance', contested the application of it to the repetition, however frequent, of the thing not 'done'. What but the 'doing' makes the thing, he would have asked, and how can a positive result from a mere iteration of negatives, or wealth proceed from the simple addition of so many instances of penury? We should here, in closer communion with him, have got into his highly characteristic and suggestive view of the fertilization of subject by form, penetration of the sense, ever, by the expression — the latter reacting creatively on the former; a conviction in the light of which he appears to have wrought with real consistency and which borrows from him thus its high measure of credit. It would undoubtedly have suffered if his books had been things of a loose logic, whereas we refer to it not only without shame but with an encouraged confidence by their showing of a logic so close. Let the phrase, the form that the whole is at the given moment staked on, be beautiful and related, and the rest will take care of itself — such is a rough indication of Flaubert's faith; which has the importance that it was a faith sincere, active and inspiring. I hasten to add indeed that we must most of all remember how in these matters everything hangs on definitions. The 'beautiful', with our author, covered for the phrase a great deal of ground, and when every sort or propriety had been gathered in under it and every relation, in a complexity of such, protected, the idea itself, the presiding thought, ended surely by being pretty well provided for.

These, however, are subordinate notes, and the plain question, in the connection I have touched upon, is of whether we would really wish him to have written more books, say either of the type of *Bovary* or of the type of *Salammbô*, and not have written them so well. When the production of a great artist who has lived a length of years has been small there is always the regret; but there is seldom, any more than here, the conceivable remedy. For the case is doubtless predetermined by the particular kind of great artist a writer happens to be, and this even if when we come to the conflict, to the historic case, deliberation and delay may not all have been imposed by temperament. The admirable George Sand, Flaubert's beneficent friend and correspondent, is exactly the happiest example we could find of the genius constitutionally incapable of worry, the genius for whom style 'came', for whom the sought effect was ever quickly and easily struck off, the book freely and swiftly written, and who consequently is represented for us by upwards of ninety volumes. If the comparison were with this lady's great contemporary the elder Dumas the disparity would be quadrupled, but that ambiguous genius, somehow never really caught by us in the *fact* of composition, is out of our concern here: the issue is of those developments of expression which involve a style, and as Dumas never so much as once grazed one in all his long career, there was not even enough of that grace in him for a fillip of the fingernail. Flaubert is at any rate represented by six books, so that he may on that estimate figure as poor, while Mme Sand, falling so little short of a hundred, figures as rich; and yet the fact remains that I can refer the congenial mind to him with confidence and can do nothing of the sort for it in respect to Mme Sand. She is loose and liquid and iridescent, as iridescent as we may undertake to find her; but I can imagine compositions quite without virtue — the virtue I mean, of sticking together — begotten by the impulse to emulate her. She had undoubtedly herself the benefit of her facility, but are we not left wondering to what extent *we* have it? There is too little in her, by the literary connection, for the critical mind, weary of much wandering, to rest upon. Flaubert himself wandered, wandered far, went much roundabout and sometimes lost himself by the way, but how handsomely he provided for our present repose! He found the French language inconceivably difficult to write with elegance and was confronted with the equal truths that elegance is the last thing that languages, even as they most mature, seem to concern themselves with, and that at the same time taste, asserting rights, insists on it, to the effect of showing us in a boundless circumjacent waste of effort what the absence of it may mean. He saw the lesson of this desert of death come back to that—that everything at all saved from it for us since the beginning had been saved by a soul of elegance within, or in other words by the last refinement of selection, by the indifference on the part of the very idiom, huge quite other than 'composing' agent, to the individual pretension. Recognizing thus that to carry through the individual pretension is at the best a battle, he adored a hard surface and detested a soft one — much more a muddled; regarded a style without rhythm and harmony as in a work of pretended beauty no style at all. He considered that the failure of complete expression so registered made of the work of pretended beauty a work of achieved barbarity. It would take us far to glance even at his fewest discriminations; but rhythm and harmony were for example most menaced in his scheme by repetition — when repetition had not a positive grace; and were above all most at the mercy of the bristling particles of which our modern tongues are mainly composed and which make of the desired surface a texture pricked through, from beneath, even to destruction, as by innumerable thorns.

On these lines production was of course slow work for him — especially as he met the difficulty, met it with an inveteracy which shows how it *can* be met; and full of interest for readers of English speech is the reflection he causes us to make as to the possibility of success at all comparable among ourselves. I have spoken of his groans and imprecations, his interminable waits and deep despairs; but what would these things have been, what would have become of him and what of his wrought residuum, had he been condemned to deal with a form of speech consisting, like ours, as to one part, of 'that' and 'which'; as to a second part, of the blessed 'it', which an English sentence may repeat in three or four opposed references without in the least losing caste; as to a third face of all the 'tos' of the infinite and the preposition; as to a fourth of our precious auxiliaries 'be' and 'do'; and as to a fifth, of whatever survives in the language for the precious art of pleasing? Whether or no the fact that the painter of 'life' among us has to contend with a medium intrinsically indocile, on certain sides, like our own, whether this drawback accounts for his having failed, in our time, to treat us, arrested and charmed, to a single case of crowned classicism, there is at any rate no doubt that we in some degree owe Flaubert's counterweight for that deficiency to *his* having, on his own ground, more happily triumphed. By which I do not mean that *Madame Bovary* is a classic because the 'thats', the 'its' and the 'tos' are made to march as Orpheus and his lute made the beasts, but because the element of order and harmony works as a symbol of everything else that is preserved for us by the history of the book. The history of the book remains the lesson and the important, the delightful thing, remains above all the drama that moves slowly to its climax. It is what we come back to for the sake of what it shows us. We see — from the present to the past indeed, never alas from the present to the future — how a classic almost inveterately grows. Unimportant, unnoticed, or, so far as noticed, contested, unrelated, alien, it has a cradle round which the fairies but scantly flock and is waited on in general by scarce a hint of significance. The significance comes by a process slow and small, the fact only that one perceptive private reader after another discovers at his convenience that the book is rare. The addition of the perceptive private readers is no quick affair, and would doubtless be a vain one did they not — while plenty of other much more remarkable books come and go — accumulate and count. They count by their quality and continuity of attention; so they have gathered for *Madame Bovary*, and so they are held. That is really once more the great circumstance. It is always in order for us to feel yet again what it is we are held by. Such is my reason, definitely, for speaking of Flaubert as the novelist's novelist. Are we not moreover — and let it pass this time as a happy hope! — pretty well all novelists now?

ÉMILE ZOLA

1903

IF it be true that the critical spirit today, in presence of the rising
tide of prose fiction, a watery waste out of which old standards
and landmarks are seen barely to emerge, like chimneys and the
tops of trees in a country under flood — if it be true that the
anxious observer, with the water up to his chin, finds himself
asking for the *reason* of the strange phenomenon, for its warrant
and title, so we likewise make out that these credentials rather fail
to float on the surface. We live in a world of wanton and importunate fable, we breathe its air and consume its fruits; yet who
shall say that we are able, when invited, to account for our prefer-
ring it so largely to the world of fact? To do so would be to make
some adequate statement of the good the product in question
does us. What does it do for our life, our mind, our manners, our
morals — what does it do that history, poetry, philosophy may
not do, as well or better, to warn, to comfort and command the
countless thousands for whom and by whom it comes into being?
We seem too often left with our riddle on our hands. The lame
conclusion on which we retreat is that 'stories' are multiplied,
circulated, paid for, on the scale of the present hour, simply because people 'like' them. As to why people *should* like anything so
loose and mean as the preponderant mass of the 'output', so little
indebted for the magic of its action to any mystery in the making,
is more than the actual state of our perceptions enables us to say.

This bewilderment might be our last word if it were not for
the occasional occurrence of accidents especially appointed to
straighten out a little our tangle. We are reminded that if the unnatural prosperity of the wanton fable cannot be adequately explained, it can at least be illustrated with a sharpness that is practically an argument. An abstract solution failing we encounter it in

the concrete. We catch in short a new impression or, to speak more truly, recover an old one. It was always there to be had, but we ourselves throw off an oblivion, an indifference for which there are plenty of excuses. We become conscious, for our profit, of a *case*, and we see that our mystification came from the way cases had appeared for so long to fail us. None of the shapeless forms about us for the time had attained to the dignity of one. The one I am now conceiving as suddenly effective — for which I fear I must have been regarding it as somewhat in eclipse — is that of Émile Zola, whom, as a manifestation of the sort we are considering, three or four striking facts have lately combined to render more objective and, so to speak, more massive. His close connection with the most resounding of recent public quarrels; his premature and disastrous death; above all, at the moment I write, the appearance of his last-finished novel, bequeathed to his huge public from beyond the grave — these rapid events have thrust him forward and made him loom abruptly larger; much as if our pedestrian critic, treading the dusty highway, had turned a sharp corner.

It is not assuredly that Zola has ever been veiled or unapparent; he had, on the contrary been digging his field these thirty years, and for all passers to see, with an industry that kept him, after the fashion of one of the grand grim sowers or reapers of his brother of the brush, or at least of the canvas, Jean-François Millet, duskily outlined against the sky. He was there in the landscape of labour — he had always been; but he was there as a big natural or pictorial feature, a spreading tree, a battered tower, a lumpish round-shouldered useful hayrick, confounded with the air and the weather, the rain and the shine, the day and the dusk, merged more or less, as it were, in the play of the elements themselves. We had got used to him, and, thanks in a measure just to this stoutness of his presence, to the long regularity of his performance, had come to notice him hardly more than the dwellers in the marketplace notice the quarters struck by the town-clock. On top of all accordingly, for our sceptical mood, the sense of his work — a sense determined afresh by the strange climax of his personal history — rings out almost with violence as a reply to our wonder. It is as if an earthquake or some other rude interference had shaken from the town-clock a note of such unusual depth as to compel attention. We therefore once more give heed, and the result of this is that we feel ourselves after a little probably as much enlightened as we can hope ever to be. We have worked round to the so marked and impressive anomaly of the adoption of the futile art by one of the stoutest minds and stoutest characters of our time. This extraordinarily robust worker has found it good enough for him, and if the fact is, as I say, anomalous, we are doubtless helped to conclude that by its anomalies, in future, the bankrupt business, as we are so often moved to pronounce it, will most recover credit.

What is at all events striking for us, critically speaking, is that, in the midst of the dishonour it has gradually harvested by triumphant vulgarity of practice, its pliancy and applicability can still plead for themselves. The curious contradiction stands forth for our relief — the circumstance that thirty years ago a young man of extraordinary brain and indomitable purpose, wishing to give the measure of these endowments in a piece of work supremely solid, conceived and sat down to *Les Rougon-Macquart* rather than to an equal task in physics, mathematics, politics or economics. He saw his undertaking, thanks to his patience and courage, practically to a close; so that it is exactly neither of the so-called constructive sciences that happens to have had the benefit, intellectually speaking, of one of the few most constructive achievements of our time. There then, provisionally at least, we touch bottom; we get a glimpse of the pliancy and variety, the ideal of vividness, on behalf of which our equivocal form may appeal to a strong head. In the name of what ideal on its own side, however, does the strong head yield to the appeal? What is the logic of its so deeply committing itself? Zola's case seems to tell us, as it tells us other things. The logic is in its huge freedom of adjustment to the temperament of the worker, which it carries, so to say, as no other vehicle can do. It expresses fully and directly the whole man, and big as he may be it can still be big enough for him without becoming false to its type. We see this truth made strong, from beginning to end, in Zola's work; we see the temperament, we see the whole man, with his size and all his marks, stored and packed away in the huge hold of *Les Rougon-Macquart* as a cargo is packed away on a ship. His personality is the thing that finally pervades and prevails, just as so often on a vessel the presence of the cargo makes itself felt for the assaulted senses. What has most come home to me in reading him over is that a scheme of fiction so conducted is in fact a capacious vessel. It can carry anything — with art and force in the stowage; nothing in this case will sink it. And it is the only form for which such a claim can be made. All others have to confess to a smaller scope — to selection, to exclusion, to the danger of distortion, explosion, combustion. The novel has nothing to fear but sailing too light. It will take aboard all we bring in good faith to the dock.

An intense vision of this truth must have been Zola's comfort from the earliest time — the years, immediately following the crash of the Empire, during which he settled himself to the tremendous task he had mapped out. No finer act of courage and confidence, I think, is recorded in the history of letters. The critic in sympathy with him returns again and again to the great wonder of it, in which something so strange is mixed with something so august. Entertained and carried out almost from the threshold of manhood, the high project, the work of a lifetime, announces beforehand its inevitable weakness and yet speaks in the same voice for its admirable, its almost unimaginable strength. The strength was in the young man's very person — in his character, his will, his passion, his fighting temper, his aggressive lips, his squared shoulders (when he 'sat up') and overweening confidence; his weakness was in that inexperience of life from which he proposed not to suffer, from which he in fact suffered on the surface remarkably little, and from which he was never to suspect, I judge, that he had suffered at all. I may mention for the interest of it that, meeting him during his first short visit to London — made several years before his stay in England during the Dreyfus trial — I received a direct impression of him that was more informing than any previous study. I had seen him a little, in Paris, years before that, when this impression was a perceptible promise, and I was now to perceive how time had made it good. It consisted, simply stated, in his fairly bristling with the betrayal that nothing whatever had happened to him in life but to write *Les Rougon-Macquart*. It was even for that matter almost more as if *Les Rougon-Macquart* had written *him*, written him as he stood and sat, as he looked and spoke, as the long, concentrated, merciless effort had made and stamped and left him. Something very fundamental was to happen to him in due course, it is true, shaking him to his base; fate was not wholly to cheat him of an independent evolution. Recalling him from this London hour one strongly felt during the famous 'Affair' that his outbreak in connection with it was the act of a man with arrears of personal history to make up, the act of a spirit for which life, or for which at any rate freedom, had been too much postponed, treating itself at last to a luxury of experience.

I welcomed the general impression at all events — I intimately entertained it; it represented so many things, it suggested, just as it was, such a lesson. You could neither have everything nor be everything — you had to choose; you could not at once sit firm at your job and wander through space inviting initiations. The author of *Les Rougon-Macquart* had had all those, certainly, that this wonderful company could bring him; but I can scarce express how it was implied in him that his time had been fruitfully passed with *them* alone. His artistic evolution struck one thus as, in spite of its magnitude, singularly simple, and evidence of the simplicity seems further offered by his last production, of which we have just come into possession. *Vérité* truly does give the measure, makes the author's high maturity join hands with his youth, marks the rigid straightness of his course from point to point. He had seen his horizon and his fixed goal from the first, and no cross-scent, no new distance, no blue gap in the hills to right or to left ever tempted him to stray. *Vérité*, of which I shall have more to say, is in fact, as a moral finality and the crown of an edifice, one of the strangest possible performances. Machine-minted and made good by an immense expertness, it yet makes us ask how, for disinterested observation and perception, the writer had used so much time and so much acquistion, and how he can all along have handled so much material without some larger subjective consequence. We really rub our eyes in other words to see so great an intellectual adventure as *Les Rougon-Macquart* come to its end in deep desert sand. Difficult truly to read, because showing him at last almost completely a prey to the danger that had for a long time more and more dogged his steps, the danger of the mechanical all confident and triumphant, the book is nevertheless full of interest for a reader desirous to penetrate. It speaks with more distinctness of the author's temperament, tone and manner than if, like several of his volumes, it achieved or enjoyed a successful life of its own. Its heavy completeness, with all this, as of some prodigiously neat, strong and complicated scaffolding constructed by a firm of builders for the erection of a house whose foundations refuse to bear it and that it is unable therefore to rise — its very betrayal of a method and a habit more than adequate, on past occasions, to similar ends, carries us back to the original rare exhibition, the grand assurance and grand patience with which the system was launched.

If it topples over, the system, by its own weight in these last applications of it, that only makes the history of its prolonged success the more curious and, speaking for myself, the spectacle of its origin more attaching. Readers of my generation will remember well the publication of *La Conquête de Plassans* and the portent, indefinable but irresistible, after perusal of the volume, conveyed in the general rubric under which it was a first installment, 'Natural and Social History of a Family under the Second Empire'. It squared itself there at its ease, the announcement, from the first, and we were to learn promptly enough what a fund of life it masked. It was like the mouth of a cave with a signboard hung above, or better still perhaps like the big booth at a fair with the name of the show across the flapping canvas. One strange animal after another stepped forth into the light, each in its way a monster bristling and spotted, each a curiosity of that 'natural history' in the name of which we were addressed, though it was

doubtless not till the issue of *L'Assommoir* that the true type of
the monstrous seemed to be reached. The enterprise, for those
who had attention, was even at a distance impressive, and the
nearer the critic gets to it retrospectively the more so it becomes.
The pyramid had been planned and the site staked out, but the
young builder stood there, in his sturdy strength, with no equipment save his two hands and, as we may say, his wheelbarrow and
his trowel. His pile of material — of stone, brick and rubble or
whatever — was of the smallest, but this he apparently felt as the
least of his difficulties. Poor, uninstructed, unacquainted, un-
introduced, he set up his subject wholly from the outside, proposing to himself wonderfully to get into it, into its depths, as he
went.

If we imagine him asking himself what he knew of the 'social'
life of the second Empire to start with, we imagine him also
answering in all honesty: 'I have my eyes and my ears — I have
all my senses: I have what I've seen and heard, what I've smelled
and tasted and touched. And then I've my curiosity and my per-
tinacity; I've libraries, books, newspapers, witnesses, the material,
from step to step, of an *enquête*. And then I've my genius — that
is, my imagination, my passion, my sensibility to life. Lastly I've
my method, and that will be half the battle. Best of all perhaps
even, I've plentiful lack of doubt.' Of the absence in him of a
doubt, indeed of his inability, once his direction taken, to entertain so much as the shadow of one, *Vérité* is a positive monument
— which again represents in this way the unity of his tone and
the meeting of his extremes. If we remember that his design was
nothing if not architectural, that a 'majestic whole', a great balanced façade, with all its orders and parts, that a singleness of
mass and a unity of effect, in fine, were before him from the first,
his notion of picking up his bricks as he proceeded becomes, in
operation, heroic. It is not in the least as a record of failure for
him that I note this particular fact of the growth of the long series
as on the whole the liveliest interest it has to offer. 'I don't know
my subject, but I must live into it; I don't know life, but I must
learn it as I work' — that attitude and programme represent, to

my sense, a drama more intense on the worker's own part than any of the dramas he was to invent and put before us.

It was the fortune, it was in a manner the doom, of *Les Rougon-Macquart* to deal with things almost always in gregarious form, to be a picture of *numbers*, of classes, crowds, confusions, movements, industries — and this for a reason of which it will be interesting to attempt some account. The individual life is, if not wholly absent, reflected in coarse and common, in generalised terms; whereby we arrive precisely at the oddity just named, the circumstance that, looking out somewhere, and often woefully athirst, for the taste of fineness, we find it not in the fruits of our author's fancy, but in a different matter altogether. We get it in the very history of his effort, the image itself of his lifelong process, comparatively so personal, so spiritual even, and, through all its patience and pain, of a quality so much more distinguished than the qualities he succeeds in attributing to his figures even when he most aims at distinction. There can be no question in these narrow limits of my taking the successive volumes one by one — all the more that our sense of the exhibition is as little as possible an impression of parts and books, of particular 'plots' and persons. It produces the effect of a mass of imagery in which shades are sacrificed, the effect of character and passion in the lump or by the ton. The fullest, the most characteristic episodes affect us like a sounding chorus or procession, as with a hubbub of voices and a multitudinous tread of feet. The setter of the mass into motion, he himself, in the crowd, figures best, with whatever queer idiosyncrasies, excrescences and gaps, a being of a substance akin to our own. Taking him as we must, I repeat, for quite heroic, the interest of detail in him is the interest of his struggle at every point with his problem.

The sense for crowds and processions, for the gross and the general, was largely the *result* of this predicament, of the disproportion between his scheme and his material — though it was certainly also in part an effect of his particular turn of mind. What the reader easily discerns in him is the sturdy resolution with which breadth and energy supply the place of penetration. He rests to his utmost on his documents, devours and assimilates them, makes them yield him extraordinary appearances of life; but in his way he too improvises in the grand manner, the manner of Walter Scott and of Dumas the elder. We feel that he *has* to improvise for his moral and social world, the world as to which vision and opportunity must come, if they are to come at all, un-hurried and unhustled — must take their own time, helped un-doubtedly more or less by blue-books, reports and interviews, by inquiries 'on the spot', but never wholly replaced by such sub-stitutes without a general disfigurement. Vision and opportunity reside in a personal sense and a personal history, and no short cut to them in the interest of plausible fiction has ever been dis-covered. The short cut, it is not too much to say, was with Zola the subject of constant ingenious experiment, and it is largely to this source, I surmise, that we owe the celebrated element of his grossness. He was *obliged* to be gross, on his system, or neglect to his cost an invaluable aid to representation, as well as one that apparently struck him as lying close at hand; and I cannot with-hold my frank admiration from the courage and consistency with which he faced his need.

His general subject in the last analysis was the nature of man; in dealing with which he took up, obviously, the harp of most numerous strings. His business was to make these strings sound true, and there were none that he did not, so far as his general economy permitted, persistently try. What happened then was that many — say about half, and these, as I have noted, the most silvered, the most golden — refused to give out their music. They would only sound false, since (as with all his earnestness he must have felt) he could command them, through want of skill, of practice, of ear, to none of the right harmony. What therefore was more natural than that, still spendidly bent on producing his illusion, he should throw himself on the strings he might thump with effect, and should work them, as our phrase is, for all they were worth? The nature of man, he had plentiful warrant for holding, is an extraordinary mixture, but the great thing was to represent a sufficient part of it to show that it was solidly, palpably, commonly the nature. With this preoccupation he doubtless fell into extravagance — there was clearly so much to lead him on. The coarser side of his subject, based on the community of all the instincts, was for instance the more practicable side, a sphere the vision of which required but the general human, scarcely more than the plain physical, initiation, and dispensed thereby conveniently enough with special introductions or revelations. A free entry into this sphere was undoubtedly compatible with a youthful career as hampered right and left even as Zola's own.

He was in prompt possession thus of the range of sympathy that he *could* cultivate, though it must be added that the complete exercise of that sympathy might have encountered an obstacle that would somewhat undermine his advantage. Our friend might have found himself able, in other words, to pay to the instinctive, as I have called it, only such tribute as protesting taste (his own dose of it) permitted. Yet there it was again that fortune and his temperament served him. Taste as he knew it, taste as his own constitution supplied it, proved to have nothing to say to the matter. His own dose of the precious elixir had no perceptible regulating power. Paradoxical as the remark may sound, this accident was positively to operate as one of his greatest felicities. There are parts of his work, those dealing with romantic or poetic elements, in which the inactivity of the principle in question is sufficiently hurtful; but it surely should not be described as hurtful to such pictures as *Le Ventre de Paris*, as *L'Assommoir*, as *Germinal*. The conception on which each of these productions rests is that of a world with which taste has nothing to do, and though the act of representation may be justly held, as an artistic act, to involve its presence, the discrimination would probably have been in fact, given the particular illusion sought, more detrimental than the deficiency. There was a great outcry, as we all remember, over the rank materialism of *L'Assommoir*, but who cannot see today how much a milder infusion of it would have told against the close embrace of the subject aimed at? *L'Assommoir* is the nature of man — but not his finer, nobler, cleaner or more cultivated nature; it is the image of his free instincts, the better and the worse, the better struggling as they can, gasping for light and air, the worse making themselves at home in darkness, ignorance and poverty. The whole handling makes for emphasis and scale, and it is not to be measured how, as a picture of conditions, the thing would have suffered from timidity. The qualification of the painter was precisely his stoutness of stomach, and we scarce exceed in saying that to have taken in and given out again less of the infected air would, with such a resource, have meant the waste of a faculty.

I may add in this connection moreover that refinement of intention did on occasion and after a fashion of its own unmistakably preside at these experiments; making the remark in order to have done once for all with a feature of Zola's literary physiognomy that appears to have attached the gaze of many persons to the exclusion of every other. There are judges in these matters so perversely preoccupied that for them to see anywhere the 'improper' is for them straightway to cease to see anything else. The said improper, looming supremely large and casting all the varieties of the proper quite into the shade, suffers thus in their consciousness a much greater extension than it ever claimed, and this consciousness becomes, for the edification of many and the information of a few, a colossal reflector and record of it. Much may be said, in relation to some of the possibilities of the nature of man, of the nature in especial of the 'people', on the defect of our author's sense of proportion. But the sense of proportion of many of those he has scandalized would take us further yet. I recall at all events as relevant — for it comes under a very attaching general head — two occasions of long ago, two Sunday afternoons in Paris, on which I found the question of intention very curiously lighted. Several men of letters of a group in which almost every member either had arrived at renown or was well on his way to it, were assembled under the roof of the most distinguished of their number, where they exchanged free confidences on current work, on plans and ambitions, in a manner full of interest for one never previously privileged to see artistic conviction, artistic passion (at least on the literary ground) so systematic and so articulate. 'Well,

I on my side', I remember Zola's saying, 'am engaged on a book, a study of the *mœurs* of the people, for which I am making a collection of all the 'bad words', the *gros mots*, of the language, those with which the vocabulary of the people, those with which their familiar talk, bristles.' I was struck with the tone in which he made the announcement — without bravado and without apology, as an interesting idea that had come to him and that he was working, really to arrive at character and particular truth, with all his conscience; just as I was struck with the unqualified interest that his plan excited. It was *on* a plan that he was working — formidably, almost grimly, as his fatigued face showed; and the whole consideration of this interesting element partook of the general seriousness.

But there comes back to me also as a companion-piece to this another day, after some interval, on which the interest was excited by the fact that the work for love of which the brave licence had been taken was actually under the ban of the daily newspaper that had engaged to 'serialise' it. Publication had definitively ceased. The thing had run a part of its course, but it had outrun the courage of editors and the curiosity of subscribers — that stout curiosity to which it had evidently in such good faith been addressed. The chorus of contempt for the ways of such people, their pusillanimity, their superficiality, vulgarity, intellectual platitude, was the striking note on this occasion; for the journal impugned had declined to proceed and the serial, broken off, been obliged, if I am not mistaken, to seek the hospitality of other columns, secured indeed with no great difficulty. The composition so qualified for future fame was none other, as I was later to learn, than *L'Assommoir*; and my reminiscence has perhaps no greater point than in connecting itself with a matter always dear to the critical spirit, especially when the latter has not too completely elbowed out the romantic — the matter of the 'origins', the early consciousness, early steps, early tribulations, early obscurity, as so often happens of productions finally crowned by time.

Their greatness is for the most part a thing that has originally begun so small; and this impression is particularly strong when we have been in any degree present, so to speak, at the birth. The course of the matter is apt to tend preponderantly in that case to enrich our stores of irony. In the eventual conquest of consideration by an abused book we recognise, in other terms, a drama of romantic interest, a drama often with large comic no less than with fine pathetic interweavings. It may of course be said in this particular connection that *L'Assommoir* had not been one of the literary things that creep humbly into the world. Its 'success' may be cited as almost insolently prompt, and the fact remains true if the idea of success be restricted, after the inveterate fashion, to the idea of circulation. What remains truer still, however, is that for the critical spirit circulation mostly matters not the least little bit, and it is of the success with which the history of Gervaise and Coupeau nestles in *that* capacious bosom, even as the just man sleeps in Abraham's, that I here speak. But it is a point I may better refer to a moment hence.

Though a summary study of Zola need not too anxiously concern itself with book after book — always with a partial exception from this remark for *L'Assommoir* — groups and varieties none the less exist in the huge series, aids to discrimination without which no measure of the presiding genius is possible. These divisions range themselves to my sight, roughly speaking, however, as scarce more than three in number — I mean if the ten volumes of the *Œuvres critiques* and the *Théâtre* be left out of account. The critical volumes in especial abound in the characteristic, as they were also a wondrous addition to his sum of achievement during his most strenuous years. But I am forced not to consider them. The two groups constituted after the close of *Les Rougon-Macquart* — *Les Trois Villes* and the incomplete *Quatre Évangiles* — distribute themselves easily among the three types, or, to speak more exactly, stand together under one of the three. This one, so comprehensive as to be the author's main exhibition, includes to my sense all his best volumes — to the point in fact of producing an effect of distinct inferiority for those outside of it, which are, luckily for his general credit, the less numerous. It is so inveterately pointed out in any allusion to him that one shrinks, in repeating it, from sounding flat; but as he was admirably equipped from the start for the evocation of number and quantity, so those of his social pictures that most easily surpass the others are those in which appearances, the appearances familiar to him, are at once most magnified and most multiplied.

To make his character swarm, and to make the great central thing they swarm about 'as large as life', portentously, heroically big, that was the task he set himself very nearly from the first, that was the secret he triumphantly mastered. Add that the big central thing was always some highly representative institution or industry of the France of his time, some seated Moloch of custom, of commerce, of faith, lending itself to portrayal through its abuses and excesses, its idol-face and great devouring mouth, and we embrace the main lines of his attack. In *Le Ventre de Paris* he had dealt with the life of the huge Halles, the general markets and their supply, the personal forces, personal situations, passions, involved in (strangest of all subjects) the alimentation of the monstrous city, the city whose victualing occupies so inordinately much of its consciousness. Paris richly gorged, Paris sublime and indifferent in her assurance (so all unlike poor Oliver's) of 'more', figures here the theme itself, lies across the scene like some vast ruminant creature breathing in a cloud of parasites. The book was the first of the long series to show the full freedom of the author's hand, though *La Curée* had already been symptomatic. This freedom, after an interval, broke out on a much bigger scale in *L'Assommoir*, in *Au Bonheur des Dames*, in *Germinal*, in *La Bête Humaine*, in *L'Argent*, in *La Débâcle*, and then again, though more mechanically and with much of the glory gone, in the more or less wasted energy of *Lourdes, Rome, Paris*, of *Fécondité, Travail* and *Vérité*.

Au Bonheur des Dames handles the colossal modern shop, traces the growth of such an organization as the Bon Marché or the Magasin-du-Louvre, sounds the abysses of its inner life, marshals its population, its hierarchy of clerks, counters, departments, divisions and subdivisions, plunges into the labyrinth of the mutual relations of its staff, and above all traces its ravage amid the smaller fry of the trade, of all the trades, pictures these latter gasping for breath in an air pumped clean by its mighty lungs. *Germinal* revolves about the coal mines of Flemish France, with the subterranean world of the pits for its central presence, just as *La Bête Humaine* has for its protagonist a great railway and *L'Argent* presents in terms of human passion — mainly of human baseness — the fury of the Bourse and the monster of Credit. *La Débâcle* takes up with extraordinary breadth the first act of the Franco-Prussian war, the collapse at Sedan, and the titles of the six volumes of The Three Cities and the Four Gospels sufficiently explain them. I may mention, however, for the last lucidity, that among these *Fécondité* manipulates, with an amazing misapprehension of means to ends, of remedies to ills, no less thickly people a theme than that of the decline in the French birth rate, and that *Vérité* presents a fictive equivalent of the Dreyfus case, with a vast and elaborate picture of the battle in France between lay and clerical instruction. I may even further mention, to clear the ground, that with the close of *Les Rougon-Macquart* the diminution of freshness in the author's energy, the diminution of intensity and, in short, of quality, becomes such as to render sadly difficult a happy life with some of the later volumes. Happiness of the purest strain never indeed, in old absorptions of Zola, quite sat at the feast; but there was mostly a measure of coercion, a spell without a charm. From these last-named productions of the climax everything strikes me as absent but quantity (*Vérité*, for instance, is, with the possible exception of *Nana*, the longest of the list); though indeed there is something impressive in the way his quantity represents his patience.

There are efforts here at stout perusal that, frankly, I have been unable to carry through, and I should verily like, in connection with the vanity of these, to dispose on the spot of the sufficiently strange phenomenon constituted by what I have called the climax. It embodies in fact an immense anomaly; it casts back over Zola's prime and his middle years the queerest gray light of eclipse. Nothing moreover — nothing 'literary' — was ever so odd as in

this matter the whole turn of the case, the consummation so logical yet so unexpected. Writers have grown old and withered and
failed; they have grown weak and sad; they have lost heart, lost
ability, yielded in one way or another — the possible ways being
so numerous — to the cruelty of time. But the singular doom of
this genius, and which began to multiply its symptoms ten years
before his death, was to find, with life, at fifty, still rich in him,
strength only to undermine all the 'authority' he had gathered.
He had not grown old and he had not grown feeble; he had only
grown all too wrongly insistent, setting himself to wreck, poet-
ically, his so massive identity — to wreck it in the very waters in
which he had formally arrayed his victorious fleet. (I say 'poet-
ically' on purpose to give him the just benefit of all the beauty of
his power.) The process of the disaster, so full of the effect, though
so without the intention, of perversity, is difficult to trace in a few
words; it may best be indicated by an example or two of its action.

The example that perhaps most comes home to me is again
connected with a personal reminiscence. In the course of some
talk that I had with him during his first visit to England I happened
to ask him what opportunity to travel (if any) his immense application had ever left him, and whether in particular he had been
able to see Italy, a country from which I had either just returned
or which I was luckily — not having the 'Natural History of a
Family' on my hands — about to revisit. 'All I've done, alas,' he
replied, 'was, the other year, in the course of a little journey to
the south, to my own *pays* — all that has been possible was then
to make a little dash as far as Genoa, a matter of only a few days.'
Le Docteur Pascal, the conclusion of *Les Rougon-Macquart*, had
appeared shortly before, and it further befell that I asked him
what plans he had for the future, now that, still *dans la force de
l'âge*, he had so cleared the ground. I shall never forget the fine
promptitude of his answer — 'Oh, I shall begin at once *Les Trois
Villes*'. 'And which cities are they to be?' The reply was finer still
— 'Lourdes, Paris, Rome.'

It was splendid for confidence and cheer, but it left me, I fear,
more or less gaping, and it was to give me afterwards the key,

critically speaking, to many a mystery. It struck me as breathing to an almost tragic degree the fatuity of those in whom the gods stimulate that vice to their ruin. He was an honest man — he had always bristled with it at every pore; but no artistic reverse was inconceivable for an adventurer who, stating in one breath that his knowledge of Italy consisted of a few days spent at Genoa, was ready to declare in the next that he had planned, on a scale, a picture of Rome. It flooded his career, to my sense, with light; it showed how he had marched from subject to subject and had 'got up' each in turn — showing also how consummately he had reduced such getting-up to an artifice. He had success and a rare impunity behind him, but nothing would now be so interesting as to see if he could again play the trick. One would leave him, and welcome, Lourdes and Paris — he had already dealt, on a scale, with his own country and people. But was the adored Rome also to be his on such terms, the Rome he was already giving away before possessing an inch of it? One thought of one's own frequentations, saturations — a history of long years, and of how the effect of them had somehow been but to make the subject too august. Was *he* to find it easy through a visit of a month or two with 'introductions' and a Baedeker?

It was not indeed that the Baedeker and the introductions didn't show, to my sense, at that hour, as extremely suggestive; they were positively a part of the light struck out by his announcement. They defined the system on which he had brought *Les Rougon-Macquart* safely into port. He had had his Baedeker and his introductions for *Germinal*, for *L'Assommoir*, for *L'Argent*, for *La Débâcle*, for *Au Bonheur des Dames*; which advantages, which researches, had clearly been all the more in character for being documentary, extractive, a matter of *renseignements*, published or private, even when most mixed with personal impressions snatched, with *enquêtes sur les lieux*, with facts obtained from the best authorities, proud and happy to co-operate in so famous a connection. That was, as we say, all right, all the more that the process, to my imagination, became vivid and was wonderfully reflected back from its fruits. There *were* the fruits — so it hadn't been pre-

sumptuous. Presumption, however, was now to begin, and what
omen mightn't there be in its beginning with such complacency?
Well, time would show — as time in due course effectually did.
Rome, as the second volume of *The Three Cities*, appeared with
high punctuality a year or two later; and the interesting question,
an occasion really for the moralist, was by that time not to recognize in it the mere triumph of a mechanical art, a 'receipt' applied
with the skill of long practice, but to do much more than this —
that is really to give a name to the particular shade of blindness
that could constitute a trap for so great an artistic intelligence.
The presumptuous volume, without sweetness, without ante-
cedents, superficial and violent, has the minimum instead of the
maximum of *value*; so that it betrayed or 'gave away' just in this
degree the state of mind on the author's part responsible for its
inflated hollowness. To put one's finger on the state of mind was
to find out accordingly what was, as we say, the matter with him.

It seemed to me, I remember, that I found out as never before
when, in its turn, *Fécondité* began the work of crowning the edifice. *Fécondité* is physiological, whereas *Rome* is not, whereas
Vérité likewise is not; yet these three productions joined hands at
a given moment to fit into the lock of the mystery the key of my
meditation. They came to the same thing, to the extent of permit-
ting me to read into them together the same precious lesson. This
lesson may not, barely stated, sound remarkable; yet without
being in possession of it I should have ventured on none of these
remarks. 'The matter with' Zola then, so far as it goes, was that,
as the imagination of the artist is in the best cases not only clarified
but intensified by his equal possession of Taste (deserving here if
ever the old-fashioned honour of a capital), so when he has luck-
lessly never inherited that auxiliary blessing the imagination itself
inevitably breaks down as a consequence. There is simply no
limit, in fine, to the misfortune of being tasteless; it does not
merely disfigure the surface and the fringe of your performance
— it eats back into the very heart and enfeebles the sources of life.
When you have no taste you have no discretion, which is the
conscience of taste, and when you have no discretion you per-

petrate books like *Rome*, which are without intellectual modesty, books like *Fécondité*, which are without a sense of the ridiculous, books like *Vérité*, which are without the finer vision of human experience.

It is marked that in each of these examples the deficiency has been directly fatal. No stranger doom was ever appointed for a man so plainly desiring only to be just than the absurdity of not resting till he had buried the felicity of his past, such as it was, under a great flat leaden slab. *Vérité* is a plea for science, as science, to Zola, is *all* truth, the mention of any other kind being mere imbecility; and the simplification of the human picture to which his negations and exasperations have here conducted him was not, even when all had been said, credible in advance. The result is amazing when we consider that the finer observation is the supposed basis of all such work. It is not that even here the author has not a queer idealism of his own; this idealism is on the contrary so present as to show positively for the falsest of his simplifications. In *Fécondité* it becomes grotesque, makes of the book the most muscular mistake of *sense* probably ever committed. Where was the judgment of which experience is supposed to be the guarantee when the perpetrator could persuade himself that the lesson he wished in these pages to convey could be made immediate and direct, chalked, with loud taps and a still louder commentary, the sexes and generations all convoked, on the blackboard of the 'family sentiment'?

I have mentioned, however, all this time but one of his categories. The second consists of such things as *La Fortune des Rougon* and *La Curée*, as *Eugène Rougon* and even *Nana*, as *Pot-Bouille*, as *L'Œuvre* and *La Joie de Vivre*. These volumes may rank as social pictures in the narrowest sense, studies, comprehensively speaking, of the manners, the morals, the miseries — for it mainly comes to that — of a bourgeoisie grossly materialised. They deal with the life of individuals in the liberal professions and with that of political and social adventures, and offer the personal character and career, more or less detached, as the centre of interest. *La Curée* is an evocation, violent and 'romantic', of the extravagant appetites, the fever of the senses, supposedly fostered, for its ruin, by the hapless second Empire, upon which general ills and turpitudes at large were at one time so freely and conveniently fathered. *Eugène Rougon* carries out this view in the high colour of a political portrait, not other than scandalous, for which one of the ministerial *âmes damnées* of Napoleon III, M. Rouher, is reputed, I know not how justly, to have sat. *Nana*, attaching itself by a hundred strings to a prearranged table of kinships, heredities, transmissions, is the vast crowded *epos* of the daughter of the people filled with poisoned blood and sacrificed as well as sacrificing on the altar of luxury and lust; the panorama of such a 'progress' as Hogarth would more definitely have named — the progress across the high plateau of 'pleasure' and down the facile descent on the other side. *Nana* is truly a monument to Zola's patience; the subject being so ungrateful, so formidably special, that the multiplication of illustrative detail, the plunge into pestilent depths, represents a kind of technical intrepidity.

There are other plunges, into different sorts of darkness; of which the æsthetic, even the scientific, even the ironic motive fairly escapes us — explorations of stagnant pools like that of *La Joie de Vivre*, as to which, granting the nature of the curiosity and the substance laboured in, the patience is again prodigious, but which make us wonder what pearl of philosophy, of suggestion or just of homely recognition, the general picture, as of rats dying in a hole, has to offer. Our various senses, sight, smell, sound, touch, are, as with Zola always, more or less convinced; but when the particular effect upon each of these is added to the effect upon the others the mind still remains bewilderedly unconscious of any use for the total. I am not sure indeed that the case is in this respect better with the productions of the third order — *La Faute de l'Abbé Mouret, Une Page d'Amour, Le Rêve, Le Docteur Pascal* — in which the appeal is more directly, is in fact quite earnestly, to the moral vision; so much, on such ground, was to depend precisely on those discriminations in which the writer is least at home. The volumes whose names I have just quoted are his express tribute to the 'ideal', to the select and the charming —

fair fruits of invention intended to remove from the mouth so far as possible the bitterness of the ugly things in which so much of the rest of his work had been condemned to consist. The subjects in question then are 'idyllic' and the treatment poetic, concerned essentially to please on the largest lines and involving at every turn that salutary need. They are matters of conscious delicacy, and nothing might interest us more than to see what, in the shock of the potent forces enlisted, becomes of this shy element. Nothing might interest us more, literally, and might positively affect us more, even very nearly to tears, though indeed sometimes also to smiles, than to see the constructor of *Les Rougon-Macquart* trying, 'for all he is worth,' to be fine with fineness, finely tender, finely true — trying to be, as it is called, distinguished — in face of constitutional hindrance.

The effort is admirably honest, the tug at his subject splendidly strong; but the consequences remain of the strangest, and we get the impression that — as representing discriminations unattainable — they are somehow the price he paid. *Le Docteur Pascal*, for instance, which winds up the long chronicle on the romantic note, on the note of invoked beauty, in order to sweeten, as it were, the total draught — *Le Docteur Pascal*, treating of the erotic ardour entertained for each other by an uncle and his niece, leaves us amazed at such a conception of beauty, such an application of romance, such an estimate of sweetness, a sacrifice to poetry and passion so little in order. Of course, we definitely remind ourselves, the whole long chronicle is explicitly a scheme, solidly set up and intricately worked out, lighted, according to the author's pretension, by 'science', high, dry, and clear, and with each part involved and necessitated in all the other parts, each block of the edifice, each 'morceau de vie', *physiologically* determined by previous combinations. 'How can I help it', we hear the builder of the pyramid ask, 'if experience (by which alone I proceed) shows me certain plain results — if, holding up the torch of my famous "experimental method", I find it stare me in the face that the union of certain types, the conflux of certain strains of blood, the intermarriage, in a word, of certain families, produces nervous conditions, conditions temperamental, psychical and pathological, in which nieces *have* to fall in love with uncles and uncles with nieces? Observation and imagination, for any picture of life,' he as audibly adds, 'know no light but science, and are false to all intellectual decency, false to their own honour, when they fear it, dodge it, darken it. To pretend to any other guide or law is mere base humbug.'

That is very well, and the value, in a hundred ways, of a mass of production conceived in such a spirit can never (when robust execution has followed) be small. But the formula really sees us no further. It offers a definition which is no definition. 'Science' is soon said — the whole thing depends on the ground so covered. Science accepts surely *all* our consciousness of life; even, rather, the latter closes maternally round it — so that, becoming thus a force within us, not a force outside, it exists, it illuminates only as we apply it. We do emphatically apply it in art. But Zola would apparently hold that it much more applies *us*. On the showing of many of his volumes then it makes but a dim use of us, and this we should still consider the case even were we sure that the article offered us in the majestic name is absolutely at one with its own pretension. This confidence we can on too many grounds never have. The matter is one of appreciation, and when an artist answers for science who answers for the artist — who at the least answers for art? Thus it is with the mistakes that affect us, I say, as Zola's penalties. We are reminded by them that the game of art has, as the phrase is, to be played. It may not with any sure felicity for the result be both taken and left. If you insist on the common you must submit to the common; if you discriminate, on the contrary, you must, however invidious your discriminations may be called, trust to them to see you through.

To the common then Zola, often with splendid results, inordinately sacrifices, and this fact of its overwhelming him is what I have called his paying for it. In *L'Assommoir*, in *Germinal*, in *La Débâcle*, productions in which he must most survive, the sacrifice is ordered and fruitful, for the subject and the treatment harmonise and work together. He describes what he best feels, and feels it more and more as it naturally comes to him — quite, if I may allow myself the image, as we zoologically see some mighty animal, a beast of a corrugated hide and a portentous snout, soaking with joy in the warm ooze of an African riverside. In these cases everything matches, and 'science', we may be permitted to believe, has had little in the business. The author's perceptions go straight, and the subject, grateful and responsive, gives itself wholly up. It is no longer a case of an uncertain smoky torch, but of a personal vision, the vision of genius, springing from an inward source. Of this genius *L'Assommoir* is the most extraordinary record. It contains, with the two companions I have given it, all the best of Zola, and the three books together are solid ground — or would be could I now so take them — for a study of the particulars of his power. His strongest marks and features abound in them; *L'Assommoir* above all is (not least in respect to its bold free linguistic reach, already glanced at) completely genial, while his misadventures, his unequipped and delusive pursuit of the life of the spirit and the tone of culture, are almost completely absent.

It is a singular sight enough this of a producer of illusions whose interest for us is so independent of our pleasure or at least of our complacency — who touches us deeply even while he most 'puts us off', who makes us care for his ugliness and yet himself at the same time pitilessly (pitilessly, that is, for *us*) makes a mock of it, who fills us with a sense of the rich which is none the less never the rare. Gervaise, the most immediately 'felt', I cannot but think, of all his characters, is a lame washer-woman, loose and gluttonous, without will, without any principle of cohesion, the sport of every wind that assaults her exposed life, and who, rolling from one gross mistake to another, finds her end in misery, drink and despair. But her career, as presented, has fairly the largeness that, throughout the chronicle, we feel as epic, and the intensity of her creator's vision of it and of the dense sordid life hanging about it is one of the great things the modern novel has been able to do. It has done nothing more completely constitutive and of a tone so rich and full and sustained. The tone of *L'Assom-*

moir is, for mere 'keeping up', unsurpassable, a vast deep steady tide on which every object represented is triumphantly borne. It never shrinks nor flows thin, and nothing for an instant drops, dips or catches; the high-water mark of sincerity, of the genial, as I have called it, is unfailingly kept.

For the artist in the same general 'line' such a production has an interest almost inexpressible, a mystery as to origin and growth over which he fondly but rather vainly bends. How after all does it so get itself *done*? — the 'done' being admirably the sign and crown of it. The light of the richer mind has been elsewhere, as I have sufficiently hinted, frequent enough, but nothing truly in all fiction was ever built so strong or made so dense as here. Needless to say there are a thousand things with more charm in their truth, with more beguilement of every sort, more prettiness of pathos, more innocence of drollery, for the spectator's sense of truth. But I doubt if there has ever been a more totally *represented* world, anything more founded and established, more provided for all round, more organised and carried on. It is a world practically workable, with every part as functional as every other, and with the parts all chosen for direct mutual aid. Let it not be said either that the equal constitution of parts makes for repletion or excess; the air circulates and the subject blooms; deadness comes in these matters only when the right parts are absent and there is vain beating of the air in their place — the refuge of the fumbler incapable of the thing 'done' at all.

The mystery I speak of, for the reader who reflects as he goes, is the wonder of the scale and energy of Zola's assimilations. This wonder besets us above all throughout the three books I have placed first. How, all sedentary and 'scientific', did he get so *near*? By what art, inscrutable, immeasurable, indefatigable, did he arrange to make of his documents, in these connections, a use so vivified? Say he was 'near' the subject of *L'Assommoir* in imagination, in more or less familiar impression, in temperament and humour, he could not after all have been near it in personal experience, and the copious personalism of the picture, not to say its frank animalism, yet remains its note and its strength. When the note had been struck in a thousand forms we had, by multiplication, as a kind of cumulative consequence, the finished and rounded book; just as we had the same result by the same process in *Germinal*. It is not of course that multiplication and accumulation, the extraordinary pair of legs on which he walks, are easily or directly consistent with his projecting himself morally; this immense diffusion, with its appropriation of everything it meets, affects us on the contrary as perpetually delaying access to what we may call the private world, the world of the individual. Yet since the individual — for it so happens — is simple and shallow our author's dealings with him, as met and measured, maintain their resemblance to those of the lusty bee who succeeds in plumping for an instant, of a summer morning, into every flower-cup of the garden.

Grant — and the generalisation may be emphatic — that the shallow and the simple are *all* the population of his richest and most crowded pictures, and that his 'psychology', in a psychologic age, remains thereby comparatively coarse, grant this and we but get another view of the miracle. We see enough of the superficial among novelists at large, assuredly, without deriving from it, as we derive from Zola at his best, the concomitant impression of the solid. It is in general — I mean among the novelists at large — the impression of the *cheap*, which the author of *Les Rougon-Macquart*, honest man, never faithless for a moment to his own stiff standard, manages to spare us even in the prolonged sandstorm of *Vérité*. The Common is another matter; it is one of the forms of the superficial — pervading and consecrating all things in such a book as *Germinal* — and it only adds to the number of our critical questions. How in the world is it made, this deplorable democratic malodorous Common, so strange and so interesting? How is it taught to receive into its loins the stuff of the epic and still, in spite of that association with poetry, never depart from its nature? It is in the great lusty game he plays with the shallow and the simple that Zola's mastery resides, and we see of course that when values are small it takes innumerable items and combinations to make up the sum. In *L'Assommoir* and in

Germinal, to some extent even in *La Débâcle*, the values are all, morally, personally, of the lowest — the highest is poor Gervaise herself, richly human in her generosities and follies — yet each is as distinct as a brass-headed nail.

What we come back to accordingly is the unprecedented case of such a combination of parts. Painters, of great schools, often of great talent, have responded liberally on canvas to the appeal of ugly things, of Spanish beggars, squalid and dusty-footed, of martyred saints or other convulsed sufferers, tortured and bleeding, of boors and louts soaking a Dutch proboscis in perpetual beer; but we had never before had to reckon with so literary a treatment of the mean and vulgar. When we others of the Anglo-Saxon race are vulgar we are, handsomely and with the best conscience in the world, vulgar all through, too vulgar to be in any degree literary, and too much so therefore to be critically reckoned with at all. The French are different — they separate their sympathies, multiply their possibilities, observe their shades, remain more or less outside of their worst disasters. They mostly contrive to get the *idea*, in however dead a faint, down into the lifeboat. They may lose sight of the stars, but they save in some such fashion as that their intellectual souls. Zola's own reply to all puzzlements would have been, at any rate, I take it, a straight summary of his inveterate professional habits. 'It is all very simple — I produce, roughly speaking, a volume a year, and of this time some five months go to preparation, to special study. In the other months, with all my *cadres* established, I write the book. And I can hardly say which part of the job is stiffest.'

The story was not more wonderful for him than that, nor the job more complex; which is why we must say of his whole process and its results that they constitute together perhaps the most extraordinary *imitation* of observation that we possess. Balzac appealed to 'science' and proceeded by her aid; Balzac had *cadres* enough and a tabulated world, rubrics, relationships and genealogies; but Balzac affects us in spite of everything as personally overtaken by life, as fairly hunted and run to earth by it. He strikes us as struggling and all but submerged, as beating over

the scene such a pair of wings as were not soon again to be
wielded by any visitor of his general air and as had not at all
events attached themselves to Zola's rounded shoulders. His be-
quest is in consequence immeasurably more interesting, yet who
shall declare that his adventure was in its greatness more successful? Zola 'pulled it off', as we say, supremely, in that he never but
once found himself obliged to quit, to our vision, his magnificent
treadmill of the pigeonholed and documented — the region we
may qualify as that of experience by imitation. His splendid economy saw him through, he laboured to the end within sight of his
notes and and his charts.

The extraordinary thing, however, is that on the single occasion when, publicly — as his whole manifestation was public —
life did swoop down on him, the effect of the visitation was quite
perversely other than might have been looked for. His courage in
the Dreyfus connection testified admirably to his ability to live
for himself and out of the order of his volumes — little indeed as
living at all might have seemed a question for one exposed, when
his crisis was at its height and he was found guilty of 'insulting'
the powers that were, to be literally torn to pieces in the precincts
of the Palace of Justice. Our point is that nothing was ever so odd
as that these great moments should appear to have been wasted,
when all was said, for his creative intelligence. *Vérité*, as I have
intimated, the production in which they might most have been
reflected, is a production unrenewed and unrefreshed by them,
spreads before us as somehow flatter and grayer, not richer and
more relieved, by reason of them. They really arrived, I surmise,
too late in the day; the imagination they might have vivified was
already fatigued and spent.

I must not moreover appear to say that the power to evoke and
present has not even on the dead level of *Vérité* its occasional
minor revenges. There are passages, whole pages, of the old full-
bodied sort, pictures that elsewhere in the series would in all
likelihood have seemed abundantly convincing. Their misfortune
is to have been discounted by our intensified, our finally fatal
sense of the *procédé*. Quarrelling with all conventions, defiant of

them in general, Zola was yet inevitably to set up his own group of them — as, for that matter, without a sufficient collection, without their aid in simplifying and making possible, how could he ever have seen his big ship into port? Art welcomes them, feeds upon them always; no sort of form is practicable without them. It is only a question of what particular ones we use — to wage war on certain others and to arrive at particular forms. The convention of the blameless being, the thoroughly 'scientific' creature possessed impeccably of all truth and serving as the mouthpiece of it and of the author's highest complacencies, this character is for instance a convention inveterate and indispensable, without whom the 'sympathetic' side of the work could never have been achieved. Marc in *Vérité*, Pierre Froment in *Lourdes* and in *Rome*, the wondrous representatives of the principle of reproduction in *Fécondité*, the exemplary painter of *L'Œuvre*, sublime in his modernity and paternity, the patient Jean Macquart of *La Débâcle*, whose patience is as guaranteed as the exactitude of a well-made watch, the supremely enlightened Docteur Pascal even, as I recall him, all amorous nepotism but all virtue too and all beauty of life — such figures show us the reasonable and the good not merely in the white light of the old George Sand novel and its improved moralities, but almost in that of our childhood's nursery and schoolroom, that of the moral tale of Miss Edgeworth and Mr Thomas Day.

Yet let not these restrictions be my last word. I had intended, under the effect of a reperusal of *La Débâcle*, *Germinal* and *L'Assommoir*, to make no discriminations that should not be in our hero's favour. The long-drawn incident of the marriage of Gervaise and Cadet-Cassis and that of the Homeric birthday feast later on in the laundress's workshop, each treated from beginning to end and in every item of their coarse comedy and humanity, still show the unprecedented breadth by which they originally made us stare, still abound in the particular kind and degree of vividness that helped them, when they appeared, to mark a date in the portrayal of manners. Nothing had then been so sustained and at every moment of its grotesque and pitiful existence lived into as the nuptial day of the Coupeau pair in especial, their fantastic processional pilgrimage through the streets of Paris in the rain, their bedraggled exploration of the halls of the Louvre museum, lost as in the labyrinth of Crete, and their arrival at last, ravenous and exasperated, at the *guinguette* where they sup at so much a head, each paying, and where we sit down with them in the grease and the perspiration and succumb, half in sympathy, half in shame, to their monstrous pleasantries, acerbities and miseries. I have said enough of the mechanical in Zola; here in truth is, given the elements, almost insupportably the sense of life. That effect is equally in the historic chapter of the strike of the miners in *Germinal*, another of those illustrative episodes, viewed as great passages to be 'rendered', for which our author established altogether a new measure and standard of handling, a new energy and veracity, something since which the old trivialities and poverties of treatment of such aspects have become incompatible, for the novelist, with either rudimentary intelligence or rudimentary self-respect.

As for *La Débâcle*, finally, it takes its place with Tolstoy's very much more universal but very much less composed and condensed epic as an incomparably human picture of war. I have been re-reading it, I confess, with a certain timidity, the dread of perhaps impairing the deep impression received at the time of its appearance. I recall the effect it then produced on me as a really luxurious act of submission. It was early in the summer; I was in an old Italian town; the heat was oppressive, and one could but recline, in the lightest garments, in a great dim room and give one's self up. I like to think of the conditions and the emotion, which melt for me together into the memory I fear to imperil. I remember that in the glow of my admiration there was not a reserve I had ever made that I was not ready to take back. As an application of the author's system and his supreme faculty, as a triumph of what these things could do for him, how could such a performance be surpassed? The long, complex, horrific, pathetic battle, embraced, mastered, with every crash of its squadrons, every pulse of its thunder and blood resolved for us, by reflection, by communication from two of the humblest and obscurest of the military units, into immediate vision and contact, into deep human thrills of terror and pity — this bristling centre of the book was such a piece of 'doing' (to come back to our word) as could only shut our mouths. That doubtless is why a generous critic, nursing the sensation, may desire to drop for a farewell no term into the other scale. That our author was clearly great at congruous subjects — this may well be our conclusion. If the others, subjects of the private and intimate order, gave him more or less inevitably 'away', they yet left him the great distinction that the more he could be promiscuous and collective, the more even he could (to repeat my imputation) illustrate our large natural allowance of health, heartiness and grossness, the more he could strike us as penetrating and true. It was a distinction not easy to win and that his name is not likely soon to lose.

PART THREE

Novels

OUR MUTUAL FRIEND

1865

Our Mutual Friend is, to our perception, the poorest of Mr Dickens's works. And it is poor with the poverty not of momentary embarrassment, but of permanent exhaustion. It is wanting in inspiration. For the last ten years it has seemed to us that Mr Dickens has been unmistakably forcing himself. *Bleak House* was forced; *Little Dorrit* was laboured; the present work is dug out, as with a spade and pickaxe. Of course — to anticipate the usual argument — who but Dickens could have written it? Who, indeed? Who else would have established a lady in business in a novel on the admirably solid basis of her always putting on gloves and tying a handkerchief 'round her head in moments of grief, and of her habitually addressing her family with 'Peace! Hold!' It is needless to say that Mrs Reginald Wilfer is first and last the occasion of considerable true humour. When, after conducting her daughter to Mrs Boffin's carriage, in sight of all the envious neighbours, she is described as enjoying her triumph during the next quarter of an hour by airing herself on the doorstep 'in a kind of splendidly serene trance', we laugh with as uncritical a laugh as could be desired of us. We pay the same tribute to her assertions, as she narrates the glories of the society she enjoyed at her father's table, that she has known as many as three copperplate engravers exchanging the most exquisite sallies and retorts there at one time. But when to these we have added a dozen more happy examples of the humour which was exhaled from every line of Mr Dickens's earlier writings, we shall have closed the list of the merits of the work before us. To say that the conduct of the story, with all its complications, betrays a long-practised hand, is to pay no compliment worthy the author. If this were, indeed, a compliment, we should be inclined to carry it further, and congratulate him on his success in what we should call the manufacture of fiction; for in so doing we should express a feeling that has attended us throughout the book. Seldom, we reflected, had we read a book so intensely *written*, so little seen, known, or felt.

In all Mr Dickens's works the fantastic has been his great resource; and while his fancy was lively and vigorous it accomplished great things. But the fantastic, when the fancy is dead, is a very poor business. The movement of Mr Dickens's fancy in Mrs Wilfer and Mr Boffin and Lady Tippins, and the Lammles and Miss Wren, and even in Eugene Wrayburn, is, to our mind, a movement lifeless, forced, mechanical. It is the letter of his old humour without the spirit. It is hardly too much to say that every character here put before us is a mere bundle of eccentricities, animated by no principle of nature whatever. In former days there reigned in Mr Dickens's extravagances a comparative consistency; they were exaggerated statements of types that really existed. We had, perhaps, never known a Newman Noggs, nor a Pecksniff, nor a Micawber; but we had known persons of whom these figures were but the strictly logical consummation. But among the grotesque creatures who occupy the pages before us, there is not one whom we can refer to as an existing type. In all Mr Dickens's stories, indeed, the reader has been called upon, and has willingly consented, to accept a certain number of figures or creatures of pure fancy, for this was the author's poetry. He was, moreover, always repaid for his concession by a peculiar beauty or power in these exceptional characters. But he is now expected to make the same concession with a very inadequate reward. What do we get in return for accepting Miss Jenny Wren as a possible person? This young lady is the type of a certain class of characters of which Mr Dickens has made a specialty, and with which he has been accustomed to draw alternate smiles and tears, according as he pressed one spring or another. But this is very cheap merriment and very cheap pathos. Miss Jenny Wren is a poor little dwarf, afflicted, as she constantly reiterates, with a 'bad back' and 'queer legs', who makes doll's dresses, and is forever pricking at those with whom she converses, in the air, with her needle, and assuring them that she knows their 'tricks and their manners'. Like all Mr Dickens's pathetic characters, she is a little monster; she is deformed, unhealthy, unnatural; she belongs to the troop of hunchbacks, imbeciles, and precocious children who have carried on the sentimental business in all Mr Dickens's novels; the little Nells, the Smikes, the Paul Dombeys.

Mr Dickens goes as far out of the way for his wicked people as he does for his good ones. Rogue Riderhood, indeed, in the present story, is villainous with a sufficiently natural villainy; he belongs to that quarter of society in which the author is most at his ease. But was there ever such wickedness as that of the Lammles and Mr Fledgeby? Not that people have not been as mischievous as they; but was any one ever mischievous in that singular fashion? Did a couple of elegant swindlers ever take such particular pains to be aggressively inhuman? — for we can find no other word for the gratuitous distortions to which they are subjected. The word *humanity* strikes us as strangely discordant, in the midst of these pages; for, let us boldly declare it, there is no humanity here. Humanity is nearer home than the Boffins, and the Lammles, and the Wilfers, and the Veneerings. It is in what men have in common with each other, and not in what they have in distinction. The people just named have nothing in common with each other, except the fact that they have nothing in common with mankind at large. What a world were this world if the world of *Our Mutual Friend* were an honest reflection of it! But a community of eccentrics is impossible. Rules alone are consistent with each other; exceptions are inconsistent. Society is maintained by natural sense and natural feeling. We cannot conceive a society in which these principles are not in some manner represented. Where in these pages are the depositaries of that intelligence without which the movement of life would cease? Who represents nature? Accepting half of Mr Dickens's persons as intentionally grotesque, where are those exemplars of sound humanity who should afford us the proper measure of their companion's variations? We ought not, in justice to the author, to seek them among his weaker — that is, his mere conventional — characters; in John Harmon,

Lizzie Hexam, or Mortimer Lightwood; but we assuredly cannot find them among his stronger — that is, his artificial creations. Suppose we take Eugene Wrayburn and Bradley Headstone. They occupy a half-way position between the habitual probable of nature and the habitual impossible of Mr Dickens. A large portion of the story rests upon the enmity borne by Headstone to Wrayburn, both being in love with the same woman. Wrayburn is a gentleman, and Headstone is one of the people. Wrayburn is well-bred, careless, elegant, sceptical, and idle: Headstone is a high-tempered, hard-working, ambitious young school-master. There lay in the opposition of these two characters a very good story. But the prime requisite was that they should *be* characters: Mr Dickens, according to his usual plan, has made them simply figures, and between them the story that was to be, the story that should have been, has evaporated. Wrayburn lounges about with his hands in his pockets, smoking a cigar, and talking nonsense. Headstone strides about, clenching his fists and biting his lips and grasping his stick. There is one scene in which Wrayburn chaffs the schoolmaster with easy insolence, while the latter writhes impotently under his well-bred sarcasm. This scene is very clever, but it is very insufficient. If the majority of readers were not so very timid in the use of words we should call it vulgar. By this we do not mean to indicate the conventional impropriety of two gentlemen exchanging lively personalities; we mean to emphasize the essentially small character of these personalities. In other words, the moment, dramatically, is great, while the author's conception is weak. The friction of two *men*, of two characters, of two passions, produces stronger sparks than Wrayburn's boyish repartees and Headstone's melodramatic commonplaces. Such scenes as this are useful in fixing the limits of Mr Dickens's insight. Insight is, perhaps, too strong a word; for we are convinced that it is one of the chief conditions of his genius not to see beneath the surface of things. If we might hazard a definition of his literary character, we should, accordingly, call him the greatest of superficial novelists. We are aware that this definition confines him to an inferior rank in the department of letters which he adorns; but we accept this consequence of our proposition. It were, in our opinion, an offence against humanity to place Mr Dickens among the greatest novelists. For, to repeat what we have already intimated, he has created nothing but figures. He has added nothing to our understanding of human character. He is master of but two alternatives: he reconciles us to what is commonplace, and he reconciles us to what is odd. The value of the former service is questionable; and the manner in which Mr Dickens performs it sometimes conveys a certain impression of charlatanism. The value of the latter service is incontestable, and here Mr Dickens is an honest, an admirable artist. But what is the condition of the truly great novelist? For him there are no alternatives, for him there are no oddities, for him there is nothing outside of humanity. He cannot shirk it; it imposes itself upon him. For him alone, therefore, there is a true and a false; for him alone it is possible to be right, because it is possible to be wrong. Mr Dickens is a great observer and a great humorist, but he is nothing of a philosopher. Some people may hereupon say, so much the better; we say, so much the worse. For a novelist very soon has need of a little philosophy. In treating of Micawber, and Boffin, and Pickwick, *et hoc genus omne*, he can, indeed, dispense with it, for this — we say it with all deference — is not serious writing. But when he comes to tell the story of a passion, a story like that of Headstone and Wrayburn, he becomes a moralist as well as an artist. He must know *man* as well as *men*, and to know man is to be a philosopher. The writer who knows men alone, if he have Mr Dickens's humour and fancy, will give us figures and pictures for which we cannot be too grateful, for he will enlarge our knowledge of the world. But when he introduces men and women whose interest is preconceived to lie not in the poverty, the weakness, the drollery of their natures, but in their complete and unconscious subjection to ordinary and healthy human emotions, all his humour, all his fancy, will avail him nothing if, out of the fullness of his sympathy, he is unable to prosecute those generalizations in which alone consists the real greatness of a work of art. This may sound like very subtle talk about a very simple matter; it is rather very simple talk about a very subtle matter. A story based upon those elementary passions in which alone we seek the true and final manifestation of character must be told in a spirit of intellectual superiority to those passions. That is, the author must understand what he is talking about. The perusal of a story so told is one of the most elevating experiences within the reach of the human mind. The perusal of a story which is not so told is infinitely depressing and unprofitable.

MIDDLEMARCH

1873

Middlemarch is at once one of the strongest and one of the weakest of English novels. Its predecessors as they appeared might have been described in the same terms; *Romola* is especially a rare masterpiece, but the least *entraînant* of masterpieces. *Romola* sins by excess of analysis; there is too much description and too little drama; too much reflection (all certainly of a highly imaginative sort) and too little creation. Movement lingers in the story, and with it attention stands still in the reader. The error in *Middlemarch* is not precisely of a similar kind, but it is equally detrimental to the total aspect of the work. We can well remember how keenly we wondered, while its earlier chapters unfolded themselves, what turn in the way of form the story would take — that of an organized, moulded, balanced composition, gratifying the reader with a sense of design and construction, or a mere chain of episodes, broken into accidental lengths and unconscious of the influence of a plan. We expected the actual result, but for the sake of English imaginative literature which, in this line is rarely in need of examples, we hoped for the other. If it had come we should have had the pleasure of reading, what certainly would have seemed to us in the immediate glow of attention, the first of English novels. But that pleasure has still to hover between prospect and retrospect. *Middlemarch* is a treasure-house of detail, but it is an indifferent whole.

Our objection may seem shallow and pedantic, and may even be represented as a complaint that we have had the less given us rather than the more. Certainly the greatest minds have the defects of their qualities, and as George Eliot's mind is preëminently contemplative and analytic, nothing is more natural than that her manner should be discursive and expansive. 'Concentration'

would doubtless have deprived us of many of the best things in
the book — of Peter Featherstone's grotesquely expectant lega-
tees, of Lydgate's medical rivals, and of Mary Garth's delightful
family. The author's purpose was to be a generous rural historian,
and this very redundancy of touch, born of abundant reminiscence, is one of the greatest charms of her work. It is as if her
memory was crowded with antique figures, to whom for very
tenderness she must grant an appearance. Her novel is a picture
— vast, swarming, deep-coloured, crowded with episodes, with
vivid images, with lurking master-strokes, with brilliant passages
of expression; and as such we may freely accept it and enjoy it. It
is not compact, doubtless; but when was a panorama compact?
And yet, nominally, *Middlemarch* has a definite subject — the
subject indicated in the eloquent preface. An ardent young girl
was to have been the central figure, a young girl framed for a
larger moral life than circumstance often affords, yearning for a
motive for sustained spiritual effort and only wasting her ardour
and soiling her wings against the meanness of opportunity. The
author, in other words, proposed to depict the career of an obscure St Theresa. Her success has been great, in spite of serious
drawbacks. Dorothea Brooke is a genuine creation, and a most
remarkable one when we consider the delicate material in which
she is wrought. George Eliot's men are generally so much better
than the usual trousered offspring of the female fancy, that their
merits have perhaps overshadowed those of her women. Yet her
heroines have always been of an exquisite quality, and Dorothea
is only that perfect flower of conception of which her predecessors
were the less unfolded blossoms. An indefinable moral elevation
is the sign of these admirable creatures; and of the representation
of this quality in its superior degrees the author seems to have in
English fiction a monopoly. To render the expression of a soul
requires a cunning hand; but we seem to look straight into the unfathomable eyes of the beautiful spirit of Dorothea Brooke. She
exhales a sort of aroma of spiritual sweetness, and we believe in
her as in a woman we might providentially meet some fine day
when we should find ourselves doubting of the immortality of

the soul. By what unerring mechanism this effect is produced —
whether by fine strokes or broad ones, by description or by narration, we can hardly say; it is certainly the great achievement of the
book. Dorothea's career is, however, but an episode, and though
doubtless in intention, not distinctly enough in fact, the central
one. The history of Lydgate's *ménage*, which shares honours with
it, seems rather to the reader to carry off the lion's share. This is
certainly a very interesting story, but on the whole it yields in
dignity to the record of Dorothea's unresonant woes. The 'love-
problem', as the author calls it, of Mary Garth, is placed on a
rather higher level than the reader willingly grants it. To the end
we care less about Fred Vincy than appears to be expected of us.
In so far as the writer's design has been to reproduce the total
sum of life in an English village forty years ago, this common-
place young gentleman, with his somewhat meagre tribulations
and his rather neutral egotism, has his proper place in the picture;
but the author narrates his fortunes with a fullness of detail which
the reader often finds irritating. The reader indeed is sometimes
tempted to complain of a tendency which we are at loss exactly to
express — a tendency to make light of the serious elements of the
story and to sacrifice them to the more trivial ones. Is it an unconscious instinct or is it a deliberate plan? With its abundant and
massive ingredients *Middlemarch* ought somehow to have depicted a weightier drama. Dorothea was altogether too superb a
heroine to be wasted; yet she plays a narrower part than the imagination of the reader demands. She is of more consequence than
the action of which she is the nominal centre. She marries enthusi-
astically a man whom she fancies a great thinker, and who turns
out to be but an arid pedant. Here, indeed, is a disappointment
with much of the dignity of tragedy; but the situation seems to us
never to expand to its full capacity. It is analysed with extraordinary penetration, but one may say of it, as of most of the
situations in the book, that it is treated with too much refinement
and too little breadth. It revolves too constantly on the same
pivot; it abounds in fine shades, but it lacks, we think, the great
dramatic *chiaroscuro*. Mr Casaubon, Dorothea's husband (of

whom more anon) embittered, on his side, by matrimonial disappointment, takes refuge in vain jealousy of his wife's relations
with an interesting young cousin of his own and registers this
sentiment in a codicil to his will, making the forfeiture of his
property the penalty of his widow's marriage with this gentleman. Mr Casaubon's death befalls about the middle of the story,
and from this point to the close our interest in Dorothea is restricted to the question, will she or will [she] not marry Will
Ladislaw? The question is relatively trivial and the implied
struggle slightly factitious. The author has depicted the struggle
with a sort of elaborate solemnity which in the interviews related
in the two last books tends to become almost ludicrously excessive.
The dramatic current stagnates; it runs between hero and heroine almost a game of hair-splitting. Our dissatisfaction here is pro-
voked in a great measure by the insubstantial character of the
hero. The figure of Will Ladislaw is a beautiful attempt, with
many finely completed points; but on the whole it seems to us a
failure. It is the only eminent failure in the book, and its defects
are therefore the more striking. It lacks sharpness of outline and
depth of colour; we have not found ourselves believing in Ladislaw as we believe in Dorothea, in Mary Garth, in Rosamond, in
Lydgate, in Mr Brooke and Mr Casaubon. He is meant, indeed, to
be a light creature (with a large capacity for gravity, for he finally
gets into Parliament), and a light creature certainly should not be
heavily drawn. The author, who is evidently very fond of him,
has found for him here and there some charming and eloquent
touches; but in spite of these he remains vague and impalpable to
the end. He is, we may say, the one figure which a masculine
intellect of the same power as George Eliot's would not have conceived with the same complacency; he is, in short, roughly speaking, a woman's man. It strikes us as an oddity in the author's
scheme that she should have chosen just this figure of Ladislaw as
the creature in whom Dorothea was to find her spiritual com-
pensations. He is really, after all, not the ideal foil to Mr Casaubon
which her soul must have imperiously demanded, and if the
author of the *Key to all Mythologies* sinned by lack of order,

Ladislaw too has not the concentrated fervour essential in the man chosen by so nobly strenuous a heroine. The impression once given that he is a *dilettante* is never properly removed, and there is slender poetic justice in Dorothea's marrying a *dilettante*. We are doubtless less content with Ladislaw, on account of the noble, almost sculptural, relief of the neighbouring figure of Lydgate, the real hero of the story. It is an illustration of the generous scale of the author's picture and of the conscious power of her imagination that she has given us a hero and heroine of broadly distinct interests — erected, as it were, two suns in her firmament, each with its independent solar system. Lydgate is so richly successful a figure that we have regretted strongly at moments, for immediate interests' sake, that the current of his fortunes should not mingle more freely with the occasionally thin-flowing stream of Dorothea's. Toward the close, these two fine characters are brought into momentary contact so effectively as to suggest a wealth of dramatic possibility between them; but if this train had been followed we should have lost Rosamond Vincy — a rare psychological study. Lydgate is a really complete portrait of a *man*, which seems to us high praise. It is striking evidence of the altogether superior quality of George Eliot's imagination that, though elaborately represented, Lydgate should be treated so little from what we may roughly (and we trust without offence) call the sexual point of view. Perception charged with feeling has constantly guided the author's hand, and yet her strokes remain as firm, her curves as free, her whole manner as serenely impersonal, as if, on a small scale, she were emulating the creative wisdom itself. Several English romancers — notably Fielding, Thackeray, and Charles Reade — have won great praise for their figures of women: but they owe it, in reversed conditions, to a meaner sort of art, it seems to us, than George Eliot has used in the case of Lydgate; to an indefinable appeal to masculine prejudice — to a sort of titillation of the masculine sense of difference. George Eliot's manner is more philosophic — more broadly intelligent, and yet her result is as concrete or, if you please, as picturesque. We have no space to dwell on Lydgate's character;

we can but repeat that he is a vividly consistent, manly figure — powerful, ambitious, sagacious, with the maximum rather than the minimum of egotism, strenuous, generous, fallible, and altogether human. A work of the liberal scope of *Middlemarch* contains a multitude of artistic intentions, some of the finest of which become clear only in the meditative after-taste of perusal. This is the case with the balanced contrast between the two histories of Lydgate and Dorothea. Each is a tale of matrimonial infelicity, but the conditions in each are so different and the circumstances so broadly opposed that the mind passes from one to the other with that supreme sense of the vastness and variety of human life, under aspects apparently similar, which it belongs only to the greatest novels to produce. The most perfectly successful passages in the book are perhaps those painful fireside scenes between Lydgate and his miserable little wife. The author's rare psychological penetration is lavished upon this veritably mulish domestic flower. There is nothing more powerfully real than these scenes in all English fiction, and nothing certainly more *intelligent*. Their impressiveness and (as regards Lydgate) their pathos, is deepened by the constantly low key in which they are pitched. It is a tragedy based on unpaid butchers' bills, and the urgent need for small economies. The author has desired to be strictly real and to adhere to the facts of the common lot, and she has given us a powerful version of that typical human drama, the struggles of an ambitious soul with sordid disappointments and vulgar embarrassments. As to her catastrophe we hesitate to pronounce (for Lydgate's ultimate assent to his wife's worldly programme is nothing less than a catastrophe). We almost believe that some terrific explosion would have been more probable than his twenty years of smothered aspiration. Rosamond deserves almost to rank with Tito in *Romola* as a study of a gracefully vicious, or at least of a practically baleful nature. There is one point, however, of which we question the consistency. The author insists on her instincts of coquetry, which seems to us a discordant note. They would have made her better or worse — more generous or more reckless; in either case more manageable. As it is, Rosamond represents, in a measure, the fatality of British decorum.

In reading, we have marked innumerable passages for quotation and comment; but we lack space and the work is so ample that half a dozen extracts would be an ineffective illustration. There would be a great deal to say on the broad array of secondary figures, Mr Casaubon, Mr Brooke, Mr Bulstrode, Mr Farebrother, Caleb Garth, Mrs Cadwallader, Celia Brooke. Mr Casaubon is an excellent invention; as a dusky *repoussoir* to the luminous figure of his wife he could not have been better imagined. There is indeed something very noble in the way in which the author has apprehended his character. To depict hollow pretentiousness and mouldy egotism with so little of narrow sarcasm and so much of philosophic sympathy, is to be a rare moralist as well as a rare story-teller. The whole portrait of Mr Casaubon has an admirably sustained grayness of tone in which the shadows are never carried to the vulgar black of coarser artists. Every stroke contributes to the unwholesome, helplessly sinister expression. Here and there perhaps (as in his habitual diction), there is a hint of exaggeration; but we confess we like fancy to be fanciful. Mr Brooke and Mr Garth are in their different lines supremely genial creations; they are drawn with the touch of a Dickens chastened and intellectualized. Mrs Cadwallader is, in another walk of life, a match for Mrs Poyser, and Celia Brooke is as pretty a fool as any of Miss Austen's. Mr Farebrother and his delightful 'womankind' belong to a large group of figures begotten of the superabundance of the author's creative instinct. At times they seem to encumber the stage and to produce a rather ponderous mass of dialogue; but they add to the reader's impression of having walked in the Middlemarch lanes and listened to the Middlemarch accent. To but one of these accessory episodes — that of Mr Bulstrode, with its multiplex ramifications — do we take exception. It has a slightly artificial cast, a melodramatic tinge, unfriendly to the richly natural colouring of the whole. Bulstrode himself — with the history of whose troubled conscience the author has taken great pains — is, to our sense, too diffusely treated; he never grasps

the reader's attention. But the touch of genius is never idle or
vain. The obscure figure of Bulstrode's comely wife emerges at
the needful moment, under a few light strokes, into the happiest
reality.

All these people, solid and vivid in their varying degrees, are
members of a deeply human little world, the full reflection of
whose antique image is the great merit of these volumes. How
bravely rounded a little world the author has made it — with how
dense an atmosphere of interests and passions and loves and enmi-
ties and strivings and failings, and how motley a group of great
folk and small, all after their kind, she has filled it, the reader must
learn for himself. No writer seems to us to have drawn from a
richer stock of those long-cherished memories which one's later
philosophy makes doubly tender. There are few figures in the
book which do not seem to have grown mellow in the author's
mind. English readers may fancy they enjoy the 'atmosphere' of
Middlemarch; but we maintain that to relish its inner essence we
must — for reasons too numerous to detail — be an American.
The author has commissioned herself to be real, her native tendency being that of an idealist, and the intellectual result is a very
fertilizing mixture. The constant presence of thought, of generalizing instinct, of *brain*, in a word, behind her observation, gives
the latter its great value and her whole manner its high superiority.
It denotes a mind in which imagination is illumined by faculties
rarely found in fellowship with it. In this respect — in that broad
reach of vision which would make the worthy historian of solemn
fact as well as wanton fiction — George Eliot seems to us among
English romancers to stand alone. Fielding approaches her, but to
our mind, she surpasses Fielding. Fielding was didactic — the
author of *Middlemarch* is really philosophic. These great qualities
imply corresponding perils. The first is the loss of simplicity.
George Eliot lost hers some time since; it lies buried (in a splendid
mausoleum) in *Romola*. Many of the discursive portions of *Middlemarch* are, as we may say, too clever by half. The author wishes
to say too many things, and to say them too well; to recommend
herself to a scientific audience. Her style, rich and flexible as it is,

is apt to betray her on these transcendental flights; we find, in our copy, a dozen passages marked 'obscure'. *Silas Marner* was a delightful tinge of Goldsmith — we may almost call it: *Middlemarch* is too often an echo of Messrs Darwin and Huxley. In spite of these faults — which it seems graceless to indicate with this crude rapidity — it remains a very splendid performance. It sets a limit, we think, to the development of the old-fashioned English novel. Its diffuseness, on which we have touched, makes it too copious a dose of pure fiction. If we write novels so, how shall we write History? But it is nevertheless a contribution of the first importance to the rich imaginative department of our literature.

FAR FROM THE MADDING CROWD

1874

MR HARDY'S novel came into the world under brilliant auspices — such as the declaration by the London *Spectator* that either George Eliot had written it or George Eliot had found her match. One could make out in a manner what the *Spectator* meant. To guess, one has only to open *Far from the Madding Crowd* at random: 'Mr Jan Coggan, who had passed the soup to Henery, was a crimson man with a spacious countenance and a private glimmer in his eye, whose name had appeared on the marriage register of Weatherbury and neighbouring parishes as best-man and chief witness in countless unions of the previous twenty years; he also very frequently filled the post of head godfather in baptisms of the subtly-jovial kind.' That is a very fair imitation of George Eliot's humorous manner. Here is a specimen of her serious one: 'He fancied he had felt himself in the penumbra of a very deep sadness when touching that slight and fragile creature. But wisdom lies in moderating mere impressions, and Gabriel endeavoured to think little of this.' But the *Spectator's* theory had an even broader base, and we may profitably quote a passage which perhaps constituted one of its solidest blocks. The author of *Silas Marner* has won no small part of her fame by her remarkable faculty as a reporter of ale-house and kitchen-fire conversations among simple-minded rustics. Mr Hardy has also made a great effort in this direction, and here is a specimen — a particularly favourable specimen — of his success:

'Why, Joseph Poorgrass, you han't had a drop!' said Mr Coggan to a very shrinking man in the background, thrusting the cup towards him.

'Such a shy man as he is,' said Jacob Smallbury. 'Why, ye've hardly had strength of eye enough to look in our young mis'ess's face, so I hear, Joseph?'

All looked at Joseph Poorgrass with pitying reproach.

'No, I've hardly looked at her at all', faltered Joseph, reducing his body smaller while talking, apparently from a meek sense of undue prominence; 'and when I see'd her, it was nothing but blushes with me!'

'Poor fellow,' said Mr Clark.

' 'Tis a curious nature for a man,' said Jan Coggan.

'Yes,' continued Joseph Poorgrass, his shyness, which was so painful as a defect, just beginning to fill him with a little complacency, now that it was regarded in the light of an interesting study. ' 'Twere blush, blush, blush with me every minute of the time when she was speaking to me.'

'I believe ye, Joseph Poorgrass, for we all know ye to be a very bashful man.'

' 'Tis terrible bad for a man, poor soul!' said the maltster. 'And how long have ye suffered from it, Joseph?'

'Oh, ever since I was a boy. Yes — mother was concerned to her heart about it — yes. But 'twas all naught.'

'Did ye ever take anything to try and stop it, Joseph Poorgrass?'

'Oh, aye, tried all sorts. They took me to Greenhill Fair, and into a great large jerry-go-nimble show, where there were women-folk riding round — standing up on horses, with hardly anything on but their smocks; but it didn't cure me a morsel — no, not a morsel. And then I was put errand-man at the Woman's Skittle Alley at the back of the Tailor's Arms in Casterbridge. 'Twas a horrible gross situation, and altogether a very curious place for a good man. I had to stand and look at wicked people in the face from morning till night; but 'twas no use — I was just as bad as ever after all. Blushes have been in the family for generations. There, 'tis a happy providence I be no worse, so to speak it — yes, a happy thing, and I feel my few poor gratitudes.'

This is extremely clever, and the author has evidently read to good purpose the low-life chapters in George Eliot's novels; he has caught very happily her trick of seeming to humour benignantly her queer people and look down at them from the heights of analytic omniscience. But we have quoted the episode because it seems to us an excellent example of the cleverness which is only cleverness, of the difference between original and imitative talent — the disparity, which it is almost unpardonable not to perceive, between first-rate talent and those inferior grades which range from second-rate downward, and as to which confusion is a more venial offence. Mr Hardy puts his figures through a variety of comical movements; he fills their mouths with quaint turns of speech; he baptizes them with odd names ('Joseph Poorgrass' for a bashful, easily-snubbed Dissenter is excellent); he pulls the wires, in short, and produces a vast deal of sound and commotion; and his novel, at a cursory glance, has a rather promising air of life and warmth. But by critics who prefer a grain of substance to a pound of shadow it will, we think, be pronounced a decidedly delusive performance; it has a fatal lack of magic. We have found it hard to read, but its shortcomings are easier to summarize than to encounter in order. Mr Hardy's novel is very long, but his subject is very short and simple, and the work has been distended to its rather formidable dimensions by the infusion of a large amount of conversational and descriptive padding and the use of an ingeniously verbose and redundant style. It is inordinately diffuse, and, as a piece of narrative, singularly inartistic. The author has little sense of proportion, and almost none of composition. We learn about Bathsheba and Gabriel, Farmer Boldwood and Sergeant Troy, what we can rather than what we should; for Mr Hardy's inexhaustible faculty for spinning smart dialogue makes him forget that dialogue in a story is after all but episode, and that a novelist is after all but a historian, thoroughly possessed of certain facts, and bound in some way or other to impart them. To tell a story almost exclusively by reporting people's talks is the most difficult art in the world, and really leads, logically, to a severe economy in the use of rejoinder and repartee, and not to a lavish expenditure of them. *Far from the Madding Crowd* gives us an uncomfortable sense of being a simple 'tale', pulled and stretched to make the conventional three volumes; and the author, in his long-sustained appeal to one's attention, reminds us of a person fishing with an enormous net, of which the meshes should be thrice too wide.

We are happily not subject, in this (as to minor matters) much-emancipated land, to the tyranny of the three volumes; but we confess that we are nevertheless being rapidly urged to a conviction that (since it is in the nature of fashions to revolve and recur) the day has come round again for some of the antique restrictions as to literary form. The three unities, in Aristotle's day, were inexorably imposed on Greek tragedy: why shouldn't we have something of the same sort for English fiction in the day of Mr Hardy? Almost all novels are greatly too long, and the being too long becomes with each elapsing year a more serious offence. Mr Hardy begins with a detailed description of his hero's smile, and proceeds thence to give a voluminous account of his large silver watch. Gabriel Oak's smile and his watch were doubtless respectable and important phenomena; but everything is relative, and daily becoming more so; and we confess that, as a hint of the pace at which the author proposed to proceed, his treatment of these facts produced upon us a deterring and depressing effect. If novels were the only books written, novels written on this scale would be all very well; but as they compete, in the esteem of sensible people, with a great many other books, and a great many other objects of interest of all kinds, we are inclined to think that, in the long run, they will be defeated in the struggle for existence unless they lighten their baggage very considerably and do battle in a more scientific equipment. Therefore, we really imagine that a few arbitrary rules — a kind of depleting process — might have a wholesome effect. It might be enjoined, for instance, that no 'tale' should exceed fifty pages and no novel two hundred; that a plot should have but such and such a number of ramifications; that no ramification should have more than a certain number of persons; that no person should utter more than a given number of words; and that no description of an inanimate object should consist of more than a fixed number of lines. We should not incline to advocate this oppressive legislation as a comfortable or ideal finality for the romancer's art, but we think it might be excellent as a transitory discipline or drill. Necessity is the mother of invention, and writers with a powerful tendency to expatiation might in this temporary strait-jacket be induced to transfer their attention rather more severely from quantity to quality. The use of the strait-jacket would have cut down Mr Hardy's novel to half its actual length and, as he is a clever man, have made the abbreviated work very ingeniously pregnant. We should have had a more occasional taste of all the barn-yard worthies — Joseph Poor-grass, Laban Tall, Matthew Moon, and the rest — and the vaga-ries of Miss Bathsheba would have had a more sensible consistency. Our restrictions would have been generous, however, and we should not have proscribed such a fine passage as this:

Then there came a third flash. Manoeuvres of the most extraordinary kind were going on in the vast firmamental hollows overhead. The lightning now was the colour of silver, and gleamed in the heavens like a mailed army. Rumbles became rattles. Gabriel, from his elevated posi-tion, could see over the landscape for at least half a dozen miles in front. Every hedge, bush, and tree was distinct as in a line engraving. In a paddock in the same direction was a herd of heifers, and the forms of these were visible at this moment in the act of galloping about in the wildest and maddest confusion, flinging their heels and tails high into the air, their heads to earth. A poplar in the immediate foreground was like an ink-stroke on burnished tin. Then the picture vanished, leaving a darkness so intense that Gabriel worked entirely by feeling with his hands.

Mr Hardy describes nature with a great deal of felicity, and is evidently very much at home among rural phenomena. The most genuine thing in his book, to our sense, is a certain aroma of the meadows and lanes — a natural relish for harvestings and sheep-washings. He has laid his scene in an agricultural county, and his characters are children of the soil — unsophisticated country-folk. Bathsheba Everdene is a rural heiress, left alone in the world, in possession of a substantial farm. Gabriel Oak is her shepherd, Farmer Boldwood is her neighbour, and Sergeant Troy is a loose young soldier who comes a-courting her. They are all in love with her, and the young lady is a flirt, and encourages them all. Finally she marries the Sergeant, who has just seduced her maid-servant. The maid-servant dies in the work-house, the Sergeant repents, leaves his wife, and is given up for drowned. But he re-appears and is shot by Farmer Boldwood, who delivers himself up to justice. Bathsheba then marries Gabriel Oak, who has loved and waited in silence, and is, in our opinion, much too good for her. The chief purpose of the book is, we suppose, to represent Gabriel's dumb, devoted passion, his biding his time, his rendering unsuspected services to the woman who has scorned him, his integrity and simplicity and sturdy patience. In all this the tale is very fairly successful, and Gabriel has a certain vividness of expression. But we cannot say that we either understand or like Bathsheba. She is a young lady of the inconsequential, wilful, mettlesome type which has lately become so much the fashion for heroines, and of which Mr Charles Reade is in a manner the inventor — the type which aims at giving one a very intimate sense of a young lady's *womanishness*. But Mr Hardy's embodiment of it seems to us to lack reality; he puts her through the Charles Reade paces, but she remains alternately vague and coarse, and seems always artificial. This is Mr Hardy's trouble; he rarely gets beyond ambitious artifice — the mechanical simulation of heat and depth and wisdom that are absent. Farmer Boldwood is a shadow, and Sergeant Troy an elaborate stage-figure. Everything human in the book strikes us as factitious and insubstantial; the only things we believe in are the sheep and the dogs. But, as we say, Mr Hardy has gone astray very cleverly, and his superficial novel is a really curious imitation of something better.

NANA

1880

M. ZOLA'S new novel has been immensely talked about for the last six months; but we may doubt whether, now that we are in complete possession of it, its fame will further increase. It is a difficult book to read; we have to push our way through it very much as we did through *L'Assommoir*, with the difference that in *L'Assommoir* our perseverance, our patience, were constantly rewarded, and that in *Nana*, these qualities have to content themselves with the usual recompense of virtue, the simple sense of duty accomplished. I do not mean, indeed, by this allusion to duty that there is any moral obligation to read *Nana*; I simply mean that such an exertion may have been felt to be due to M. Zola by those who have been interested in his general attempt. His general attempt is highly interesting, and *Nana* is the latest illustration of it. It is far from being the most successful one; the obstacles to the reader's enjoyment are numerous and constant. It is true that, if we rightly understand him, enjoyment forms no part of the emotion to which M. Zola appeals; in the eyes of 'naturalism' enjoyment is a frivolous, a superficial, a contemptible sentiment. It is difficult, however, to express conveniently by any other term the reader's measure of the entertainment afforded by a work of art. If we talk of interest, instead of enjoyment, the thing does not better our case — as it certainly does not better M. Zola's. The obstacles to interest in *Nana* constitute a formidable body, and the most comprehensive way to express them is to say that the work is inconceivably and inordinately dull. M. Zola (if we again understand him) will probably say that it is a privilege, or even a duty, of naturalism to be dull, and to a certain extent this is doubtless a very lawful plea. It is not an absolutely fatal defect for a novel not to be amusing, as we may see by the

274

example of several important works. *Wilhelm Meister* is not a
sprightly composition, and yet *Wilhelm Meister* stands in the
front rank of novels. *Romola* is a very easy book to lay down, and
yet *Romola* is full of beauty and truth. *Clarissa Harlowe* dis-
courages the most robust persistence, and yet, paradoxical as it
seems, *Clarissa Harlowe* is deeply interesting. It is obvious, therefore, that there is something to be said for dullness; and this something is perhaps, primarily, that there is dullness and dullness.
That of which *Nana* is so truly a specimen, is of a peculiarly un-
redeemed and unleavened quality; it lacks that human savour,
that finer meaning which carries it off in the productions I just
mentioned. What *Nana* means it will take a very ingenious apolo-
gist to set forth. I speak, of course, of the impression it produces
on English readers; into the deep mystery of the French taste in
such matters it would be presumptuous for one of these to attempt
to penetrate. The other element that stops the English reader's
way is that monstrous uncleanness to which — to the credit of
human nature in whatever degree it may seem desirable to determine — it is probably not unjust to attribute a part of the facility
with which the volume before us has reached, on the day of its
being offered for sale by retail, a thirty-ninth edition. M. Zola's
uncleanness is not a thing to linger upon, but it is a thing to speak
of, for it strikes us as an extremely curious phenomenon. In this
respect *Nana* has little to envy its predecessors. The book is, perhaps, not pervaded by that ferociously bad smell which blows
through *L'Assommoir* like an emanation from an open drain and
makes the perusal of the history of Gervaise and Coupeau very
much such an ordeal as a crossing of the Channel in a November
gale; but in these matters comparisons are as difficult as they are
unprofitable, and *Nana* is, in all conscience, untidy enough. To
say the book is indecent, is to make use of a term which (always,
if we understand him,) M. Zola holds to mean nothing and to
prove nothing. Decency and indecency, morality and immorality,
beauty and ugliness, are conceptions with which 'naturalism' has
nothing to do; in M. Zola's system these distinctions are void,
these allusions are idle. The only business of naturalism is to be

— natural, and therefore, instead of saying of *Nana* that it contains a great deal of filth, we should simply say of it that it contains a great deal of nature. Once upon a time a rather pretentious person, whose moral tone had been corrupted by evil communications, and who lived among a set of people equally pretentious, but regrettably low-minded, being in conversation with another person, a lady of great robustness of judgment and directness of utterance, made use constantly, in a somewhat cynical and pessimistic sense, of the expression, 'the world — the world'. At last the distinguished listener could bear it no longer, and abruptly made reply: 'My poor lady, do you call that corner of a pig-sty in which you happen to live, *the world*?' Some such answer as this we are moved to make to M. Zola's naturalism. Does he call that vision of things of which *Nana* is a representation, *nature*? The mighty mother, in her blooming richness, seems to blush from brow to chin at the insult! On what authority does M. Zola represent nature to us as a combination of the cesspool and the house of prostitution? On what authority does he represent foulness rather than fairness as the sign that we are to know her by? On the authority of his predilections alone; and this is his great trouble and the weak point of his incontestably remarkable talent. This is the point that, as we said just now, makes the singular foulness of his imagination worth touching upon, and which, we should suppose, will do much towards preserving his works for the curious contemplation of the psychologist and the historian of literature. Never was such foulness so spontaneous and so complete, and never was it united with qualities so superior to itself and intrinsically so respectable. M. Zola is an artist, and this is supposed to be a safeguard; and, indeed, never surely was any other artist so dirty as M. Zola! Other performers may have been so, but they were not artists; other such exhibitions may have taken place, but they have not taken place between the covers of a book — and especially of a book containing so much of vigorous and estimable effort. We have no space to devote to a general consideration of M. Zola's theory of the business of a novelist, or to the question of naturalism at large — much further than to say that the system on which the series of *Les Rougons-Macquart* has been written, contains, to our sense, a great deal of very solid ground. M. Zola's attempt is an extremely fine one; it deserves a great deal of respect and deference, and though his theory is constantly at odds with itself, we could, at a pinch, go a long way with it without quarrelling. What we quarrel with is his application of it — is the fact that he presents us with his decoction of 'nature' in a vessel unfit for the purpose, a receptacle lamentably, fatally in need of scouring (though no scouring, apparently, would be really effective), and in which no article intended for intellectual consumption should ever be served up. Reality is the object of M. Zola's efforts, and it is because we agree with him in appreciating it highly that we protest against its being discredited. In a time when literary taste has turned, to a regrettable degree, to the vulgar and the insipid, it is of high importance that realism should not be compromised. Nothing tends more to compromise it than to represent it as necessarily allied to the impure. That the pure and the impure are for M. Zola, as conditions of taste, vain words, and exploded ideas, only proves that his advocacy does more to injure an excellent cause than to serve it. It takes a very good cause to carry a *Nana* on its back, and if realism breaks down, and the conventional comes in again with a rush, we may know the reason why. The real has not a single shade more affinity with an unclean vessel than with a clean one, and M. Zola's system, carried to its utmost expression, can dispense as little with taste and tact as the floweriest mannerism of a less analytic age. Go as far as we will, so long as we abide in literature, the thing remains always a question of taste, and we can never leave taste behind without leaving behind, by the same stroke, the very grounds on which we appeal, the whole human side of the business. Taste, in its intellectual applications, is the most human faculty we possess, and as the novel may be said to be the most human form of art, it is a poor speculation to put the two things out of conceit of each other. Calling it naturalism will never make it profitable. It is perfectly easy to agree with M. Zola, who has taken his stand with more emphasis than is necessary; for the matter reduces itself to a question of application. It is impossible to see why the question of application is less urgent in naturalism than at any other point of the scale, or why, if naturalism is, as M. Zola claims, a method of observation, it can be followed without delicacy or tact. There are all sorts of things to be said about it; it costs us no effort whatever to admit in the briefest terms that it is an admirable invention, and full of promise; but we stand aghast at the want of tact it has taken to make so unreadable a book as *Nana*.

To us English readers, I venture to think, the subject is very interesting, because it raises questions which no one apparently has the energy or the good faith to raise among ourselves. (It is of distinctly serious readers only that I speak, and *Nana* is to be recommended exclusively to such as have a very robust appetite for a moral.) A novelist with a system, a passionate conviction, a great plan — incontestable attributes of M. Zola — is not now to be easily found in England or the United States, where the storyteller's art is almost exclusively feminine, is mainly in the hands of timid (even when very accomplished) women, whose acquaintance with life is severely restricted, and who are not conspicuous for general views. The novel, moreover, among ourselves, is almost always addressed to young unmarried ladies, or at least always assumes them to be a large part of the novelist's public. This fact, to a French storyteller, appears, of course, a damnable restriction, and M. Zola would probably decline to take *au sérieux* any work produced under such unnatural conditions. Half of life is a sealed book to young unmarried ladies, and how can a novel be worth anything that deals only with half of life? How can a portrait be painted (in any way to be recognizable) of half a face? It is not in one eye, but in the two eyes together that the expression resides, and it is the combination of features that constitutes the human identity. These objections are perfectly valid, and it may be said that our English system is a good thing for virgins and boys, and a bad thing for the novel itself, when the novel is regarded as something more than a simple *jeu d'esprit*, and considered as a composition that treats of life at large and helps us to *know*. But under these unnatural conditions and insufferable restrictions a variety of admirable works have been produced; Thackeray, Dickens, George Eliot, have all had an eye to the innocent classes. The fact is anomalous, and the advocates of naturalism must make the best of it. In fact, I believe they have little relish for the writers I have mentioned. They find that something or other is grievously wanting in their productions — as it most assuredly is! They complain that such writers are not serious. They are not so, certainly, as M. Zola is so; but there are many different ways of being serious. That of the author of *L'Assommoir*, of *La Conquête de Plassans*, of *La Faute de L'Abbé Mouret* may, as I say, with all its merits and defects taken together, suggest a great many things to English readers. They must admire the largeness of his attempt and the richness of his intention. They must admire, very often, the brilliancy of his execution. *L'Assommoir*, in spite of its fetid atmosphere, is full of magnificent passages and episodes, and the sustained power of the whole thing, the art of carrying a weight, is extraordinary. What will strike the English reader of M. Zola at large, however, and what will strike the English reader of *Nana*, if he have stoutness of stomach enough to advance in the book, is the extraordinary absence of humour, the dryness, the solemnity, the air of tension and effort. M. Zola disapproves greatly of wit; he thinks it is an impertinence in a novel, and he would probably disapprove of humour if he *knew* what it is. There is no indication in all his works that he has a suspicion of this; and what tricks the absence of a sense of it plays him! What a mess it has made of this admirable *Nana*! The presence of it, even in a limited degree, would have operated, to some extent, as a disinfectant, and if M. Zola had had a more genial fancy he would also have had a cleaner one. Is it not also owing to the absence of a sense of humour that this last and most violent expression of the realistic faith is extraordinarily wanting in reality? Anything less illusory than the pictures, the people, the indecencies of *Nana*, could not well be imagined. The falling-off from *L'Assommoir* in this respect can hardly be exaggerated. The human note is completely absent, the perception of character, of the way that people feel and think and act, is helplessly, hopelessly at fault; so that it becomes almost grotesque at last to see the writer trying to drive before him a herd of figures that never for an instant stand on their legs. This is what saves us in England, in spite of our artistic levity and the presence of the young ladies — this fact that we are by disposition better psychologists, that we have, as a general thing, a deeper, more delicate perception of the play of character and the state of the soul. This is what often gives an interest to works conceived on a much narrower programme than those of M. Zola — makes them more touching and more real, although the apparatus and the machinery of reality may, superficially, appear to be wanting. French novelists are at bottom, with all their extra freedom, a good deal more conventional than our own; and *Nana*, with the prodigious freedom that her author has taken, never, to my sense, leaves for a moment the region of the conventional. The figure of the brutal *fille*, without a conscience or a soul, with nothing but devouring appetites and impudences, has become the stalest of the stock properties of French fiction, and M. Zola's treatment has here imparted to her no touch of superior verity. He is welcome to draw as many figures of the same type as he finds necessary, if he will only make them human; this is as good a way of making a contribution to our knowledge of ourselves as another. It is not his choice of subject that has shocked us; it is the melancholy dryness of his execution, which gives us all the bad taste of a disagreeable dish and none of the nourishment.

BIBLIOGRAPHICAL NOTE

'The Art of Fiction', *Longman's Magazine*, September 1884, reprinted in *Partial Portraits*, 1888.

'The Great Form', letter to the Deerfield Summer School, published in the New York *Tribune*, 4 August 1889.

'The Future of the Novel', preface to Vol. 28 of *The Universal Anthology*, 1899.

'The Lesson of Balzac', *Atlantic Monthly*, August 1905, reprinted in *The Question of Our Speech*, 1905.

'Anthony Trollope', *Century Magazine*, July 1883, reprinted in *Partial Portraits*, 1888.

'Robert Louis Stevenson', *Century Magazine*, April 1888, reprinted in *Partial Portraits*, 1888.

'Guy de Maupassant', *Fortnightly Review*, March 1888, reprinted in *Partial Portraits*, 1888.

'Turgenev and Tolstoy', originally titled 'Turgenev', in Vol. XXV, *Library of the World's Best Literature*, 1897.

'Nathaniel Hawthorne', Vol. XII, *Library of the World's Best Literature*, 1897.

'Gustave Flaubert', preface to *Madame Bovary*, 1902, reprinted in *Notes on Novelists*, 1914.

'Émile Zola', *Atlantic Monthly*, August 1903, reprinted in *Notes on Novelists*, 1914.

The reviews of the four novels were printed unsigned as follows: *Our Mutual Friend*, the *Nation*, 21 December 1865; *Middlemarch*, the *Galaxy*, March 1873; *Far from the Madding Crowd*, the *Nation*, 24 December 1874, and *Nana*, the *Parisian*, 26 February 1880.

INDEX

Alva, Duke of, 102
Archer, William, 116, 118, 126
Aristotle, 271
Arnold, Matthew, 9
Austen, Jane, 15, 18, 45, 62, 63, 71, 207, 265

Balzac, Honoré de, 15–18, 60–85, 102, 111, 133, 189, 192, 245
  La Comédie Humaine, 64, 68, 71, 74, 75
  Le Curé de Village, 81
  Eugénie Grandet, 65, 81
  Les Parents Pauvres, 77
  Le Père Goriot, 81, 83
Besant, Sir Walter, 23, 26, 28, 30, 33, 35, 38, 39, 40, 42, 43, 44
Brontë, Charlotte, 15, 18, 63, 64, 71
  Jane Eyre, 63
Brontë, Emily, 63, 64
  Wuthering Heights, 63
Byron, George Gordon, 6th Baron, 193

Carlyle, Thomas, 101
Cervantes Saavedra, Miguel de, 31
Cherbuliez, Victor, 192
Chopin, Frédéric, 18
Coleridge, Samuel Taylor, 9
Colet, Louise, 191

Darwin, Charles, 267
Daudet, Alphonse, 106, 165
Day, Thomas, 247
Dickens, Charles, 15, 18, 23, 31, 45, 56, 67, 71, 89, 92, 101, 253–8, 265, 279
  Bleak House, 253
  David Copperfield, 18
  Little Dorrit, 253
  Our Mutual Friend, 18, 253–8
Dostoievsky, Fyodor, 18
Dreyfus, Alfred, 223, 234, 246

Dryden, John, 9
Du Camp, Maxime, 190, 197
Dumas, Alexandre, 45, 71, 84, 95, 132, 217, 228
  The Three Musketeers, 133
Dumas, Alexandre, fils, 84
Dupee, F. W., 10

Edgeworth, Maria, 247
Eliot, George, 15, 18, 42, 71, 79, 89, 92, 93, 259–67, 268, 269, 275, 279
  Middlemarch, 18, 259–67
  Romola, 259, 264, 266, 275
  Silas Marner, 267
Eliot, T. S., 9, 10, 11, 14

Faguet, Émile, 187, 195, 198, 200, 201
Feuillet, Octave, 192
Fielding, Henry, 56, 70, 207, 263, 266
Flaubert, Gustave, 10, 14, 16, 36, 45, 106, 140, 158, 162, 165, 187–219
  Bouvard et Pécuchet, 194, 204, 210
  Le Candidat, 197
  L'Éducation Sentimentale, 162, 193, 194, 195, 199, 200, 201, 202, 203, 204, 206, 207, 210, 213
  Madame Bovary, 194, 195, 196, 197, 198, 199, 200, 201, 205, 206, 207, 209, 210, 212, 214, 216, 219
  Salammbô, 190, 193, 194, 195, 206, 207, 208, 209, 210, 212, 214, 216
  La Tentation de Sainte-Antoine, 190, 194, 195, 206, 207, 209, 210, 212
  Trois Contes, 36, 194, 207

Garnett, Constance, 171
Garrick, David, 102
Gautier, Théophile, 193
Gibbon, Edward, 26
Goethe, Johann Wolfgang von, 193, 275
  Wilhelm Meister, 275

Goldsmith, Oliver, 101, 267
Goncourt, Edmond de, 41, 165, 208
  Chérie, 41
Goncourt, Jules de, 165

Haggard, Sir H. Rider, 158
Hardy, Thomas, 268–73
Harte, Bret, 152
Hawthorne, Nathaniel, 15, 16, 19, 36,
  71, 152, 176–86
  The American Note Books, 185
  The Blithedale Romance, 36, 182, 185
  The Dolliver Romance, 185
  The Grandfather's Chair, 177
  The House of the Seven Gables, 180,
    181, 182, 185
  The Marble Faun, 183, 184, 186
  Mosses from an Old Manse, 177
  Our Old Home, 183, 185
  The Scarlet Letter, 177, 179, 180, 181
  Septimius Felton, 185
  The Snow Image, 177
  Tanglewood Tales, 177
  Twice-Told Tales, 176
  The Wonder Book, 177
Heine, Heinrich, 193
Hogarth, William, 239
Huxley, T. H., 267

Irving, Washington, 186

James, Henry, *An International Episode*,
  40
  Essays in London, 12, *The Painter's
    Eye*, 9, *The Scenic Art*, 9
Jonson, Ben, 9

Kemble, John, 102

Lemaître, Jules, 147
Leopardi, Giacomo, 193
Longfellow, H. W., 176
Lubbock, Percy, 19

Macaulay, Thomas Babington, 26, 63,
  102
Margot la Balafrée, 40
Mathilde, Princess, 191, 208

Maupassant, Guy de, 14, 16–17, 139–67
  Bel-Ami, 140, 147, 161
  Boule de Suif, 140, 154
  La Maison Tellier, 140, 145, 153, 155
  Miss Harriet, 154
  Mont-Oriol, 148, 158
  Pierre et Jean, 139, 142, 147, 161,
    164, 165
  Une Vie, 158, 161, 162, 163
Melville, Herman, 19
Meredith, George, 67, 71, 131, 133
  The Ordeal of Richard Feverel, 133
Millet, Jean-François, 221
Moore, George, 10
Motley, John L., 102
Musset, Alfred de, 18

Oliphant, Margaret, 90

Pall Mall Gazette, 40, 42, 44
Pater, Walter, 207
Pierce, Franklin, 176, 183, 185
Poe, Edgar Allen, 152, 154
Pushkin, Alexander, 193

Racine, Jean, 10
Reade, Charles, 263, 273
Renan, Ernest, 192
  Revue des Deux Mondes, La, 192
Richardson, Samuel, 56, 70, 275
  Clarissa Harlowe, 275
Royal Institution, 23

Sand, George, 18, 62, 67, 71, 90, 140,
  190, 217, 247
Sainte-Beuve, C. A., 9, 10, 11, 15
Sardou, Victorien, 16
Scott, Sir Walter, 56, 67, 95, 121, 228
Shakespeare, William, 67, 76, 110
Shaw, G. Bernard, 10
  Spectator, The, 268
Spencer, Herbert, 116
Stevenson, Robert Louis, 41, 52, 114–
  138
  A Child's Garden of Verses, 117, 119,
    120, 122
  Doctor Jekyll and Mr Hyde, 117, 119,
    126, 131, 133, 134, 135, 138

The Dynamiter, 130, 133
An Inland Voyage, 121, 122, 128, 129
Kidnapped, 119, 121, 124, 125, 128, 133, 136, 137
Memories and Portraits, 125
The Merry Men, 125, 129, 136
The New Arabian Nights, 117, 126, 128, 131, 133
The Pavilion on the Links, 122
Prince Otto, 117, 118, 119, 126, 131
The Rajah's Diamond, 122
The Silverado Squatters, 126, 130, 131
The Suicide Club, 133
Travels With a Donkey, 125, 127, 128
Treasure Island, 41, 117, 119, 126, 128, 132, 134
Virginibus Puerisque, 117, 120, 121, 125, 126
Stowe, Harriet Beecher, *Uncle Tom's Cabin*, 169
Sweeney, John L., *The Painter's Eye*, 9

Taine, Hyppolite, 77, 192
Tennyson, Alfred Lord, 193
Thackeray, W. M., 18, 23, 32, 67, 71, 77, 78, 89, 92, 103, 108, 111, 137, 159, 263, 279
Denis Duval, 18
The History of Henry Esmond, Esq., 137
The Newcomes, 103
Pendennis, 78, 159
Thackeray, Anne (Lady Ritchie), *The Story of Elizabeth*, 32
Titian, 41
Tolstoy, Count Leo, 18, 79, 168–75, 248
Anna Karénina, 169
War and Peace, 169, 170
Trollope, Anthony, 16, 26, 89–113
The American Senator, 104
Barchester Towers, 89, 98, 99, 101, 103, 108
The Bertrams, 109
Can You Forgive Her?, 89
Doctor Thorne, 112
The Duke's Children, 104, 105
Framley Parsonage, 89

He Knew He Was Right, 89, 103, 110
John Caldigate, 104
The Last Chronicle of Barset, 104
Linda Tressel, 110
Nina Balatka, 110
Orley Farm, 89, 104, 111
Phineas Finn, 104
Phineas Redux, 104
The Prime Minister, 104
Ralph the Heir, 112
The Small House at Allington, 104
The Three Clerks, 99
The Vicar of Bullhampton, 96, 97, 98, 106
The Warden, 89, 98, 101, 102, 108
The Way We Live Now, 89
Turgenev, Ivan, 18, 36, 168–75, 190
Fathers and Children, 173
A House of Gentlefolk, 170, 173
On the Eve, 170, 173
Rudin, 173
Smoke, 170
A Sportsman's Sketches, 169, 172
Spring Floods, 173
Virgin Soil, 173

Wade, Allan, 9
Wells, H. G., 10
William of Orange, 102

Zola, Émile, 10, 14, 16, 37, 45, 74, 75, 76, 79, 106, 131, 165, 192, 220–249, 274–80
L'Assommoir, 76, 226, 229, 231, 232, 233, 236, 241, 242, 243, 244, 247, 274, 275, 279
L'Argent, 233, 234, 236
La Bête Humaine, 233, 234
Au Bonheur des Dames, 225, 279
La Conquête de Plassans, 225, 279
La Curée, 238
La Débâcle, 233, 234, 236, 241, 245, 247, 248
Le Docteur Pascal, 235, 239, 240
Eugène Rougon, 238, 239
La Faute de l'Abbé Mouret, 239, 279
Fécondité, 233, 234, 237, 238
La Fortune des Rougon, 238

Germinal, 229, 233, 234, 241, 244, 245, 247, 248
La Joie de Vivre, 238
Lourdes, 233, 247
Nana, 238, 239, 274–80
L'Œuvre, 247
Une Page d'Amour, 239
Paris, 233
Pot-Bouille, 238
Les Quatres Évangiles, 232

Le Rêve, 239
Rome, 233, 237, 238, 247
Les Rougon-Macquart, 74, 75, 222, 223, 224, 225, 227, 232, 234, 235, 236, 240, 244, 277
Travail, 233
Les Trois Villes, 232, 235, 237
Vérité, 224, 226, 233, 234, 237, 238, 244, 246, 247
Le Ventre de Paris, 229, 233